ANGELS AT DAWN

University of Philippines Agriculture School, Los Baños, Luzon, PI

ANGELS AT DAWN
The Los Baños Raid

Lt. Gen. Edward M. Flanagan, Jr. USA (Ret.)

PRESIDIO

This book was originally published with the title:
The Los Baños Raid

This edition printed 1999

Published by Presidio Press
505 B San Marin Drive, Suite 300
Novato, CA 94945-1340

Library of Congress Cataloging-in-Publication Data

Flanagan, E. M., 1921–
    The Los Baños Raid.
    Bibliography: p. 271
    Includes index.
    1. Los Baños (Los Baños, Laguna, Phipippines: Concentration camp) 2. World War, 1939–1945—Prisoners and prisons, Japanese. 3. United States. Army. Airborne Division, 11th—History. 4. World War, 1939–1945—Aerial operations, American. 5. World War, 1939–1945—Campaigns—Philippines. I. Title.
D805.P6F58   1986   94054'4973   86–3268
ISBN 0-89141-687-0 (paperback)

Printed in the United States of America

For all the valiant "Angels," the soldiers of the 11th Airborne Division in World War II—particularly those who raided the Los Baños Internment Camp on 23 February 1945 and freed 2,122 internees.

"Nothing could be more satisfying to a soldier's heart than this rescue. I am deeply grateful. God was certainly with us today."

Douglas MacArthur
General of the Army
Special Communique
24 February 1945
(The day after the Los Baños raid)

Contents

Acknowledgements

Writing a book of this sort entails two distinct but not necessarily time-separated procedures: research and writing. I am deeply indebted to two different groups of people for assistance in each of these phases.

In the research phase, I relied heavily on Hank Burgess's "Reminiscences" which he graciously allowed me to quote from, or to paraphrase, as I wanted. But over the months of writing, as I got deeper and deeper into the story, I wrote him many letters asking for specific answers to specific questions. He answered my queries promptly and in detail. I also talked to him about the raid during the 1984 11th Airborne Division Reunion in Clearwater, Florida, and at General Swing's funeral in Arlington, VA in December of 1984. He commented wisely and helpfully on my first rough draft of the manuscript. Without his detail memory of events pertaining to Los Baños, I could never have written this book with the accuracy I wanted.

John Ringler was also most helpful, both in letters and in person when we discussed the raid at the Clearwater reunion. In 1968 and 1969, he worked for me when I commanded the John F. Kennedy Center for Military Assistance (the training center at Fort Bragg for the Special Forces—Green Berets—and Psychological Warfare troops) but, unfortunately, at that time, I had no idea that I would write a book about Los Baños and thus never discussed the operation with Colonel Ringler then.

More recently, however, he provided details of the raid which no other man could have done, and he also gave me names of other soldiers who had important roles in the raid. I am most grateful to John Ringler for his assistance.

Colonel Jay D. Vanderpool read the chapter on the guerrillas and steered me on the right track in my discussion of the part they played in the raid. I also used his letters to me in answer to my detailed questions. He was most helpful and supportive.

Colonel Dave Blackledge answered my questions and also wrote a number of letters on Los Baños to the *Voice of the Angels,* the quarterly newspaper of the 11th Airborne Division Association. I relied on them for accuracy and clarification of many controversial points. I am indebted to Dave Blackledge for his memories of life in Los Baños as a teenager.

John Fulton was a storehouse of information which he shared freely with me. He, of all of the 11th Airborne men involved in the raid, knew personally the part played by the guerrillas; he was insistent that they be given full credit for their commendable and considerable assistance to the troopers of the 11th, particularly the Recon Platoon, and the initial attack on the guards around the camp perimeter.

Bob Kennington, an old friend of the 11th from World War II days, and particularly later in Sapporo during the occupation of Japan, sent me papers he had written on the raid after the war at the Infantry School. These papers filled the blanks in my knowledge of the maneuvers of the Soule Task Force as it came down Highway One, providing a formidable diversion against any Japanese troops who might have decided to move toward the internment camp while the attack and evacuation were going on.

Colonel Alan H. Chenevert filled me in on the part played by the elements of the 127th Airborne Engineer Battalion which jumped in with "B" Company.

Arthur J. Coleman, formerly of the Amphibian Battalion, was of great assistance in helping me understand the characteristics of amtracs and the role they played in the rescue.

Martin Squires wrote me a number of letters detailing the activities of the Recon Platoon both before and during the raid.

He also sent me a copy of a short history of the recon platoon which contained some details of the platoon's operations which were recorded nowhere else.

Letters to *The Voice of Angels* from participants in the raid, both 11th Airborne and guerrillas, were a great source of personal anecdotes and recollections. For example, Jim Holzem's story about Oscar, John Fulton's reminiscences, and Dave Blackledge's recollections about his life in Los Baños were printed in *The Voice*. Tabo Ingles, Kit Quesada, and Antonio Nieva, among other ex-guerrillas, wrote letters to *The Voice* or sent copies of articles about Los Baños which had been reprinted in *The Voice*. I used these sources on many occasions.

Jasper Bryan Smith and the late "Moose" Mason were also kind enough to write to me about their parts in the raid; Bill Abernathy cleared up the puzzle of how "B" Company was selected to make the jump.

A number of ex-internees were most gracious and cooperative in sharing their experiences. Without the contribution and the letters of Ben Edwards, I would have missed a great part of the story, not only of the internees, but also of the guerrillas with whom he collaborated before and during the raid. He wrote over twenty-six long letters to clarify points I raised. He read and commented upon the original draft of the manuscript. I am most indebted to Ben Edwards.

Sister Miriam Louise Kroeger sent me copies of her reminiscences written just after the liberation and also wrote letters to me again in answer to specific questions. She very kindly permitted me to use her writings in whole or in part.

Father William R. McCarthy not only permitted me to quote from his pamphlets about the raid, but also answered a number of my questions.

Bill Rivers wrote a number of times to fill me in on details which I needed. He has a great memory for detail from which I benefited.

Grace Nash gave me permission to quote from her book about her days in the Los Baños Camp, *That We Might Live*. It is a very nostalgic story of her life immediately after the Japanese invasion of Luzon and of her family's incarceration in Los Baños.

The ex-guerrillas were extremely cooperative. Frank Quesada sent me copies of the Hunters' documents as well as a copy of *Terry's Hunters*, the history of the Hunters-ROTC Guerrillas in the fight against the Japanese. He also wrote numerous letters, again responding to my questions. He is a stalwart member of the Hunters-ROTC Association which strives to keep alive their motto: "Once a Hunter, Always a Hunter" and to try to see to it that the guerrillas are given their just due.

Gustavo C. Ingles very kindly wrote me a number of times from Manila clarifying points which only he could know about. I am most grateful for his cooperation.

Reverend George J. Williams, SJ, wrote a detailed article about the raid which appeared in a Manila newspaper in February of 1947 and which was later reprinted in *The Voice*.

Charles Richard Anderson's diary, published in the Chicago *Times* on March 17, 1945, gave some almost on the spot details of the raid and the rescue.

Anthony Arthur, who has recently completed a book on the raid, very generously sent me copies of the transcript of the Konishi trial.

In spite of the help in research from the people I mentioned above, any inaccuracies which remain in the book are my responsibility.

For assistance in writing the book, I would be most remiss if I did not mention the editorial help given me by the Editor-in-Chief of Presidio Press, Adele Horwitz. After she read my first attempt, she critiqued it in three pages of very valuable comments. In effect, she told me to "put it back through my typewriter." I did that and followed her suggestions as nearly to the letter as possible. I am most grateful for her very professional help and advice.

Cheri Elliott, a secretary at the Dowling Law Firm where I used to work, typed and retyped the manuscripts with speed and great good cheer. She learned to translate the scribbled notes on my typewritten pages with skill.

I know that I have omitted, however inadvertently, a number of people who helped me put together this story of the Los Baños Raid. But I am most grateful to them as well as to the people I have mentioned. But to Hank Burgess, Ben Edwards, and Adele Horwitz, I must give special added thanks and my heartfelt appreciation. Without them, there would have been no book.

Introduction

Worl War II was a drama of colossal proportions; it was enacted on a vast stage with a cast of millions in prominent roles and with millions more in supporting parts. The action raged from the sprawling, swirling tank battles in the deserts of North Africa to the titanic clashes of far-flung armadas thundering their guns across the far reaches of the Pacific; from the massive, thousand-plane bombing assaults on Germany to the relentless, but fruitless, siege of the frozen, unconquerable bastions of Stalingrad; from amphibious invasion and airborne strike in the pre-H-hour darkness of D-day to the scores of Marine assaults on the hitherto anonymous islands in the remote stretches of the Pacific; from the searing heat of the jungles of New Guinea to the frozen battlefields of northern Europe; from the monstrous sins of the oven tenders at Dachau, Belsen, and Buchenwald to the solitude and misery of the POWs in the Philippines and Japan; and from the lonely rifleman with his M1 to the Enola Gay and its war-ending single weapon that ushered in the nuclear age. The world was the stage for World War II; its population was the cast. There were few persons, military or civilian, who were not touched by the drama, organization, and prodigies of production, transportation, and technology that marked the progress of the war as nations geared up for their parts in the enormous struggle.

Tucked away from the footlights, in unseen corners of that global stage, were relatively unapplauded scenes within the main drama. Those byplays were largely overlooked and were, for the most part, unreported by the press, which was, quite reasonably, concerned with the big picture, the grand strategy, the battles that would influence the outcome of the war: the blitzkrieg, the Maginot Line, the Battle of Britain, Pearl Harbor, Alamein, Algeria, Sicily, Salerno, Coral Sea, Midway, Guadalcanal, Iwo Jima, the Bulge, the Philippines, Okinawa, Hiroshima, and Nagasaki. Some of the smaller scenes of the war were, however, of momentous importance, particularly to the people involved in them.

It is significant that the mission or motivation for some of the minor acts of the war was not, as it was for the larger battles, the reduction of yet another enemy obstacle that was blocking the movement of troops toward a strategic objective, nor the requirement to kill thousands of the enemy before an area could be declared secure, nor the pulverization of a factory complex by bombing or sinking the major elements of the enemy fleet. The mission of some of the small-scale actions had a far more humane and soul-satisfying goal: the rescue of prisoners of war or civilian internees. Civilian internees, imprisoned for years in concentration camps, after all, were guilty only of the "crime" of being citizens of a country with which another nation was at war.

Throughout the area of the world that the Japanese had overrun in their initially successful efforts to form the Greater East Asia Co-Prosperity Sphere, they had established POW and internee camps to confine the thousands of military prisoners and civilians captured in their early drives. The suffering and anguish of military prisoners at the hands of the Japanese has been well recorded in books and motion pictures. Of the movies, *The Bridge Over the River Kwai* is probably one of the most dramatic. In every POW camp British and American POWs were treated abominably by the Japanese. Torture was common. The terrible conditions imposed on the British who built the railroad in Burma, at a cost of 15,000 lives, is a grim illustration of the fate of POWs at the hands of the Japanese.

In the Philippines the Japanese had captured thousands of soldiers and forced them into primitive camps without adequate food or water. The Bataan Death March, when the facts became known, highlighted for the world the brutality of the Japanese toward the soldiers they conquered. On 6 May 1942 the white flags went up over the few remaining flagpoles on Corregidor. The next day the Japanese started the 11,000 captives of Corregidor and those captured on Bataan on that long, brutal march. Before the sixty-five-mile walk was over, nearly 25,000 prisoners had lost their lives from beatings, disease, starvation, and executions. Another 22,000 would die during the first two months at Camp O'Donnell.

The Japanese had established a POW prison on Palawan, another island in the Philippine chain; and when the American forces sailed from Leyte to Mindoro, the Japanese on Palawan mistakenly thought they were headed for their island. In a reaction of terror and fear, they forced the U.S. POWs into underground shelters, poured gasoline on them, and set them afire. Those who did not burn to death were machine-gunned as they tried to escape. In that incident 140 POWs died.

The treatment of the prisoners in Burma and on Palawan was indicative of the heinous treatment meted out by the Japanese captors to their defeated enemy. As the empire shrank, the Japanese tried to move their prisoners to the homeland in brutally overcrowded transports. Many of these floating "death chambers" were sunk by unknowing Americans in planes and submarines, and hundreds of prisoners drowned or were machine-gunned by the Japanese as they tried to swim ashore. Many more prisoners died after they landed in Japan; in some cases they were frozen by water hosed on them in subzero weather. In the case of one POW ship that landed at Moji, Japan, on 29 January 1945, only one-fourth of those who began the trip survived; and of 110 deathly ill prisoners of those survivors who were carried ashore, only 10 survived.

Less well documented is the story of the civilians interned by the Japanese in the conquered territories. In the Philippines there were several such camps, notably at Santo Tomas and Los

Baños, both on the main island of Luzon. Life in Los Baños and the camp's eventual liberation by a combined force of guerrillas and 11th Airborne paratroopers produce the story of this book.

The role played by one of the leading actors in World War II, Gen. Douglas MacArthur, has been well recorded in books and articles. What is less well known, perhaps, is the depth of the feeling General MacArthur had for the men and women who were captured, both those who were fighting for the United States and those who were rounded up and interned by the Japanese in the months after the fall of Manila and the Philippines.

General MacArthur's role in World War II and, for that matter, before and after World War II, is highly controversial. He performed bravely and masterfully in World War I.[1] But as Chief of Staff of the Army in 1932, during the Depression, his use of force against the "bonus marchers" was something less than benevolent. The Bonus Expeditionary Force (BEF, or bonus marchers) was a group of some 25,000 World War I vets and their families who had come to Washington to plead for a cash bonus from the government. As their ranks began to swell in an unauthorized shantytown across the Anacostia from Washington, D.C., President Hoover sent word to MacArthur through Secretary Hurley to evict the BEF. MacArthur, who believed that 90 percent of the BEF were fakes (in fact, a Veteran's Administration survey held that 94 percent were bona fide veterans), took to his task with perhaps unwarranted enthusiasm. In uniform he personally led Army troops to the camp and ordered them to put the torch to the shacks, tents, and lean-tos.

MacArthur skillfully and masterfully performed his role in occupying Japan and restructuring its constitution and government after World War II. This undoubtedly formed the basis for the subsequent renaissance of Japan as a world power. In Korea, once again he demonstrated his military genius by ordering the surprise landings at Inchon, but he displayed his defiance of authority in his controversy with President Truman over

---

1. During World War I, General MacArthur earned two Distinguished Service Crosses, the Distinguished Service Medal, seven Silver Stars, and two Purple Hearts; he received the Medal of Honor in World War II.

the conduct of the Korean War, an episode that led to his relief as Supreme Commander Allied Powers and relief from active duty in April 1951—at age seventy-one.

In spite of his controversial nature, his obvious flamboyancy, his supreme ego, his forthright defiance of authority, his unwillingness to admit a mistake, General MacArthur had a genuine fondness for and deep interest in the welfare of the people of the Philippines. He developed that encompassing loyalty through his long association with the people and military forces of the Philippines and the American forces that served there.

From 1930 until 1935, General MacArthur was the Chief of Staff of the United States Army, the highest military position a U.S. soldier could hold. Although the tour was normally for four years, President Roosevelt held him on for the fifth year, "to his surprise," General MacArthur noted modestly.

In 1935, the Philippines was about to become a Commonwealth of the United States; Manuel Quezon was the president-elect. Quezon came to the United States in 1935 to discuss the future national defense of the Philippines after that country obtained its independence. He contacted General MacArthur and asked him his opinion of the defensibility of the islands. MacArthur told him that "any place could be defended if sufficient men, munitions, and money were available, and above all, if there was sufficient time to train the men, to provide the munitions, and to raise the money." Then Quezon asked MacArthur a question—will you accept the task of organizing the defense of the Philippines?—the answer to which would affect the destiny of the Philippines, the conduct of the coming war, and MacArthur's own fate, fortunes, and future. MacArthur said yes, but he emphasized to Quezon that it would require ten years and much help from the United States. Years later MacArthur wrote, "As it turned out, neither was forthcoming. War came in five years, and American help came too late and too little."

General MacArthur sailed for the Philippines in the fall of 1935, still a four-star general on active duty in the United States Army. About a year later, on 24 August 1936, Quezon appointed him a field marshal of the Philippine army. By 1937, however, relations between Roosevelt and Quezon were cooling; in addition, Roosevelt's interests were focusing on Europe and the defenses of Hawaii and the west coast of the United States. According to General MacArthur, Roosevelt asked him to return to Hawaii to take command of the defenses of the Hawaiian islands and the Pacific coast of the United States. MacArthur, however, had promised Quezon that he would stay with him for Quezon's full six-year term of office, which still had about three years to run. But MacArthur also felt, and relayed his feeling to the President, that by staying on the active ranks of the Army as a full general, he was blocking the promotion of other generals. Therefore, according to his book *Reminiscences*, "I settled both problems by retiring from the Army as a four-star general." President Roosevelt accepted his resignation from the Army's active list effective 31 December 1937. MacArthur continued his service to Quezon and the Philippines with the rank of field marshal.

On 1 September 1939 war broke out in Europe when Hitler invaded Poland. By 1939 the Sino-Japanese War had been raging for two years, and the Japanese had occupied not only coastal regions of China but important cities in the interior as well. World War II was well underway but without direct U.S. military involvement. Gradually, the United States was being drawn in on the side of its allies and was more and more concerned with its own defenses.

On 26 July 1941 President Roosevelt established the United States Forces Far East Command and assigned to it "the forces of the Commonwealth of the Philippines called into the service of the United States and such other forces as may be assigned to it." The U.S. War Department named the command Headquarters, United States Forces Far East; ordered it established in Manila; and designated General MacArthur its commander. By that order General MacArthur was brought back on the active roles of the Army at age 61—not in his former rank of general but as a major general. Twenty-four hours later, however, he was promoted to lieutenant general. Of that rank he wrote, "I had reached a stage of life when I cared little for the reasons of administrators." Nonetheless, six months later the War Department restored him to four-star status.

Then came Pearl Harbor, the successful Japanese attack on the Philippines, the fall of Manila, the Bataan collapse, and the seemingly long erosion of the stalwart defense of Corregidor. Before the fall of Bataan, President Roosevelt ordered General MacArthur from Corregidor to Australia to prepare to retake the territory lost to the Japanese. In Australia General MacArthur developed and directed the strategy that defended Australia in New Guinea, which saw his forces hop and skip up the Pacific island chain until, by January of 1945, his troops were once again fighting for the capital of the Philippines. This time, however, he had victory rather than defeat in his sights.

General MacArthur's long service in and to the Philippines made him most understanding and sympathetic to the plight of the thousands of soldiers and civilians who were being held captive in POW camps and internee compounds throughout the islands. He knew many of the civilians from his days in Manila. He had many friends, compatriots, and loyal followers among the soldiers who were being held by the Japanese; he had trained them and fought with them. Now he was back, determined to liberate them as quickly and as safely as possible.

In *Reminiscences* General MacArthur wrote:

> I was deeply concerned about the thousands of prisoners who had been interned at the various camps on Luzon since the early days of the war. Shortly after the Japanese had taken over the islands, they had gathered Americans, British, and other Allied nationals, including women and children, in concentration centers without regard to whether they were actual combatants or simply civilians. I had been receiving reports from my various underground sources long before the actual landings on Luzon, but the latest information was most alarming. With every step that our soldiers took toward Santo Tomas University, Bilibid, Cabanatuan, and Los Baños, where these prisoners were held, the Japanese soldiers guarding them had become more and more sadistic. I knew that many of these half-starved and ill-treated people would die unless we rescued them promptly. The thought of their destruction with deliverance so near was deeply repellent to me.

By early 1945 the stage was set for General MacArthur's return to Luzon and for the culmination of his three-year effort to fulfill his dramatic prophecy: "I shall return." By the time he arrived on Luzon, he had imbued his headquarters staff not only with the necessity for keeping casualties to a minimum, but also with the need for speed in liberating the POWs and internees.

General MacArthur's headquarters, therefore, made certain that, through the assignment of specific missions and orders, POW camps and internee compounds would be freed as soon as possible. Late in January 1945, for example, after the initial landing at Lingayen Gulf, Sixth Army was in the process of moving south toward Manila. At that time the 6th Ranger Battalion was under the direct command of the Sixth Army commander, Gen. Walter Krueger, and he directed the battalion to free some 500 prisoners at Pangatian, a POW camp about 5 miles east of Cabanatuan, a city about 100 miles north of Manila. On 28 January the Rangers launched their attack, rescued the prisoners (about 200 of whom were in very poor physical condition), and evacuated them 20 miles to the main lines of the Sixth Army.

Another prisoner liberation involved the 8th Cavalry Regiment of the 1st Cavalry Division. As the lead elements of that division were entering Manila from the north, the first mission assigned to the 8th Cavalry was the rescue of the civilian internees held on the campus of Santo Tomas University in Manila. The 8th assaulted the campus and quickly freed more than 3,500 prisoners. The attack, however, was not without its difficulties. The Japanese commander of the camp held 275 more prisoners hostage and announced that he would release them only if he and his camp guards were granted safe passage out of the university grounds. To spare the lives of the hostages, the commander of the 8th allowed the former Santo Tomas commander and his staff to head for the hills; later they were hunted down and eliminated.

On 4 February the 8th Cavalry freed another 500 internees and approximately 800 U.S. and Allied POWs from the Old Bilibid Prison in Manila. General MacArthur visited the prisoners recovered from Bilibid shortly after their release. Later he wrote:

> I will never know how the 800 prisoners there survived for three long years. The food given them was generally full of worms

and skimpy even by Oriental standards. The men who greeted me were scarcely more than skeletons.

The military prisoners had been kept separate from the civilians. The soldiers had maintained their sense of discipline all through those long years. Somehow, every man dragged himself to his feet to stand beside his cot in some semblance of attention. They remained silent, as though at inspection. I looked down the lines of men, bearded and soiled, with hair that often reached below their shoulders, with ripped and soiled shirts and trousers, with toes sticking out of such shoes as remained, with suffering and torture written on their gaunt faces. Here was all that was left of my men of Bataan and Corregidor. The only sound was the occasional sniffle of a grown man who could not fight back the tears. As I passed slowly down the scrawny, suffering column, a murmur accompanied me as each man, barely speaking above a whisper, said, "You're back" or "You made it" or "God bless you." I could only reply, "I'm a little late, but we finally came."

When the 11th Airborne Division waded ashore at Nasugbu and parachuted onto Tagaytay Ridge on 3 and 4 February 1945, it was the major unit of the Eighth Army in that area of Luzon.[2] But on 10 February, while the 11th was investing Manila and its defenses from the south, General MacArthur's headquarters transferred the 11th from the Eighth to the Sixth Army and assigned it to the XIV Corps so that the entire attack on Manila would have "unity of command," a proven principle of war. Therefore, the attack on Manila was conducted from both the north and the south by the same commander, Gen. Oscar Griswold, commanding general of the XIV Corps. North of Manila he had the 1st Cavalry, the 37th Infantry, and the 40th Infantry divisions; pushing up from the south the 11th Airborne Division. By 13 February the 11th had linked up with the elements of XIV Corps in the north, but it still was involved in difficult and bloody fighting all along the Genko Line until late in February.

---

2. When the 11th Airborne made its jump on Tagaytay Ridge on 4 February, the author jumped with them. He was then Captain Flanagan, Battery Commander, B Battery, 457th parachute FA Battalion. On the day of the raid he was on the dried rice paddies outside Fort McKinley, supporting the 187th Infantry.

Previously, on 4 February, General Headquarters, Southwest Pacific Area (GHQ/SWPA)—General MacArthur's headquarters—had assigned to the 11th Airborne Division the mission of rescuing the internees at the Los Baños Internment Camp. General MacArthur and GHQ/SWPA realized that the 11th was otherwise engaged in the attack on Manila and that the raid on Los Baños would have to be deferred. GHQ/SWPA, therefore, approved the request of Maj. Gen. Joseph M. Swing, the 11th's commanding general, to postpone the Los Baños mission until he could free enough troops to accomplish the rather delicate task. GHQ/SWPA realized that Los Baños held "no strategic importance," and its liberation could thus be delayed, but it directed General Swing, nonetheless, to liberate Los Baños with all possible speed, for humanitarian reasons.

And so the 11th's staff, even while directing the fight against Manila and the Genko Line, had, in the back of its collective mind, the mission assigned to it by GHQ/SWPA: get the internees out of Los Baños and get them out before the Japanese can commit another atrocity. Most of the time the 11th's staff fought the big battle against the defenses of Manila; but part of the time, albeit a small part, the staff considered, planned for, and sought intelligence about a place it barely knew existed: Los Baños.

What follows is the story of that raid on Los Baños Camp. It is a story of intricate and resourceful staff planning; well-trained, disciplined, battle-tested troops; extraordinary heroism by brave, young internees; heroics by fractious guerrilla bands; and appropriate and reasoned decision making by tactically sound commanders on the ground. It is an operation performed under the stress of battle, with commanders wary of the fact that at any moment their small units might suddenly be engulfed by a much larger enemy force. It is an account of commanders working under extreme pressure of time and distance with an unruly mob of excited, hilarious civilians, suddenly free and unaware of the dangers that persisted even though the big, suntanned, exuberant Americans had arrived.

On the surface the plan was relatively simple: surround the camp during the night before the raid with a force of some 60 guerrillas and 30 U.S. 11th Airborne reconnaissance men; drop a parachute company of about 125 men a few hundred yards from the compound at first light; have the recon platoon and the guerrillas attack the guards around the camp as soon as the first parachute opens; bring in a battalion (less the parachute company) in amtracs across a large lake and move it the two miles overland into the camp, arriving a few minutes after the parachute drop; round up the internees and transport them back across the lake to U.S. lines; then bring out the attacking force.

The plan sounds uncomplicated, the execution easy; however, remember that the raid had to take place 25 miles behind the Japanese lines, that there were thousands of Japanese forces within a short march of the camp; and that U.S. troop commanders had little knowledge of the condition of the internees. Nonetheless, it worked. The paratroopers, the guerrillas, and the recon platoon hit the camp in unison; they wiped out the guards or sent them scurrying to the hills; they rounded up the internees and forced them, with various ruses, to move swiftly to the amtracs; they evacuated all of the internees safely; and they brought out all of the raiding force. Specific results of the raid? All of the 2,122 internees (one as young as three days old) were rescued and moved back behind U.S. lines; not a single U.S. soldier in the raiding force was lost.

In reality it is a story with three tracks: (1) the tale of the internees and their forced relocation from comfortable homes and prosperous businesses, from convents and rectories, hospitals and orphanages, to an internment camp, where most of them made the best of a miserable situation; (2) the chronicle of an unusual group of dedicated men, trained to enter combat by parachute or glider; disciplined during months of hard training from Camp Mackall, North Carolina, to Camp Polk, Louisiana, to Dobodura, New Guinea; hardened in combat in Leyte and Luzon; and, (3) the saga of an ill-equipped, loosely organized ragtag group of guerrilla bands united for once by a benevolent and satisfying mission. The three tracks of the tale are widely separate until they converge suddenly with dramatic results on 23 February 1945.

It is a story, on the one hand, of patience, oppression, and misery; on the other hand, it is a tale of heroics, intelligence, training, calmness under pressure, discipline, combat readiness, and, perhaps, above all, motivation. It is a story of an operation that the raiders to this day savor for an important reason: They marked their success, for a change, not by the number of the enemy killed or the amount of ground seized, but by the number of fellow citizens they saved from almost certain death.

CHAPTER I: The Roundup

The Los Baños Internment Camp was located about two miles from the town of Los Baños,[1] a small village near the southern shore of Laguna de Bay, a large, freshwater, three-pronged lake southeast of Manila on the main island of Luzon in the Philippines. Twenty-three February 1945 began routinely and monotonously for the 2,122 civilian internees incarcerated in the Los Baños Internment Camp. As usual, they woke up and began to stir shortly after 0530. Then, obeying their captors' standing orders, the internees rounded up the children, filed out of their bamboo and sawali barracks, and at the sound of a gong shortly before 0700 lined up for roll call in a semiorderly formation. After the Japanese guards counted them and issued additional instructions or harangued them about their conduct around the camp, the internees shuffled along in four long lines to the kitchen areas for the usual inadequate, in fact, nearly starvation-inducing breakfast of unhusked rice (palay) and ersatz coffee. The breakfast practice and roll-call formation were tedious

---

1. In Spanish Los Baños means "The Baths." Near the southern shore of Laguna de Bay were a number of hot springs around which the Filipinos had built "health spas," hence the name "Los Baños."

and obligatory. Over the months of their imprisonment, the internees had become fatalistically inured to them.

Thus began for the internees of Los Baños another in a seemingly endless number of humdrum days, waiting for deliverance, praying for some small sign of hope, wondering how they and their families could survive for yet another dawn. Their days were filled with despair, spiced occasionally with a promising rumor of good news or the sight of U.S. planes overhead. For months they had carried on by making themselves take the days "one at a time."

The prisoners who stumbled weakly about the camp early that morning hardly dared to think optimistically about their release. Mostly they thought about how to survive another day on rations that had become progressively meager as the Japanese fortunes of war ground inexorably toward final disaster. After each defeat of the Imperial Army, it seemed, the camp commander reduced the rice ration. By February 1945 the Japanese were suffering one defeat after another all over their contracting empire, the shattered remnants of the once formidable Greater East Asia Co-Prosperity Sphere; the rice ration in Los Baños proportionately dwindled to levels that barely sustained life.

True, the prisoners had begun to receive some hopeful news of the war. The relentless rice ration reduction was a positive, if malevolent, sign. Additionally, a few prisoners had managed to keep and hide forbidden radios over which they had learned of the recent American forces landings at Lingayen Gulf on Luzon. But the sign that raised morale the highest, one of the signals for which the internees had been waiting throughout the long months, was the roar and sight of American aircraft overhead. The internees saw planes that they could not identify by type; but the aircraft flew low enough so that they could see the U.S. Army Air Corps markings on them. In the dogfighting that ensued, the Americans were always the victors in the eyes of the biased prisoners. The Japanese guards had boasted to them for months about the invincibility of their "Wild Eagles," but P-51s, although the internees did not know them by that description, "simply ate Jap planes in seconds," according to one internee observer.

Unfortunately, the appearance of American aircraft over the

compound made life more difficult for the prisoners because the Japanese, resentful, fearful, and furious at the success of the American aircraft in particular and mindful of the war's overall deterioration in general, ordered the internees back into their barracks at the first sign of American aircraft and forbade the inmates to wave at the planes or even to look at them in the skies. Punishment for so doing could mean death to the offender. In spite of such orders, many internees watched the planes and dogfights surreptitiously.

In the early morning hours the air temperature was still cool; later the heat of the day would warm the air and the camp. But at a few minutes before seven in the morning, the smog of the cooking fires mixed with the heavy, humid air of Luzon in February cast a funereal pall over the nipa-roofed, bamboo-sided barracks in which the internees lived.

By 0700 this morning the Japanese guards were divided and scattered about the camp performing their routine duties. One guard relief manned the various pillboxes and walking posts that completely surrounded the camp. Another relief prepared to go on duty. Most of the rest of the guards, off duty, began, as usual, to fall out and line up in front of their barracks just across from the main guard house on Pili Lane. The ritualistic formation was for calisthenics, and the Japanese were in loincloths and without weapons, a fact that would prove highly significant very shortly. Other Japanese noncoms conducted the internee roll call. The prisoners, bony and haggard, raggedly dressed in torn, endlessly patched clothes, and wearing handmade sandals and shoes, little knew that an attempt to rescue them would begin in just two or three minutes.

The prisoners of Los Baños were, for the most part, civilians of many nationalities who had been working in various business, service, commercial, educational, and religious pursuits in the Philippines before the war. There were even some dependents of U.S. military men who for various reasons had not left the Philippines. One such family was the Blackledges.

Dave Blackledge was eleven years old in December 1941. At that time his father was a captain stationed at Nichols Field outside Manila. The last time that Dave Blackledge saw his father was on Christmas Eve 1941.

After MacArthur declared Manila an "open city" on 26 December 1941, he ordered the bulk of the U.S. forces on Luzon to Bataan Peninsula; Captain Blackledge was among them. With the fall of Bataan, where he had been a company commander, Captain Blackledge, along with thousands of other Americans, was captured. For refusing to hand over his wedding ring to a Japanese soldier, he was bayoneted but not killed. Because of his wound, he missed the famous Bataan Death March. Later, in early 1945, Captain Blackledge was put on a Japanese transport to be evacuated from Manila to Japan. U.S. aircraft sank the transport just off the coast of Luzon, and the Japanese on shore machine-gunned the prisoners who tried to reach the beach. Nonetheless, Captain Blackledge eventually made it to shore and was later put on a ship bound for Japan. On 29 January 1945, when he arrived in Moji, Japan, he was one of the prisoners who was hosed with freezing sea water. He died there on 3 February 1945 at age thirty-nine.

After the Japanese occupied Manila on 2 January 1942, Dave Blackledge, his mother, and his six-year-old brother, Robert, hid out with friends in Manila. Shortly, though, Mrs. Blackledge found out that the Japanese knew where they were, and she surrendered the family in mid-1942. At first they were sent to Santo Tomas, but in mid-1943 they were transferred to Los Baños. The family had not gone back to the States because, as Dave Blackledge remembers it, "We never envisioned that the Japanese would be able to successfully invade the islands."

That same line of reasoning accounted for the presence of most of the other civilians who were living in the Philippines when the Japanese occupied the islands. The civilians, obviously to their regret, had discounted the rumors and talk of war, had had great faith in their various governments, and thus did not try to leave the Philippines before 7 December 1941.

Bill Rivers, who had been in Manila on a temporary business assignment and had been scheduled to fly out on 7 December 1941, remembers:

The residents and indigenous peoples were really carefully

advised of the progress of events, so that they would maintain confidence in the ability of the USAFFE (United States Armed Forces Far East) and the "Philippine Scouts" to protect the islands from invasion. A strong, positive thought seemed to emanate from the American High Commissioner's office, which painted a bright picture of the war in its early stages, and never seemed to cease conveying the thought: Don't drop everything and go home, as that will rob the Filipino people of the inspirational link to the United States.

With this kind of semiofficial encouragement, the trusting Allied civilians went about their business with faith and misplaced confidence.

A great many of the prisoners at Los Baños were from various religious orders throughout the islands. Before the war one group of Maryknoll Sisters in the Philippines operated St. Paul's Hospital in Manila. On 8 December 1941 their quiet routine was interrupted by the ominous sounds of battle, mainly Japanese aircraft bombing targets in Manila. They heard the American antiaircraft artillery firing at the enemy and watched Manila come under air attack. A few days later, while Manila was still in American hands, the U.S. Army took over their hospital, and the Sisters moved all of their possessions and equipment to the Philippine Women's University. A month later the Japanese overran Manila. After occupation of the city, the Japanese made repeated calls at the university but consistently refused the Sisters' offer to continue to care for the wounded.

Next, the Japanese moved the nuns to the Assumption Convent in Manila. Mother Rose of the convent and her community (neutrals) received the nuns with warmth and generous hospitality. Finally, on the night of 7 July 1944, the Japanese Military Police, on orders from the occupation force commander, swarmed into Manila and rounded up for internment all enemy aliens still at large. Included were other religious in other areas and the Sisters at Assumption Convent. As a result of the sweep, 250 Catholic priests, seminarians, scholastics, and Sisters and an equal number of Protestant missionaries were moved to Los Baños, where the Japanese assigned them to barracks in the upper part of the camp. The nuns, undaunted, and with their sense of humor still intact, christened their area "Vatican City." They referred to the lower half, occupied by lay internees, as "Hell's Half-Acre." One barracks in Vatican City housed the Catholic chapel, which had twenty-six cubicle altars. There were so many priests interned in Vatican City that more than 130 masses were offered daily in the makeshift chapel.

Another group of eight Maryknoll nuns had taught school before the war in Baguio, the summer capital of the Philippines. In the first few days after Pearl Harbor, the nuns saw and heard the war first hand. Their convent was located a few blocks from Camp Hay, an Army recreational center in the mountains near Baguio. At 0820 on 8 December 1941, just fifteen minutes after the nuns had heard on their radio that the Japanese had bombed Pearl Harbor, they saw a group of silver aircraft over Baguio. At first they thought that they must be American; their hopes were shattered when bombs began to fall on Camp Hay. There was no opposition from the rec center. During the next few weeks, the Japanese planes were overhead almost daily, bombing Hay and Baguio and killing hundreds of civilians in the area. On 28 December 1941 Japanese ground troops arrived in Baguio. For the next thirty-eight months the nuns would be under the surveillance and control of the Japanese.

In the next few weeks the Japanese moved the nuns from one place to another but finally returned them to confinement in their own convent in Baguio. On 13 November 1942, however, the Japanese again moved them to a "formal concentration center" at Camp Holmes, where their home was a small room with seventy-nine other people, some of whom had been their pupils. In May 1943 the Japanese relocated the nuns once again— this time to "semi-internment" in the Assumption Convent in Manila.

Because they could move about the city to some extent while they lived in Assumption Convent, the nuns could observe some of the conditions of life in Manila during the Japanese occupation. Sister Miriam Louise Kroeger was one of the Baguio nuns. Shortly after the war, she returned to Baguio and wrote about those days in Manila in 1943 and 1944:

> Lawlessness was rampant. Robberies were going on twenty-
> four hours a day; graves were opened and corpses relieved of

jewelry, clothing, and gold teeth; people were murdered and their bodies thrown in front of the police station to flaunt the authorities; for the sake of a few pesos, friend betrayed friend to the Japanese Kempiti. Over and above that, there was the constant threat of Japanese brutality. One of their most feared acts was the occasional roundup of hundreds of civilians, rich or poor, who were taken to the torture house at Fort Santiago. Death after months of ill treatment was a happy finale to an existence that before the war was inconceivable.

Sister Kroeger and the four remaining nuns from Baguio were among those moved from Assumption Convent to Los Baños in July of 1944. She says that they were shipped there as "public examples of espionage, insincerity, dishonesty, and a list of various other crimes."

Fr. William R. McCarthy, a Maryknoller ordained on 16 June 1940, was sent initially by his order to a Maryknoll mission in Cebu City; he became a prisoner of the Japanese when they captured that city early in 1942. Along with 120 other captives, he was incarcerated at first in the Cebu Provincial Jail, where, he says, "the bedbugs outnumbered us by a hundred to one." A couple of weeks later he was transferred to a camp at the University of the Philippines, still on Cebu. After about six months there, he was moved to the clubhouse of the Philippine Golf Club. There he celebrated his forty-fifth birthday. He remembers that day well because the prisoners received an extra ladle of rice; he is sure, however, that the Japanese were not celebrating his birthday. Rather, in those early days of the war the Japanese were still expanding the Greater East Asia Co-Prosperity Sphere, winning victory after victory on land and sea in their headlong, euphoric conquest of every area their forces attacked. Consequently, they fed their civilian prisoners adequately, with an extra ration to mark an especially important victory.

In December 1942 the Japanese loaded their Cebu prisoners onto a freighter bound for Manila and for Santo Tomas University, which by that time had become an internee camp. After about five months, when the Japanese decided to use Santo Tomas as a hospital, they selected some 800 unattached males from Santo Tomas and sent them to the Agricultural College of the

University of the Philippines, located near Los Baños. That was the birth of the Los Baños Internment Camp.

On 16 May 1943 Father McCarthy unfolded his cot on the floor of the basketball court of the gymnasium. His cot was separated from the next ones by eighteen inches. He lived in that confined space for months, until eventually the Japanese moved all prisoners from the gymnasium and cottages to newly constructed barracks. The crowded conditions still prevailed, however, in the barracks.

Among the other internees were: Les Yard, a Hollywood newspaperman, and, after the war, a member of the staff of the *Hollywood Reporter*. He regaled Father McCarthy and the others with stories of the fabulous studios of Hollywood. Clarence Cumming, both before and after the war, was in the business of exporting leather to the Far East. Paul Danner had been a representative of the Asia Life Insurance Company in New York. Ray Cronin was an Associated Press correspondent; he spent two years in Los Baños. Clyde DeWitt had been an outstanding lawyer in Manila. Darley Downes was a Presbyterian minister who had been in Japan before the war and who could speak Japanese fluently; when necessary he spoke with the guards and camp administrators. Alex Calhoun had been a Manila banker before the war. Bill Spencer had been with Pan American World Airways. And Mike O'Brien was an export brewer with San Miguel Brewery in Manila.

There were also many American business and professional people: a refrigeration engineer from the Merchant Marines, a merchandise broker and importer, an employee of Republic Steel Corporation, a minister and missionary for the American Bible Society, a merchant seaman, an employee of the Philippine Long Distance Telephone Company, a branch manager for General Motors Overseas Operations, a lubrication engineer for Associated Tidewater Oil Company, a tobacco buyer for Liggett and Myers Tobacco Company, a representative of the Export Department for Montgomery Ward and Company, and an employee of Union Oil Company.

Of the families that were at Los Baños the Whitakers were typical. Jock, the father, was a naturalized American of British birth. Before the Japanese invasion of the Philippines, he directed the field division of the Philippines Sugar Administration, and he and his family—his wife, Evelyn, and their two teenage daughters, Margaret and Betty—lived in Manila. They, too, had no place to hide nor any way to escape the island when war came.

Initially, the Whitakers were interned, along with thousands of other civilians swept up by the Japanese early in the war, within the 300-year-old walls of Santo Tomas University in Manila. The first week of December 1944 the Japanese commander of Santo Tomas ordered the Whitakers and about 150 other prisoners in Santo Tomas to move to Los Baños by train. All they could say of Los Baños was that it was at least more spacious than Santo Tomas.

The Nashes, also Americans, were gathered up by the Japanese shortly after their occupation of Manila. Ralph Nash was an engineer who by 1935 had lived in the Orient for ten years. While home on leave in 1936, he fell in love with Grace Chapman whom he had met on a train between Cleveland and Chicago. Nine months later, in September 1936, Grace Chapman boarded a ship to Manila to become the bride of Ralph Nash. After their marriage, they lived in the Pasay section of Manila, about five miles from the U.S. Army Air Corps' Nichols Field. Their first son was born in October 1936, and their second thirteen months later. The Nashes lived a comfortable life in Manila with a chauffeur, an amah for the boys, cooks, and housegirls. Grace was an accomplished concert violinist who played with the Manila Symphony and who also performed as a soloist. She was the only American and the only woman in the orchestra. She also belonged to a chamber music group that met each week and presented a series of radio programs. In addition, she taught music classes at the American school, directed the all-city junior orchestra, and was the music critic for the *Manila Daily Bulletin*. Her husband worked long, hard hours at his job; she was obviously equally energetic.

In the days leading up to the outbreak of war, the Nashes were ambivalent about whether Grace and the boys should return to the States. Ralph would not leave his company, which he had singlehandedly rescued, and Grace would not go without him. So they continued their pleasant life in the Philippines:

Ralph dedicated to his work and Grace filling her days with classes, concerts, and writing.

The good mood and high confidence that was evident in Manila just before the war was highlighted by a conversation Grace Nash had with a U.S. Navy officer at the Palm Garden of the Manila Hotel after a Friday night concert. It was 5 December 1941, a U.S. Navy captain had joined them at their table. The night was quite clear, and someone in the group remarked somewhat darkly that it would be a great night for a surprise bombing. The captain said, with what everyone present thought was consummate authority, that the U.S. Navy could sink the Japanese navy over the weekend. Thus reassured, the group relaxed and enjoyed the drinks; it would prove to be the last Friday night for more than three years they would be free to do so.

With the Japanese occupation the Nashes fell under the authority of the occupying troops and, with thousands of other Americans, spent time—sometimes separate, sometimes together—in Santo Tomas and Assumption Convent (where both of the Nash boys were deathly ill); in April 1944 they were transferred to Los Baños. By then there were five Nashes: Roy was born in June 1943.

Benjamin Franklin Edwards, who was later to prove his bravery both before and during the rescue operation, came to the Philippines as a mechanic for Pan American World Airways on 8 October 1941, shortly before his 23rd birthday. At the outbreak of the war, he was working at the Pan Am base situated on the coast of Manila Bay between Sangley Point and Cavite Naval Base, on a peninsula that jutted into. Manila Bay about ten miles from Manila. He did not know that the war had started until 0700, Monday, 8 December, which was 1300, Sunday, 7 December 1941, Honolulu time. When he heard the news, he immediately went to the Pan Am terminal, where the Pan Am guard at the gate verified that the Japanese had indeed attacked Pearl Harbor. Ben Edwards was not particularly surprised because he had recognized the deterioration of the situation in the short time he had been in the Philippines. In November 1941, for example, he had seen a number of Japanese ships dock in Manila and take on hundreds of Japanese civilians. He had noted also the number of American families who were leaving or planning to leave Manila. But with the general optimism that prevailed in the Philippines at the time, he felt that the war would be over in a few months—at the outside.

His optimism was shattered in just two days. Pan Am had a communications network throughout the Philippines for collecting weather reports. Shortly after the declaration of war, Pan Am set up a watch schedule at the Cavite terminal to relay incoming teletype messages to the U.S. Navy installation at Sangley Point. Ben Edwards was on the 10 December watch and received and telephoned the following message to a U.S. Navy commander at Sangley Point: "Fifty-six twin-engine enemy bombers over San Fernando [to the north of Manila] heading toward Manila with another wave following." The message came in at 1219. When he received the message, the commander at Sangley Point said half to himself and half to Ben, "I wonder if they're going to hit *us* this time?"

His musing was prescient. In thirty minutes the Japanese bombers hit the Cavite Naval Base and Sangley Point, heavily damaging both installations and killing about 2,200 people in a half-hour raid. Over 2,000 of the fatalities were Filipino and about 100 were American. Most of the dead were at the Cavite Naval Base. The Pan Am base was not hit; still Ben was not altogether happy sitting out the raid in a circle of sandbags at the Pan Am installation.

After the raid, the Pan Am bosses decided that their personnel should go to Manila because the Philippine government had ordered the evacuation of the town of Cavite. Ben and several of his friends found rooms at the Manila YMCA. The next day, when he tried to enlist in the Army, he was told that the Army had no need for aircraft mechanics. He spent the next several nights (the Japanese planes were all over Manila in the daylight) loading barges with food and medical supplies for Corregidor.

On Christmas Eve 1941 he and several other Pan Am employees went back to their base near Cavite to destroy it. They set up candles on the floor of the various shops and administrative buildings near drums of Avgas. Then they lighted the candles, backed off to the doorway, and fired rifles at the drums of gasoline. Their crude, but eminently successful demolition system effectively destroyed all of their shops and the equipment in them.

Ben and his arsonist friends then went back to the Manila Hotel for the last Christmas party that famous hotel would host for the next four years. During the evening, Ben met a lovely Spanish girl who was staying in a suite in the hotel with her mother and sister. A day or so later the mother of the girls asked Ben to stay in the suite with the girls because she had to go home to look after other children. Naturally he agreed. The family, as he soon discovered, was politically powerful; and the suite belonged to an aide to President Quezon, Manuel Nieto, who had let the family use the suite in his absence. It was well stocked with liquor, clothes, and food. Ben, who had left the Pan Am base with little or no belongings or clothes, found, much to his delight, that Nieto's clothes fit him perfectly.

On 31 December 1941 the U.S. High Commissioner asked Ben and his friend Bill Rivers to assist the local Filipino police in controlling the Filipino civilians who were looting business establishments, government warehouses, and other sources of goods, food, liquor, and jewelry. The police deputized Ben and Bill and gave them police badges. That night the two deputies worked with the police and persuaded many of the civilians in their assigned area to go home, using the logical and sensible argument that the looters might very well be shot when the Japanese arrived and found them milling about the streets. After their work with the police, Edwards and Rivers went back to the hotel to await the arrival of the Japanese army. And arrive it did, on New Year's Day; and many of its conquering soldiers rode in on bicycles.

Three days after the arrival of the Japanese, the Philippine Secretary of the Interior came to Nieto's suite and escorted the Spanish girls to the home of their mother.[2] Shortly thereafter, the Japanese decided that they wanted the Nieto suite for themselves, because, among other reasons, it contained a rare com-

---

2. During the liberation of Manila, the Japanese killed the mother and her two daughters; a Japanese soldier slashed a son with a samurai sword and left him for dead, but he survived.

fort: air-conditioning. However, since Ben had been occupying the suite, the Japanese assumed he was an important person and so assigned him another, in the non-air-conditioned side of the hotel. Finally, on 6 January the Japanese ordered him to Manila's Santo Tomas University for "registration" and told him to take three days' supply of food. Those three days of registration stretched into three years of incarceration.

In February (1942) Rivers and Edwards decided that they would be better off in either Corregidor or Bataan than at Santo Tomas. Before daylight one morning they went over the wall. They had walked only a few blocks when a Japanese sentry stopped them. They were able to convince the sentry that they were Spanish and eventually made their way to the home of their Spanish friends, where they explained their desire to get to Bataan or Corregidor. One of the houseboys made a reconnaissance for a boat to take the escapees to Corregidor but discovered instead that the trip was impossible. Edwards and Rivers returned to Santo Tomas, climbed with great difficulty over the twelve-foot wall, and made the evening roll call with only minutes to spare.

A couple of days after Rivers' and Edwards' return, the Japanese apprehended three British subjects on the outskirts of Manila after they had escaped from Santo Tomas. They were hauled back to the camp, beaten severely, then shot.

Edwards and Rivers "languished" in Santo Tomas until 14 May 1943, when they went along with the 800 "able-bodied young men" and 12 U.S. Navy nurses captured on Corregidor who were shipped to Los Baños. It would prove to be their home for the next twenty-one months.

The twelve Navy nurses were the only military prisoners on the roster of the Los Baños internees. Mary Harrington Nelson was one of the nurses—and one of only eighty-one American military women to be held captive as POWs during World War II. At Los Baños she and other nurses set up a makeshift hospital in the old college infirmary, where they found a few medicines and drugs. They assisted the captured doctors in surgery, childbirth, general medicine, and other medical tasks. They formed a library with books they found in the old college buildings and with books some of the internees had managed to bring to the camp. Along with interned university faculty members, they helped teach some college courses. Before long they, too, were victims of the skimpy rations. Mary Harrington remembers that the hungrier you got the more you smoked, and "dried eggplant leaves stretched tobacco nicely."

Eventually, the Los Baños Internment Camp was crowded with the second largest concentration of Allied internees in the Philippines: men, women, and children ranging in age at the time of their liberation from three days (a baby girl was born on 20 February) to seventy years. They represented ten nationalities. The bulk of them (1,575) were Americans, but there were also 320 British, 89 Netherlanders, 56 Canadians, 33 Australians, 22 Poles, 10 Norwegians, 15 Italians (the Japanese may not have known who was fighting whom on the other side of the world), 1 Nicaraguan, and 1 Frenchman—Jules Dreyfus. (See Appendix B for a complete list of the internees.)

All of them will remember 23 February 1945; that date will tug at their hearts, put a smile on their lips, and cause a quickening of their pulses.

CHAPTER II: Life in Los Baños

The Agricultural College of the University of the Philippines at Los Baños was, as the itik flies, some forty miles to the southeast of Manila in a lush lowland area, highly suitable for the basic mission of the college: studying and improving the growing and farming techniques for fruits and vegetables of many varieties. In pre–World War II days the college area was surrounded by hundreds of cultivated plots and experimental gardens. To the west, in the foothills of Mount Maquiling, were located the houses and cottages of the faculty; they were referred to as Faculty Hill.

The College of Veterinary Science was near the Agricultural College; a Forestry School was situated in the foothills of Mount Maquiling. The Agricultural College covered a sixty-acre area and consisted originally of some fifteen concrete school buildings, five large two-story dormitories (all of which were heavily damaged by Japanese bombs prior to the capitulation of the Philippines), some thirty or so small cottages for the faculty, and a sugar mill. The first internees to arrive lived in several of the existing buildings. Some of the 800 men who arrived in early May 1943 set up their living quarters in the gymnasium (Baker Hall), the YMCA, and a few of the cottages around the campus.

At the beginning of their confinement, the internees were permitted to use the football and baseball fields and the track. As was their wont, the Japanese followed what seemed to be their formula for the treatment of internees (but not for prisoners of war): good war, good treatment.

Early in the war, to emphasize to internees its policy toward them, the Japanese government sent a career diplomat, Mr. Kodaki, on a tour of the various internee camps in the Philippines. His message to each assembled group of internees was the same: "As long as we're victorious, we can afford to be and will be magnanimous." In his speeches Mr. Kodaki made no provision for the unlikely prospect that the Japanese might find their huge empire being rolled back to its core: Japan. Nor did he spell out how his government would treat the internees in such an eventuality.

Sometime in 1944 General Ko, the Japanese military commander of all the internee camps in the Philippines, sent Japanese civilian contractors to Los Baños to construct a barracks area in the open fields of the Agricultural College campus. The contractors built the barracks in military camp fashion with dirt roads between rows of aligned barracks.

The thirty or so buildings were poorly constructed (several collapsed even before they were occupied) of wood frames with nipa roofs and sawali sidings. Nipa is a plant with fronds similar to those of the coconut tree and was commonly used by Filipinos as roofing material. (As was to prove very useful later, nipa roofs are highly flammable when dried out.) Sawali is bamboo split thinly then woven to form mats, walls, and sidings. The floors of some of the barracks were dirt, others were concrete, and still others were raised bamboo. The barracks were about 40 feet wide and 150 feet long and housed about 75 to 100 prisoners. Some barracks, but not all, were subdivided variously into fifteen or sixteen cubicles partitioned by sawali screens. Each such room had six bunks and each prisoner a space of 3 by 3 by 7 feet.

Families set up their own areas within their assigned barracks as best they could. Some of them had brought mattresses and mosquito nets—hardly a luxury item in this mosquito and malaria-infested area of Luzon. Others, more fortunate or perhaps more perspicacious, had managed to bring to Los Baños such items as cooking stoves, extra clothes, musical instruments, books, toys for children, and canned foods. Primitive washing facilities and latrines were in separate huts between each barracks.

After the completion of the barracks area, the Japanese gradually increased the population of the camp until it reached a maximum of 2,144 inmates. (The figure, of course, varied from day to day because of a few births and the deaths of internees, which increased toward the end of the internment.) Life in the camp varied from week to week, depending for the most part on the fortunes of the Japanese military forces and the moods and personalities of the camp commanders and their staff. Initially, for example, the Japanese permitted the internees to have gardens, but later the gardens ceased to exist because the camp commandant whittled away the garden space for other uses and because the camp supply officer refused to allow the internees to collect their crops.

As the months wore on, food and survival became the all-encompassing, totally consuming preoccupation of the internees. In the early days of the camp, the internees ate three meals a day, but in the final few months they were down to two meals—generally one at 0700, the other at 1700. At meal times the internees formed four long lines at the ringing of a gong. Each internee had a meal ticket, which a Japanese guard punched to prevent internees from rejoining the line for a second helping. For breakfast there was rice and coffee; in the evening there was a ladle of rice and a ladle of stew, with the meat, rarely available, well concealed in talinum greens. (Talinum was known among the internees as New England spinach; when cooked, it tasted slimy and metallic.) Finally, the internees were trying to survive on only unhusked rice, and that in totally inadequate quantities.

Father McCarthy remembers:

> Our meals became progressively worse . . . during our last month of imprisonment. The struggle for survival forced us to eat weeds, flowers, vines, salamanders, the pulpy insides of banana trees, and juicy black bugs, called slugs or grubs, found in

the damp soil. Deaths mounted to two a day in January 1945. At the time of our rescue, the camp doctor told me that most of the prisoners would have died of starvation within another month.

The Japanese chicken yard, located in a fenced-in area within the Japanese barracks, was fair game for the enterprising internees who would take great personal risks to obtain food for themselves and their families and sick friends. The Japanese had apparently failed to notice that even when they clipped both wings of a Filipino chicken, it could still fly, at least over the fence. Once the chicken was over the fence, an alert internee would grab it, wring its neck, and run back to his barracks area, ever alert for Japanese guards. There were few chickens, however; eventually dogs and cats made their way into the cooking pots. Some prisoners even went so far as to kill, skin, cook, and eat rats.

One of the most well known internees was Gypsy, a big, raw-boned man with a scraggly beard who had been a jack-of-all-trades in Manila before the war. His sense of humor and lively personality helped keep up the spirits of those who knew him. He had been a bartender, taxi driver, roustabout, and, just before his capture, a merchant seaman. Before most meals Gypsy asked the cook (one of the internees) what was on the menu. The cook usually replied, "Cat and dog stew." The prisoners thought that the cook was only joking. One day, however, near the end of their captivity, when the food supplies were dwindling to the vanishing point, the cook answered Gypsy's usual query with one word: Brownie. The prisoners within earshot blanched. Brownie was a large shepherd dog, a favorite of all the prisoners, the beloved pet of the Currans. Mr. Curran had been a professor of forestry at the university before the war, was interned in his own house on the campus, and remained there throughout the war. In spite of their emaciated condition, the prisoners lost their appetites that day. Gypsy never again asked the cook what he was about to serve.

By December 1944, when Jock Whitaker and his family arrived at Los Baños from Santo Tomas, the rice ration doled out to the prisoners was insufficient to maintain life. As the weeks

Internment Camp Number 2
Los Baños, Luzon

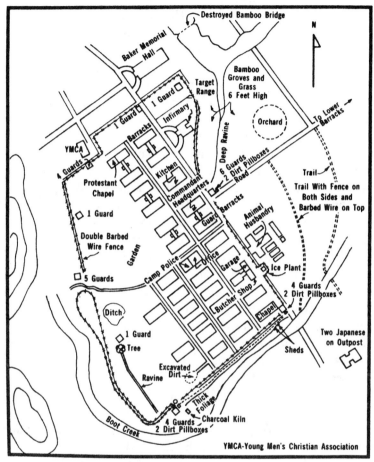

Sources: *Combat Notes Number 7*, Assistant Chief of Staff, G3, Headquarters, Sixth Army, May 1945, p 37; and *After Action Report, Mike I Operation*, US Army, Headquarters, XIV Corps, 29 July 1945, p 163. The latter reference has a slightly different version of the map with arrows and approximate yardages to Los Baños and the drop zones. It also notes in the map legend, "Compiled from guerrillas, escaped internees and civilians."

dragged on, Margaret and Betty, the Whitakers' teenage daughters, became more and more concerned for the lives of their parents, who were growing weaker by the day. "Our rice supply will run out on Monday, February 19th," Margaret recorded in her diary. "Then we'll really begin to starve. We're starving now, but it's kind of a chronic ailment."

During the periodic inspections by the Japanese guards, Margaret carefully concealed her forbidden diary. Another entry said, "I weigh 83 pounds, which could be worse. Another man died this AM. Two yesterday." Her last diary entry was dated 19 February. "The grave diggers are working overtime," she wrote. "The Army must come soon."

Within a small, confined area housing some 2,000 frustrated people, people not accustomed to discipline in the military sense, not organized in any governable manner, not in the least happy with their circumstances, and not necessarily of a mind to share, there had to be some kind of governing body to control the daily chores and to prevent anarchy and chaos. And so at the beginning of their internment the internees established a committee to administer and govern the camp within the rules set up by the Japanese. The committee operated with Japanese consent, if not with their total support and cooperation.

The internees elected the committee, who, in turn, appointed monitors for each barracks to enforce its and the Japanese rules. The committee also set up an internee police force. The committee had a number of purposes: to deal almost daily with the Japanese camp commandant and his staff; to maintain law and order among the internees; to develop plans and schemes for their release; to establish, clandestinely, through Filipino guerrillas, some sort of liaison with the American forces and to barter for food as best they could with the Filipinos in the area.

Murray B. Heichert of General Motors Corporation was the last chairman of the Administrative Committee of the Civilian Internees, and George Gray was the secretary. Alex Calhoun, manager of the National City Bank of Manila, was the head of the prisoners' governing committee. (See Appendix C for the last committee report.) Each man played an important role in the eventual liberation of the camp.

One rather surprising but actually necessary action by the committee to control the internees was the establishment of a jail within the camp itself. Some of the prisoners thought that such a control device was ironic and absurd since they were already behind barbed wire. But the effervescent Gypsy, who apparently had had more experience in various civilian jails before the war than most of the businessmen who were his fellow inmates in Los Baños, explained that being separated from your friends, even in a jail within a jail, was punishment enough to make one toe the line and follow the committee's rules. In addition to maintaining discipline, the committee doled out food, organized and provided work crews, and bought goods and food on the black market from local Filipinos. As the fortunes of war worsened for the Japanese, however, the Japanese in control of the camp restricted outside sources of food to a trickle, then brought them to a full stop. The committee also tried to control rumors, unearth valid news of the outside world, and, just before the raid, control the undercover contact with the guerrillas outside the camp.

The ways in which the prisoners received news of the progress of the war were varied and sometimes ingeniously developed and interpreted from unlikely sources. For example, a Filipino who was friendly to the prisoners smuggled into the camp a handful of shiny, new American dimes, obviously obtained from someone in recent contact with the American forces. A returning escapee brought back fresh American cigarettes—not only a long-absent luxury but a sure sign that American forces were nearby.

Another source of information was the local Filipinos who came into the camp to deliver bananas and other food to the Japanese officers. Unfortunately, that news passed from person to person orally and by the time it got to the fifth person was hardly recognizable.

The devaluation of Japanese money was an indicator of the progress of the war. Father McCarthy remembers that when he first went to Los Baños, one could buy a water buffalo for $60 in Japanese pesos (printed by Japanese for Philippines), but after the Americans landed on Leyte, the price rose to $10,000. Thereafter, the Japanese peso was as worthless as, in the words of internees and Filipinos alike, "Mickey Mouse money."

Still another, and an unlikely, source of news was the Japanese newspaper, the Manila *Shinbun*—when it was available. The news contained in it required interpretation by an expert in Japanese misinformation. According to the *Shinbun*, the Japanese never lost a battle on land or sea, and the Americans never won one. When the Americans seized a Japanese-held island, for example, the *Shinbun* would report euphemistically that the Japanese had given up another island for which they had no further use. Father McCarthy said that "once the technique of reading such a paper was mastered, we could interpret the outcome of battles by the relative size and importance of a reported Japanese victory. For instance," he said, "they would report the sinking of an American ship without any Japanese losses and conclude with the remark, 'A squadron of planes dove into the enemy ships and has not yet returned to its base.'"

A few prisoners had radios, which they concealed from the guards with care and deviousness because radios were strictly forbidden. If the guards found a radio, the owner fully expected torture and death. With the concealed radios, though, the internees knew of the landings on Leyte and the invasion of Luzon, but they did not know the details of the fighting in and around Manila, actions which were of paramount importance to them. Mail, packages, Red Cross parcels, and the like were rarely delivered to the internees. In late 1943 the Japanese finally permitted one Red Cross package per internee, plus other supplies, to come into the camp.

The Japanese commanders of the camp were a varied lot. Prior to 1 June 1944 the commandant was Colonel Urabi, who, according to Edward J. Gray, a refrigeration engineer in the Merchant Marines, was not a bad sort and was "better" than his successor. Urabi "would try to get us food," said Gray, a condition that would not prevail under the regime of Major Iwanaka, who succeeded Urabi as the camp commandant on 1 June 1944. The culprit during Iwanaka's command was not Iwanaka himself, but his warrant officer, Sadaaki Konishi, Imperial Japanese Army, ISN 51J-104279, who arrived in August 1944. Konishi's arrival was a black day for the internees, but they were not to find that out until some time later.

Major Iwanaka was described by one of the internees as "an old, doddering imbecile, running around from morning to night in pajamas tending his garden, which was his busiest occupation. He was in his late fifties, neither speaking nor understanding English." Another internee said that Iwanaka "was a rather weak character who never seemed to want to make any definite decisions and was very much influenced and overridden by . . .

Konishi." With the advent of Iwanaka and Konishi, the internees' food rations decreased steadily.

Warrant Officer Konishi, twenty-nine years old at the time of the Los Baños operation, was from Fukuoka Prefecture in Japan. He arrived in the Philippines on 2 January 1942 with the 65th Infantry Brigade at Lingayen then marched with the brigade to Baguio. He apparently developed tuberculosis shortly after his arrival in the Philippines because he was confined for two months in the hospital at Baguio with that disease. Next he was ordered to the headquarters of General Ko in Manila. Then Konishi spent some five months in the hospital at Santo Tomas before he was sent to Los Baños in August 1944. Konishi was an intendance officer in the army, a member of a branch of service that is a combination of the U.S. Army's Finance and Quartermaster Corps. At Los Baños Konishi was with the finance section of the camp and in charge of finance and supply affairs: purchasing food, maintaining accounts for supplies and money, and distributing the food supply from the commissary to the internees' kitchens.

Konishi was universally despised by the internees. He was about 5'7" tall, with a scarred face and a generally "mean" look. The internees felt that he had "an intense hatred for the white race," that he was "very cunning," that he was a "sadistic individual," "ferocious," "the rascal of the camp," "an ignorant, brutal type of person." He "had a vast effect over the commandant and definitely influenced Iwanaka, not only within his own sphere, which was food and supply, but also in other matters of camp administration." An internee in Santo Tomas who knew Konishi there was emphatic, "He was the most hated man ever to enter Santo Tomas, a squat, sloppy, filthy-bodied little Jap."

Mrs. Francisca Esguerra Gianzon, who was a resident of one of the small villages near Los Baños and who had had dealings with Konishi while he was stationed at the Los Baños Camp, said that "Konishi was about 5'6" or 5'7" and had a fairly light complexion. He always exhibited the sarcastic Japanese smile when dealing with Filipino residents near the internment camp. His mannerisms were typically Japanese. He spoke very little English and did not understand or speak a word of Tagalog. He was always accompanied by an interpreter in his dealings with the Filipinos."

Konishi may also have been a drug addict and an alcoholic. But there is no question that he hated the Americans with a consuming passion. He vowed at one point that "they would be eating dirt before he was through with them." He said that they were getting too much to eat, and he told them repeatedly that food supplies were not available, that the ration should be reduced. Paraphrasing a remark supposedly made by Marie Antoinette, he said, "Let them starve."

Konishi was as good as his word. In September 1944 the rice ration had been 400 grams per day; by January 1945, under Konishi's orders, the ration was 150 grams of unhulled rice per day. He refused to permit Filipinos to bring additional food supplies into the camp. He denied the camp committee permission to barter with or buy food from the local civilians. He wiped out the camp garden in October 1944 and thus caused bushels of vegetables to rot on the ground. He barred the internees from feeding some pigs they had bartered for earlier, and the pigs died of starvation. On Thanksgiving Day 1944 Konishi turned back Filipinos with wagonloads of food at the camp gate. He offered, however, to sell a sack of sugar to an internee for 50,000 pesos. By January 1945 the internees were reduced to trading with the Japanese guards whatever remained of their jewelry, watches, fountain pens, and anything else of value for food of any kind. The internees believed, with some justification and evidence, that Iwanaka and Konishi were getting a cut of the bartered goods from the guards.

The irony of the situation was not lost on the internees. They knew that the Japanese guards had ample food, they knew that there were tons of food in the storage sheds, and they knew that the land around Los Baños was highly productive. After all, it had been an agricultural college. They could see "miles of coconut and banana trees." They knew that there were poultry and produce farms in the neighborhood. And until September 1944 the internees had run a canteen where large amounts of fruit and vegetables, bought through the Japanese, were sold. But Konishi, by raising the price of the food sold in the canteen, made the operation prohibitively expensive, and the internees were forced to close it down.

The Japanese used the food supply as a means of enforcing discipline. Paul Iddings, an internee, and a representative of General Motors in Manila before the war, said that "we had to bow to Japanese soldiers on guard. When any of the internees were guilty of any infraction of the rules, such as being out of bounds, or failing to bow, the Japs said nothing but took a portion of our rations from us. This was the big hold Konishi thought he had over us."

As the months from August 1944 to February 1945 dragged on the physical condition of the internees visibly deteriorated. Seventy percent of the internees suffered from beriberi, dysentery, and malnutrition. By Christmas 1943 deaths averaged one per day in the camp, and by February 1945 the death rate had doubled. Many of the internees had lost fifty pounds or more. Konishi was living up to his threats.

His sadism, brutality, and hatred of Americans is best exemplified by his treatment of George Louis. George Louis had been a Pan Am mechanic before the war. On the night of 27 January 1945, he made his way out of the camp to get food, and while trying to slip back into the camp about 0645 on the morning of the 28th he was detected by a guard who shot him through the shoulder. Shortly, a group of Japanese soldiers came out of their barracks and put Louis on a sawali door frame. A Catholic priest and the camp doctor requested permission to help Louis, but the Japanese denied the request. Then the soldiers carried Louis through the guardhouse on the southeast corner of the camp and put him on the ground beside it.

Paul Hennesen, a State Department employee and an internee, witnessed what happened next from the camp chapel, which was on a slight rise and near the southeast guard post. Hennesen went there after having seen the guards carry off Louis. About an hour after the Japanese had laid Louis on the ground beside the guardhouse, Hennesen saw Iwanaka and Konishi arrive at the spot where Louis was lying. Konishi called for some soldiers, and they hurried over to him. According to Hennesen, "Konishi called out again, took a white-handled gun out of his holster, and gave it to a soldier. The soldier went up to Louis and blew his brains out." The guards later turned the body over to the camp physician, Dr. Dana Nance, who reported in his autopsy that Louis was dead from "a bullet that entered his skull in the left occipital region and blew out his brains. . . ."

A number of internees, including George Gray, Bill Rivers, and Ben Edwards, had known that several internees were outside looking for food that night of 27 January. Apparently the Japanese also had been aware of the escape because they had doubled the guards and increased patrols that night. Ben Edwards, who lived in Barracks #12 on the southeast side of the camp, had assumed that some internees would try to reenter the camp in front of his barracks. Edwards, Gray, and Rivers had spent the night trying to communicate with those outside the fence to warn them that the Japanese were on the alert. They had talked loud enough to be heard by anyone outside the fence, and they had also sung songs using words of warning. Unfortunately, George Louis either had not heard them or had not correctly interpreted the warnings.

In spite of the general Japanese penchant for cruelty and sadism, they were not entirely without some compassion and human kindness. Lieutenant Kodi, one of the first Los Baños commanders, appeared in a Catholic chapel one Sunday morning while Father McCarthy was saying mass and stood at respectful attention throughout. Later Father McCarthy received a note ordering him to report to the commandant's office. He knew that such a trip was not usually for the purpose of engaging in small talk or to discuss the weather. Father McCarthy duly reported to Lieutenant Kodi's office.

"After a slight pause, Kodi threw out his chest in a military manner," Father McCarthy remembers, "and I knew that the purpose of the command visit would be explained. But his next question caught me off guard, and I had to ask the interpreter to repeat it. Again I heard the interpreter ask, 'Do you have enough mass supplies?' I told him that the priests were short of wine, that we had limited the amount used for each mass to an eyedropper full, but that the supply was very short. He made no reply, but after two pointless questions our meeting was concluded."

On the way back to his barracks, Father McCarthy tried to

figure out why Kodi had called him to his office. "Certainly he was not concerned about my welfare," reasoned Father McCarthy, "nor about the war, nor with the shortage of mass supplies. The only solution that appeared reasonable was that he would seize our limited supply of wine to prevent our daily mass. Still, he had not appeared angry or harsh. I decided to wait for his next move.

"I did not have to wait very long, for three days later one of the guards delivered six bottles of mass wine to the chapel. A note attached said that they were obtained from a Spanish monastery in Manila. I made a mental apology to the commandant and remembered him in the next mass I offered. I never saw Lieutenant Kodi again. He was transferred shortly afterwards, in keeping with the Japanese practice of rotating the officers and guards at our camp from time to time."

Another example of a break from the usual image of Japanese POW wardens was a guard who was able to speak enough English to carry on simple conversations with the internees. His greatest pleasure was to whip out a picture of his wife and three children and show them to the prisoners. He explained endlessly that he had been a school teacher in a small town in Japan and longed to return there to his family and his teaching.

Another Japanese guard was nicknamed "St. Louis" by the prisoners. St. Louis's knowledge of the United States was rather limited. Nonetheless, he delighted in explaining that after the Japanese had won the war he was going to that state (St. Louis), where he would "be one of the ten electoral votes from St. Louis pledged to cast their ballots for Tojo for President."

Father McCarthy recalled one other small act of charity. He noticed a guard leaving the mess hall with a plate of rice. The guard walked over to four prisoners who were pawing over refuse in a garbage pail, trying to pick out the shriveled eggplants. The guard hastily scraped his rice into a dirty handkerchief held by one of the men then walked quickly away. Unfortunately, though, the Japanese kindnesses, especially as the war ground down, were fewer and farther between.

In the early days of their confinement, the internees found that life was not entirely grim and humorless. On one occasion, in the days long before Konishi, some Red Cross packages did arrive at Los Baños after making their tortuous way through the labyrinth of Japanese obstacles, administrative and military. The internees opened the packages with great hopes, but it became readily obvious that the packages had been destined for somewhere other than the tropical climate of the Philippines. When the internees broke open the boxes, they found "long-sleeved underwear, long British-type shorts, and seersucker nightgowns." Nevertheless, after the first shock of opening the packages and discovering their contents had worn off, the internees made the best of the ludicrous situation.

They celebrated by organizing two softball teams, one dressed in long underwear, shirts, and ties; the other in long shorts, shirts, and ties. The girls of the camp dressed in seersucker nightgowns and led the cheers; the umpire wore top hat and tails. After several innings of serious softball, Edwards said, "I pitched a third strike overhand, and the umpire called the batter out even though it was an illegal pitch. From then on no one paid any attention to the rules, and the game was finally called with everyone laughing so hard we could no longer play. The crowd loved it, but the Japanese thought we were all crazy."

On another occasion one of the camp commandants decided that the internees would play softball against a team made up of Japanese office staff. The committee, concerned about the welfare of the internees, felt that the internees should play to lose; Ben Edwards, one of the players, disagreed and insisted that the team play to win. The players eventually won the argument and agreed to play the Japanese. Even though the game was played with a Japanese ball—the size of a baseball—the internees routed the Japanese through four innings. Thereupon, the Japanese commandant abruptly called the game. The Japanese never again mentioned that game nor suggested a rematch.

The internees did their best to amuse themselves and the children in the camp. During the time the internees had the use of the basketball court, baseball diamond, and other recreational facilities, they kept up a steady effort to organize sports and other entertainment. But toward the latter part of 1944, the Japanese restrictions on the use of the recreational facilities made it almost impossible for the internees to continue those activities on a large scale.

Because there were a number of school-age children in the camp and because there were some teachers and very interested parents, routine school classes for elementary and high school students continued on nearly a full-scale basis. Many of the internees who had managed to bring books with them from their Manila homes turned them over to the teachers who put them to good use in the schools. Thus, the children got a large part of their education from reading. Once freed, most of the children had no difficulty picking up in their proper grades in Stateside schools.

Hugh Hosking Williams was a retired British ship captain who had owned a small salvage vessel that he had operated in Manila Harbor before the war. During the initial Japanese attack on the Manila area, Williams's boat had been bombed and sunk, and he was subsequently interned by the Japanese. Eventually, he turned up in Los Baños.

Grace Chapman Nash related the story of "The Gallant Buccaneer of Los Baños" in a *Reader's Digest* "First Person Award" story. One morning as she was on her way to her daily work assignment, cleaning the latrines, her two boys walked with her, carrying their mops like rifles. The boys, five and six, pulled their two-month-old brother, Roy, in a crude wagon. Stan, the six-year-old, suddenly whispered to his mother, "Look at that man, Mommy—he looks just like a pirate."

Mrs. Nash turned and looked at what she describes as a "gaunt apparition: a bony, hollow-cheeked man of sixty-odd years whose seaman's uniform hung upon him in rags. Yet his bristling white mustache, spiked beard, and burning gray eyes gave him a look of ferocious dignity."

The stranger, overhearing the young boy's comment, said, "And a terrible pirate I once was, buckoes!"

From then on the old seaman raised the spirits of the boys with his tales of life on the high seas as a pirate. He would stand on the bridge of an imaginary ship and bark orders to the boys, "Boom, boom! Show 'em our colors, mates—run up the Jolly Roger! Give 'em another broadside! B-o-o-m!"

The boys loved the games with the buccaneer, and they looked happier than they had in months. As the tedious and monotonous days wore on and the rations were cut more and more, the skipper's stories became wilder and more entertaining. As the situation became more desperate, however, even the skipper could not sustain the morale of the boys.

Mrs. Nash wrote:

As the fall of 1944 approached, my breast milk was failing, and we were all developing the stiff, aching joints of beriberi. Death lurked close now. Roy, his head pathetically large for his shrunken little body, had scarcely enough energy left to cry. The boys, slumping against the barracks wall for support, talked weakly and endlessly about food.

By Christmas, I had all but given up hope. All real nourishment for Roy was gone. For once, not even the skipper could think of anything to say. I know now it was because he was making his big decision.

The next morning I was standing wearily in the water line, Roy in one arm and clay jug in the other, when the skipper walked up and handed me a newspaper-wrapped package. "For the wee one," he said casually. "I've been saving it for him."

It was a whole can of powdered milk, saved from the one Red Cross shipment that had got through to us more than a year earlier. It was enough to make a gallon of strength—two gallons the way we diluted it. "No, Skipper," I stammered. "You'll need it yourself."

"Never touch the stuff," he said gruffly. He looked at Roy for a long moment, then turned away. In tears I called after him, "How can I ever repay you?" Half-jokingly he called back, "Just play me 'Danny Boy' at your next concert."

On New Year's Day I made a last feeble effort at giving a recital. Skipper didn't show up to take the front-row camp chair I had reserved for him. Omitting encores, I rushed to the infirmary—too late. Hugh Williams was gone. The prison doctor said he had died from acute colitis. "An all-milk diet might have saved him," he added.

Adults organized language classes for each other. The Japanese tried to get into the act by setting up Japanese language classes, but discontinued them after the first attempt because no students showed up at the classroom.

In addition to the sports events, the internees also played poker, bridge, chess, and backgammon; those who had brought musical instruments were especially popular for camp entertainment.

There were, of course, isolated instances of fraternization between the internees, both male and female, and the Japanese guards for the purpose of better rations, better accommodations, and more privileges. However, for the most part, almost all of the internees distanced themselves rigidly from the Japanese.

The internees organized themselves into various work crews for the general welfare of the camp. Ben Edwards was in charge of a twenty-five man work crew that gathered wood for the cooking fires. The crew worked a five-hour day and got double rations for their efforts. There were also crews for the latrines, for policing the camp, for working the gardens when they were permitted, and for maintaining the barracks and the kitchen. Others worked in the schools, the hospital, and in camp administration.

Ben Edwards said:

"It is very difficult to say who worked hardest for the internees, but my vote would go to those serving on the camp committee. They had to keep the Japanese semihappy, yet protect, to the greatest extent possible, the internees. In many instances their efforts were less than appreciated by both sides. Another group that I developed a great deal of respect for was the Catholic priests. They were always available when extra hands were needed, and they were always cheerful. As I also had charge of moving firewood into the camp, which was accomplished by utilizing every able-bodied man in camp on a rotation basis (by barracks), it was very apparent that the priests would move at least twice the amount of wood as their counterparts in other walks of life. I also think George Gray did an outstanding job. Had it not been for him having the courage to go against the desires of the committee and make contact with the guerrillas, things could have been much different."

Toward the middle of February, the internees saw the Japanese working on a project that caused them the greatest anguish. The Japanese were digging a huge hole near the southwest guard post. The internees' fears in this case were unfounded; the hole was an excavation for a new barracks. But the rumor spread speedily through the camp that the Japanese were planning to massacre all of them, throw them into the ditch, and abandon the camp. Even the guerrilla headquarters in southern Luzon had that word. A message sent on 21 February to Major Vanderpool, the American coordinating the guerrillas, said that the guerrilla "Red Lion Division" had "received reliable information that the Japs have Los Baños scheduled for massacre."

As 1945 began, the days were beginning to grind down for the prisoners; they began to sense that something was up, but they did not know when or where or what. The nuns prayed, the priests celebrated masses, the camp committee conspired, and the bulk of the internees struggled on, hoping for good news, more food, and eventual deliverance.

On 9 January 1945 the Sixth U.S. Army waded ashore in Lingayen Gulf; on 31 January the glider elements of the 11th Airborne Division landed amphibiously at Nasugbu in southern Luzon; on 3 and 4 February the parachute elements of the 11th Airborne Division, the 511th Parachute Infantry Regimental Combat Team, jumped onto Tagaytay Ridge ahead of the amphibious elements and astride the main southern route to Manila.

The paths of two main elements in the Los Baños operation, the internees and their rescuers, were still far apart; but, unknown to both of them, their destinies were beginning to converge.

CHAPTER III: The 11th Airborne Attack on Manila and the Genko Line

T he 11th Airborne Division, the eventual liberators of Los Baños, was one of five airborne divisions born, bred, and bled during World War II. The 82d and the 101st came first; they had been standard infantry divisions that went "airborne" on 15 August 1942, then on to much-deserved fame and glory on European battlefields. Then came the 11th Airborne, activated from scratch in February 1943. These three were followed by the 13th, which, although alerted a number of times for combat jumps in Europe, never did see combat as a division, and the 17th, which fought extensively as a ground unit during the Battle of the Bulge and, with the British 6th Division, made the jump across the Rhine on 24 March 1945.

The 11th was the only airborne division to fight in the Pacific theatre. (The 503d Airborne Regimental Combat Team was, however, also in the Pacific.) The division trained at Camp Mackall, North Carolina, from its activation until January 1944, when it headed for Camp Polk, Louisiana, for postgraduate training and final readiness exams in the infamous Calcasieu Swamps through which it maneuvered and waded, and upon which it heaped raucous and well-deserved calumnies. The War Department finally declared the division fit to fight and totally prepared to try its skills against the real enemy—Japan—and ordered it on its way. After fighting the Calcasieu Swamps of Louisiana, the division felt that fighting Japanese would be a "piece of cake."

The division sailed from Camp Stoneman, up the Bay from San Francisco, out under the Golden Gate Bridge on 2 May 1944, and headed across the vast Pacific for a point unknown. The troopers in the division whiled away the boring hours on the transports with endless talk of their eventual destination. Some lesser gung-ho types opted for Australia; the fighter types, or perhaps the realists, hoped for China, India, or Burma. Finally came the word: New Guinea.

In late May, twenty-seven days after leaving Stoneman, the transport ships carrying the division docked briefly at Milne Bay to take on water but not, unfortunately, to discharge the thoroughly bored and restless troops. The transports weighed anchor and sailed again for Oro Bay, up the coast of New Guinea, where they finally docked. The troops unloaded over the sides via rope-net ladders into a fleet of DUKWs, amphibious taxis, that carried them inland some forty miles to Dobodura, an abandoned U.S. Army Air Corps airfield. There they unloaded, and the steaming, heavy, humid air of New Guinea bore down like a hot, wet, heavy blanket, engulfing and enervating them.

The division troopers built a pyramidal tent city they were to call home for the next six months. Dobodura took the Los Baños raiders one step closer to their rendezvous with a throng of internees, many of whom were at that very time being rounded up in Manila by the Japanese Military Police and herded onto trains for their trip to Los Baños.

In New Guinea the division acclimatized itself to the heat and the jungle—valuable assets for later combat—and trained, trained, trained. Glider-riders became paratroopers and paratroopers learned that riding a rickety, vibrating oversize kite of sticks and canvas is a far less preferable way to get into combat than by flying in a C-47 and jumping out over a drop zone. As they said, they would rather fight to jump and jump to fight than get "roped into it."

The troops rapidly became accustomed to the heat and humidity; practiced surviving on Australian bully beef, dehydrated potatoes and eggs, and tropical butter, which had the consistency of axle grease and a melting point far higher than a human's digestive tract; learned to march and maneuver through the jungles and kunai grass, an accomplishment that would stand them in good stead in the jungled mountains of Leyte; and turned yellow from the Atabrine that held the ever-present malaria in check. Finally, trained to a fine edge, the division sailed for Leyte and combat on 18 November 1944.

Basically the airborne divisions of World War II started out with the same organization—one-third paratroopers and two-thirds glider-riders. With the exigencies of combat and the varying tactical situations into which they were about to be thrust, however, the division organizations frequently changed to meet the situation. One division might have an extra parachute regiment attached, another an extra battalion of artillery. The 11th, however, stuck rather closely to the original scheme, although in the New Guinea and Philippine jump schools many gliderists became paratroopers. Essentially, the division was very light in men and equipment. Its strength totaled only 8,321 officers and men, roughly just over half the size of a conventional infantry division, a fact that would necessitate the 11th's fighting without a reserve when it got to the heavy combat on Leyte and Luzon.

In essence, the division had three regiments of infantry: one was parachute-qualified with three line battalions; the other two were glider-borne and organized with only two line battalions. Thus, the division at full strength had only seven very light and slender infantry battalions. The rest of the division was organized to support the basic paratrooper/glider-rider concept: one parachute and two glider elements. The artillery had one parachute artillery battalion equipped with three four-howitzer pack-75 mm firing batteries and two glider-borne battalions, each with two firing batteries of six pack–75s each. Additionally, there were the usual support elements: an engineer battalion with very light parachutable and gliderable equipment; an antiaircraft, antitank battalion; a quartermaster company; a signal company; an ordnance company; a medical company; a military police platoon; and, finally, in the heat of combat, a recon platoon, which would play such a vital part at Los Baños. Even though the 11th's task force, which eventually made the raid on Los Baños, was rel-

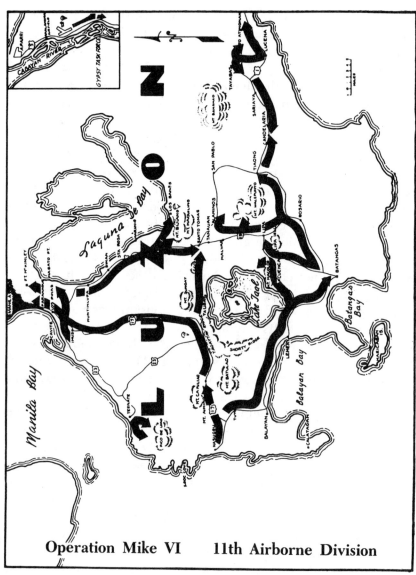

Operation Mike VI   11th Airborne Division

atively small, many elements from the units mentioned above participated.

By the time the division debarked on Leyte's Bito Beach, it had acquired its nickname: The Angels. Its origin is somewhat obscure at this point, but it is clear that it did not derive, as even some men in the division commonly believe, from the drop of the paratroopers at Los Baños. (One nun is reported to have said that the paratroopers looked like "angels come to free us.") The true version holds that the pseudonym stems from the division's work details that were sent to unload ships on the docks in New Guinea. All units there had to take their turn at stevedore work; the 11th was no exception. Airborne troopers were perhaps a bit more lively and light-fingered than most troops and made off with far more plunder from the unloading docks than the regular units. Therefore, an irate port commander took to task the 11th Airborne Division commander, Gen. Joe Swing, for the pilfering proclivity of his troops. One senior commander, aware of the 11th's unequal distribution of ships' cargoes (the bulk to the 11th) even referred to the division as "Swing and his 8,000 Thieves." General Swing is reputed to have said, with tongue in cheek (and probably apocryphally) that his troops couldn't possibly have stolen anything because they were such a "bunch of angels." Hence the nickname.

On Leyte the division developed an innovative style of solving combat problems that it would put to good use in planning for and in executing the Los Baños raid. For example, the division's 511th Parachute Infantry Regiment was committed to combat three days after it unloaded on Bito Beach. The regiment fought its way across the muddy mountains of Leyte (the monsoon rainy season was at hand) against stiff Japanese dug-in resistance. Nonetheless, the regiment rapidly ran out of the range of artillery support.

The 11th's commander came up with a solution: drop a battery of pack-75s into a clearing near the regiment. The problem was that the battery needed twelve C-47s; not nearly that many C-47s could be found on Leyte. The answer was to find one and have it make twelve trips. The parachute artillery battalion commander did just that. Lt. Col. Nicholas G. Stadtherr found an Air-Sea Rescue C-47 on the San Pablo Strip and persuaded the cooperative pilot to work for him between rescue missions. And so it came to pass. The C-47 was fitted with six pararacks under its fuselage to hold a pack-75 artillery howitzer broken down into its six basic loads. The battalion commander ordered the division parachute maintenance officer to send him the necessary personnel and equipment chutes for one battery. Then he alerted the 457th Parachute Field Artillery Battalion's A Battery to move to San Pablo Strip ready to jump into the mountains with their howitzers.

Finally, on 4 December 1944 the battalion commander and one gun crew took off from San Pablo for a forty-minute flight to a drop zone some 150 feet wide and 500 feet long surrounded on three sides by cliffs and mountains. Undaunted, Stadtherr dropped them onto the drop zone from 500 feet, a very low altitude, but one which prevented scattering paratroopers and equipment. Because the field was so short, Colonel Stadtherr restricted each jump to five men on a pass and made four or five passes per trip. In all, he made thirteen trips and personally jumpmastered each one. Thus, unspectacularly and on the most modest of scales, the 11th Airborne made its first combat jump. More important, thereafter, A Battery of the 457th was able to provide 360-degree artillery support for all of the division's infantry fighting in the Leyte Hills.

The division continued to fight its way west through the rain-soaked mountains of central Leyte along slippery jungle trails and against cleverly camouflaged and heavily dug-in enemy positions. Because the trails were so narrow, slippery, and steep—even the carabao, or water buffalo, refused to haul supplies along them—the division commander resorted to what was to become a standard improvisation. He pressed into service as jump aircraft the fleet of eleven artillery spotter planes (Cubs or L-4s)[1] to drop men and supplies to the troops in the hills.

Manarawat, the site of the artillery drop zone, became the hub of the division's support. Medics, engineers, surgeons, signal troops, and their equipment were all ferried to the area and dropped on the small drop zone. The medics, imaginative and persevering, set up a primitive hospital, complete with an operating room in a nipa hut at Manarawat. The hospital was good enough to permit Dr. Nester, a surgeon with the 11th, to perform brain surgery on a wounded company commander.

---

1. A Cub was a very light, two-passenger aircraft with two seats—pilot in front, passenger in rear. The gas tank was in front of the pilot beyond the windshield. The gas gauge, primitive but effective, was a wire on a cork float that slid down into the tank through the tank cap as the gas supply dwindled. When the cork hit bottom and no more wire was visible, the pilot knew he was in a glide mode.

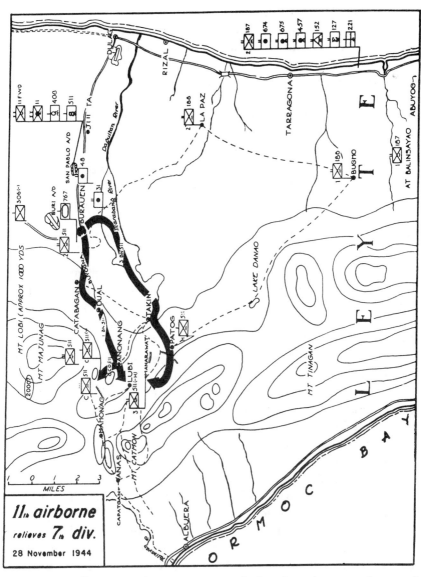

Eventually, enough engineers with hand tools were dropped into the drop zone to extend the clearing far enough for a Cub to land. Thereafter, a Cub with a piece of plywood lying flat over the back seat and just touching the back of the pilot's neck, could ferry out the seriously wounded men who could not make it back down the trails under their own power.

During the battle for Leyte, the division commander, General Swing, continued to prove himself a master of impromptu and unusual solutions, a talent that would help later on to insure the success of the Los Baños operation. By early December 1944 the division had established a command post at Leyte's San Pablo airfield, at the foothills of the central mountain range. The airfield was lightly defended with the division's AA-AT Battalion (.50-caliber machine guns on antiaircraft mounts), some support units, and clerks from division headquarters. At dusk on 6 December 1944, the Japanese struck San Pablo in a most unusual and unexpected fashion. They dropped about 275 paratroopers of the Katori Shimpei Force on the field in an effort apparently aimed at blocking the flow of supplies and men that daily flew out of that field in the Cub aircraft to support the troops fighting in the hills.

General Swing's solution to this most surprising development was to use everything and every man near his headquarters, no matter his basic function, to wipe out the paratroopers. He ordered the 674th Glider Field Artillery Battalion from Bito Beach to San Pablo without its pack-75s; he mobilized the engineer battalion as leg infantry; and he personally led those two noninfantry battalions across the airfield in a sweeping ground attack reminiscent of Civil War maneuvers. The assault cleared the airfield and permitted General Swing to reorganize his base of operations at San Pablo and to resume flying supplies to his troops in the mountains.

After much heavy fighting in the central mountains, the division emerged, blooded but successful, on the west coast of Leyte in mid-January 1945. Shortly thereafter the division was pulled back to Bito Beach for a short break. By 22 January 1945, however, the division was attached to General Eichelberger's relatively new Eighth Army and was ordered to prepare for a landing on southern Luzon with a D-day of 31 January 1945. This was yet another step closer to the division's rendezvous with the Los Baños internees.

Shortly after the 11th landed amphibiously at Nasugbu in southern Luzon and by parachute on Tagaytay Ridge forty miles or so farther inland, General MacArthur's Headquarters alerted

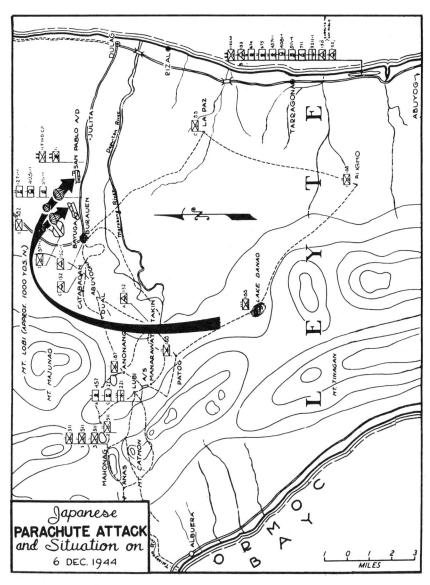

Japanese
PARACHUTE ATTACK
and Situation on
6 DEC. 1944

General Eichelberger, commanding general of Eighth Army who had come ashore with the 11th, to the pressing need to rescue POWs and interned civilians in the various camps throughout the Eighth's area of operations. GHQ/SWPA gave Eighth Army no set timetable for the rescue operations because of the obvious need to defeat the main enemy forces first. Combat operations necessarily had first priority. The freedom of the prisoners, civilian and military, had a very close second priority in General MacArthur's strategy.

On or about 3 February General Eichelberger passed the Los Baños part of the mission to General Swing and the 11th; Los Baños was in their zone of operations, and at the time the 11th was the major element of the rather threadbare Eighth Army. Before General Swing could even begin to think about Los Baños, however, he and the 11th had a formidable amount of hard fighting ahead of them.

The 11th Airborne Division was an unusual unit in an unconventional theatre in an unconventional atmosphere commanded by an unconventional commanding general. It was the only airborne division in the Pacific theatre, and, because it was "airborne," it had only just over half of the men and firepower of the conventional infantry divisions fighting in that theatre. With Napoleonic mimicry, it equalized its small size and light equipment by its self-imposed, imagined and real, superior fighting quality. Nonetheless, because it was a division, commanded by a major general just as were the standard infantry and mechanized divisions, the senior commanders under whom it fought (MacArthur, Eichelberger, Griswold) thought of it as a division and gave it full-size division missions. Thus, the 11th, in all of its months of fighting on Leyte and Luzon, never enjoyed the extravagance afforded to the other divisions in combat—units in reserve. The conventional triangular fighting concept of "two up and one back" was a luxury the 11th simply could not afford. The division was indeed unconventional.

The Pacific was an unconventional theatre—if there really is such a thing—as compared to the European theatre, for example. The Pacific theatre's area was vast, mostly ocean, and its islands were thousands of miles apart. If one superimposed a map of the United States on the Pacific, San Francisco would be near Leyte in the Philippines and New York would be near Kwajalein. The war in the Pacific featured an island-hopping campaign punctuated with what will probably be the last of the great naval battles, pitting our battleships and cruisers against similar dreadnoughts of the enemy. There were, of course, aircraft carriers on both sides that gave distance to the blue water navy's reconnaissance, long-range firepower from its aircraft, and wide-ranging airborne protection from enemy planes.

The ground war in the Pacific also was unconventional, first of all, because of the terrain and climate. The Pacific war was highlighted by amphibious landings that were so numerous they became routine; by the Marines' bloody, frontal assaults against firmly entrenched enemy positions supported by vast firepower; by infantry attacks that pushed, step by slogging step, through steaming jungles and over slippery rain-soaked mountains; by vast transport armadas of ships carrying thousands of troops to yet another island for yet another fight; and by MacArthur's brilliant, successful, man-saving strategy of "benign neglect," that is, bypassing Japanese-held islands to let them wither and die, using the U.S. Navy to cut off their waterborne, logistical support.

There were no great tank battles such as there were on the plains of Europe because the terrain rarely opened enough for one and because the enemy had few tanks deployed. There were no airborne attacks of the size of the invasion of Normandy (3 airborne divisions), the airborne attack on Nijmegen and Arnhem ($3\frac{1}{2}$ airborne divisions), or the crossing of the Rhine (2 airborne divisions). The biggest parachute operations in the Pacific were the regimental-size drops of the 503d Regimental Combat Team at Nadzab and Noemfoor, New Guinea, the 503d attack on Corregidor, and the 11th Airborne's 511th Regimental Combat Team parachute landing on Tagaytay Ridge, Luzon.

The unconventional atmosphere of the war in the Pacific derived from the enemy's tactics, from his fanaticism and his willingness to self-destruct for his Emperor, his country, and his religion. In Europe, for example, there were generally front lines behind which most support units were relatively safe from attack (except in such cases as the German 1944 Battle of the Bulge offensive). For the most part the front lines in Europe were relatively linear and fairly solid. As the Allies moved forward, they overran enemy positions and killed, captured, or drove back the defenders. In the Pacific theatre, however, there were no such conventional front lines. The area between the U.S. infantry and the supporting artillery was a no-man's-land, and the artillery and troops farther to the so-called rear had to protect themselves, especially at night, with their own 360-degree perimeter well dug in and defended with scrounged-up machine guns and even, as in the case of the 457th FA Battalion, captured Japanese "knee" mortars. When an infantry unit stopped attacking for the night, it had to dig in, bring in protective mortar and artillery fires around itself, and prepare for the often-suicidal attacks of small groups of the enemy foot troops, laden with bombs and grenades. This was especially true on Luzon when the enemy began to realize that he was not winning the war.

The division was commanded by an unconventional, shrewd tactician who felt that, because his troops were so good and so well trained, they could and would do all that was asked of them—and more. Who else but General Swing would have tried and succeeded in moving an artillery battery to an area totally inaccessible by road by borrowing a C-47 Air-Sea-Rescue ship and parachuting his howitzers and men into the area? Who else would have the foresight and temerity to use his augmented fleet of sixteen Cub aircraft (normally for FA aerial observers) to establish an airborne logistical tramway to back up his troops that were fighting without a land-based logistical tail? (At peak operation, the sixteen Cubs carried twenty-one tons a day to their airhead at Manarawat on Leyte.) Who else would divorce an artillery battalion and engineers and other assorted noninfantry types from their guns, miniature bulldozers, D-handled shovels, and typewriters and use them to attack an elite Japanese parachute battalion that had had the effrontery to drop on the headquarters of the 11th Airborne Division at Burauen, Leyte? Who else had the confidence in his men to know that, without a doubt, such an attack would succeed? Who else would accept as perfectly normal and without discussion or question the mission of invading southern Luzon by amphibious and parachute attack as the sum total of the Eighth Army? And who else would accept as perfectly routine and unremarkable the task of freeing and evacuating over 2,000 civilian prisoners held in a secure environment some forty-five miles deep in enemy-held territory, guarded by perhaps as many as 250 Japanese security forces, with between 8,000 and 15,000 more Japanese forces within a couple of hours' march to the camp? Maj. Gen. Joseph

M. Swing, the unconventional commander of the 11th, that's who.

After slugging, slipping, and sloshing its way across the mountains of Leyte, parts of the division finally emerged on the western side of the island, near Albuera on Ormoc Bay. About 15 January 1945, General Swing ordered the division to reassemble once again on Leyte's Bito Beach. There the division settled briefly into its base camp, dried out, licked its wounds, sloughed off its mud-caked fatigues and rotting boots, cleaned weapons, bathed in the clear streams near the bivouac areas, integrated some replacements, trained, guarded its perimeter, and talked endlessly of what would be its next operation.

There they also had hot, real food for the first time in about seven months. One of the advantages of moving to a combat zone was the improvement in the food. In New Guinea the division ate canned food, Australian bully beef, dehydrated eggs and potatoes, and other delicacies that the Quartermaster Corps tried unsuccessfully to pass off as food on the not-so-gullible troops. At least in the combat zone, there were occasional fresh items (even if they were from Filipino chicken coops and gardens) and real meat. Even the "new" 10-in-one rations, one meal for ten troops, or such other arrangement as an enterprising mess sergeant might devise were far preferable to the K and C rations on which the division had lived for so long in the mountains. But the R and R on the beach was to be short-lived. The invasion of Luzon was about to begin.

To reconquer Luzon and to defeat General Yamashita's 275,000 men lying in wait on that island, General MacArthur formed his 280,000 men into two armies: the Sixth with four divisions would land at Lingayen Gulf on 9 January 1945 and attack south toward Manila; the Eighth would land the 11th Airborne Division minus its parachute regimental combat team at Nasugbu on 31 January 1945 and would attack to the east and the north toward Manila. General MacArthur had told General Eichelberger before the attack that he wanted him to "undertake a daring expedition against Manila with a small mobile force using tactics that would have delighted Jeb Stuart."

On 22 January Eighth Army implemented MacArthur's directive and issued Field Order No. 17, which ordered the 11th

Airborne Division to land two regimental combat teams amphibiously on the Pacific beaches near Nasugbu, Luzon, on 31 January and to seize and defend the beachhead; to drop the 511th Parachute Regimental Combat Team on Tagaytay Ridge, some thirty-five miles inland to the east of Nasugbu, but only when, in the division commander's judgment, he could link up the two forces within twenty-four hours; and to unite the two elements and prepare for further action to the north and the east as directed by the commanding general of Eighth Army. Thus General Eichelberger sought to delight Jeb Stuart.

On 31 January 1945 the 11th carried out the Eighth Army order. The 1st Battalion of the 188th Glider Regiment waded ashore near Nasugbu. The division commander had selected the 1st Battalion of the 188th to make the initial assault because its battalion commander, Lt. Col. Ernie LaFlamme, had been stationed at Fort McKinley, Luzon, before the war, and he and his wife had spent many weekends on the beaches of Nasugbu. Sometimes a person's innocent and happy past comes back to haunt him.

The remainder of the two glider regimental combat teams followed the 1/188th ashore, assaulted out of the beachhead, and attacked inland and uphill through the defiles and Japanese positions guarding Tagaytay Ridge. By 2 February General Swing felt that if the 511th dropped the next day, he could contact it with the forces he had ashore and thus fulfill the conditions of General Eichelberger's directive. He ordered the 511th Regimental Combat Team to mount up.

The 511th Regimental Combat Team had previously moved to Mindoro from Leyte and was ready and waiting on the airstrip on Mindoro for the launch order. But because of a shortage of C-46 and C-47 paratroop transports, the combat team had to fly to Luzon in two echelons, the infantry units on 3 February and the 457th Parachute Field Artillery Battalion and other supporting units on the 4th.

From the date of the drop on Tagaytay Ridge, less than three weeks were left before elements of the 11th would find themselves at Los Baños; but in those nineteen days the division had to move and fight as it never had moved and fought before. By the evening of 3 February, the glider units had joined the 511th paratroopers on Tagaytay Ridge, and the division readied itself for the next phase of the operation, the attack on Manila from the south.

The route from Nasugbu had not been easy. The glider units had had to fight uphill to Tagaytay Ridge through the Mount Cariliao–Mount Batulao defile and across Shorty Ridge (so named for the diminutive commander of the 188th Regiment, Colonel "Shorty" Soule, who had earned the Distinguished Service Cross by leading the point attack against the Japanese positions on that ridge). The Japanese had honeycombed Shorty Ridge with caves and tunnels and fought their usual "defend to the death" battle to block the U.S. attack. But the 188th, after pounding the area with air strikes, mortars, and artillery, overran the position with a final infantry assault. The success cleared the way for the 188th to link up with the 511th on the ridge. After that, it was on to Manila.

The division commander, General Swing, and the Eighth Army commander, General Eichelberger, had moved forward with the lead elements of the 188th, and after the battle for Shorty Ridge had cleared Highway 17 all the way to the top of the ridge, the two senior commanders established a makeshift joint command post in the Manila Hotel Annex on the top of Tagaytay Ridge, overlooking the magnificently scenic Lake Taal. One wag dubbed the attack up the ridge as a "spearhead tipped with brass." Because Highway 17 was then clear from Nasugbu to Tagaytay, the division commander was able to bring forward from the beachhead enough $2\frac{1}{2}$ ton trucks to get elements of the 511th mounted up and on the move to Manila.

At that stage of the operations, Lt. George Skau and his provisional division reconnaissance platoon came front and center. (Skau was to play an important role in the raid on Los Baños in a few weeks' time.) General Swing ordered Lieutenant Skau to move out after dark on the 3d, preceding the 511th on Highway 17 to Manila, to reconnoiter the route and to report on the Japanese defenses along the highway. At 0400 on the 4th, Lieutenant Skau reported back that the road was secure to Imus (just south of Manila) but that the Japanese had blown a bridge and set up a defensive line. He added that he had found a dirt road which bypassed Imus and which had a suitable bridge but

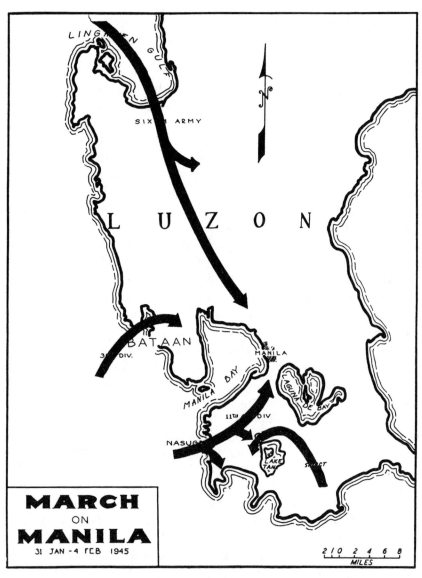

MARCH
ON
MANILA
31 JAN - 4 FEB 1945

which was mined. He added somewhat casually that he and his platoon had removed the charges. Based on his report, General Swing then ordered one battalion of the 511th to proceed to bypass Imus, to leave a holding force at the bridge, and to halt only when the enemy forced them to dismount and fight. Then one truck-mounted battalion of paratroopers led by a jeep patrol and Col. "Rock" Haugen, the intrepid commander of the 511th, set off for Manila. The rest of the regiment began the thirty-mile march on foot.

Some units of the 11th stayed on the ridge for a time to keep Highway 17 open and to fight and defend against the Japanese who had been pushed back from the ridge. From Tagaytay Ridge, the troopers of the 11th initially could see Manila shining white in the bright Luzon sun. (Shortly afterwards it would become a blackened pyre.) They could trace the curved forefinger of Cavite as it hooked into Manila Bay where Corregidor, still in Japanese hands and the symbol of the United States' surrender in 1942, lay curiously and ominously dormant. On 16 February Corregidor came back to life. The 503d Airborne Regimental Combat Team parachuted onto two tiny drop zones on Top Side; the 34th Regiment of the 24th Division landed amphibiously on beaches at the foot of Malinta Hill. Expecting to find some 850 Japanese defenders, the attackers eventually found and defeated nearly 5,000 determined Japanese.

Shortly after the U.S. landings on Corregidor, the Japanese defenders of "The Rock" tried to blast their way out of the U.S. vise. Their bomb-planting experts badly miscalculated, however, and on 21 February and again on 26 February, two gigantic, earth-shattering explosions blew up large chunks of Malinta Hill and trapped and killed hundreds of Japanese in caves inside. The second explosion was so gargantuan that it shook the entire island as if by earthquake and showered rock and debris on ships in the harbor. It was the last effort made by the Japanese on Corregidor; shortly Corregidor was in American hands.

Still, Manila had not been recaptured. On 3 February the troopers on Tagaytay Ridge could see fires breaking out all over the city as the Japanese methodically and ruthlessly began to destroy the "Pearl of the Orient," the city General MacArthur had left "open" in 1942 because he did not want it destroyed needlessly in battle. But the Japanese command structure had failed, and Manila suffered wanton, cruel, needless destruction.

Once he determined that he could not successfully hold Manila, General Yamashita, the overall Japanese commander on Luzon, had evacuated the city with the bulk of his troops and declared the city "open." Unfortunately for Manila, there were still about 30,000 Japanese sailors and marines under the command of Rear Admiral Iwabuchi manning and guarding the Japanese-controlled port facilities and naval warehouses. Admiral Iwabuchi's boss, Rear Admiral Okochi, ordered him to destroy the naval facilities. And even before the battle for Manila began, Iwabuchi and his men went on a rampage of destruction, devastation, atrocity, rape, and pillage, totally ignoring Yamashita's directive to leave Manila an "open city." Either Iwabuchi had not received Yamashita's order or, because of frustration and revenge, had chosen to ignore it. He and his men laid the city to waste and continued to defend it. Then came the battle for Manila.

The attacking American forces had to fight and blast their way street by street, house by house, and even floor by floor to dislodge the fanatical, suicidal Japanese. When the battle was finally over, General Eichelberger said that "Manila had ceased to exist except for some places that the Japanese thought were not worth defending or where our American troops got in by surprise."

In *American Caesar*, William Manchester wrote:

> The devastation of Manila was one of the great tragedies of World War II. Of Allied cities in those war years, only Warsaw suffered more. Seventy percent of the utilities, 75 percent of the factories, 80 percent of the southern residential district, and 100 percent of the business district were razed. Nearly 100,000 Filipinos were murdered by the Japanese. Hospital beds were set afire after their patients had been strapped to their beds. The corpses of males were mutilated, females of all ages were raped before they were slain, and babies' eyeballs were gouged out and smeared on walls like jelly. The middle class, the professionals, the white-collar workers suffered most.

The troopers on Tagaytay Ridge could see the beginning of the destruction. The troopers of the 11th were attacking Manila, but it would be some weeks before they could drive the Japanese out completely. On 31 January the division had hit the beaches at Nasugbu; by the night of the 4th, the 511th had advanced as far as the Parañaque River Bridge on the southern boundary of Manila. Although the bridge had not been completely destroyed, the Japanese had the north bank studded with machine-gun emplacements and concrete pillboxes from whose narrow slits protruded automatic weapons. The battle for the Parañaque River Bridge marked the end of the division's free-wheeling, rapid drive to the north.

The division had "a beachhead sixty-nine miles long and 100 yards wide" and had run up against the formidable Genko Line, which formed the southern defenses of the city. The Japanese had been building the Genko Line since their occupation began in 1942. It was there that the slugging match began.

The Genko Line was a formidable, defensive network of interlocking, mutually supporting emplacements. It consisted of a series of concrete pillboxes, and the portion of the line in front of the 511th extended in depth 6,000 yards through the Manila Polo Club. From that fortified position on the west, it stretched east across Nichols Field and anchored itself on its eastern end on the high ground of Mabato Point along Laguna de Bay. The rear of the line was based on the high ground on Fort Mc-Kinley, a prewar U.S. Army post. All along the line five- and six-inch guns and 150-mm. mortars were set in concrete emplacements, facing south, and 20-, 40-, and 90-mm. antiaircraft guns were tactically deployed to fire horizontally against attacking ground troops. Many of the concrete pillboxes were two and three stories deep. Some of the forts were constructed of stone, had dome-shaped roofs piled high with sod and soggy dirt, and were so overgrown with tangles of weeds that they could be recognized only from a few feet away. Many of the pillboxes were defended by two men and either a .50-caliber machine gun or a 20-mm. automatic weapon. Some positions were occupied by only one man, who stayed at his post until he was killed.

The force manning the Genko Line was the Southern Unit, Manila Defense Force, some 6,000 strong. In the line there were over 1,200 pillboxes, 44 120-mm. coastal defense guns used as field artillery, 164 antiaircraft guns sighted to fire parallel to the ground against infantry attacks, and hundreds of machine guns, 333 of which were captured by the division in its attack on the line. The concrete and steel line was further reinforced with 245 100-pound bombs and 35 antisubmarine depth charges, em-

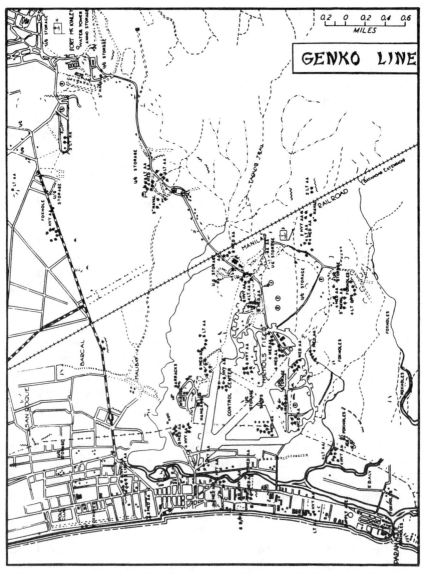

placed and rigged as land mines. All roads leading to the line were heavily mined with 500-pound aerial bombs armed with low-pressure detonators.

All night 4/5 February, the 511th was held up at the Parañaque River Bridge. That the division's "spearhead was tipped with brass" was unfortunately proven that night when the chief of staff of the division, Col. Irving R. Schimmelpfennig, was killed by machine-gun fire as he and General Swing tried to reconnoiter a route to bypass the bridge.

For the next sixteen days the division attacked the massive and stubbornly defended Genko Line with artillery and air attacks, but in the final determination it was the movement of the infantry on the ground that reduced the defenses. In those sixteen days the division units, and by then almost all of the division's strength was engaged in the operation, killed some 5,210 defenders. The fighting was brutal, with slow-moving, treacherous house-to-house fighting in the suburbs of Manila and valiant infantry attacks across open terrain along the line between Nichols Field and Fort McKinley.

By 13 February the 511th had reduced the western bastion of the line and had swung eastward, north of Nichols Field, to join the battle for the airfield and Fort McKinley. The 511th, with the 2d Battalion of the 187th attached, had pushed through the left end of the line by battering its way through block after block of the crumbled, burning, debris-littered streets of Manila, then turned east to continue the attack on Nichols Field and Fort McKinley. Meanwhile the 188th and the 1st Battalion of the 187th had swung across the pillbox-studded Nichols Field and had joined up with the 511th as it was coming east. Finally Nichols Field fell, and the three regiments headed east to Fort McKinley.

On 17 February the division attacked Fort McKinley from the east and the south. It was an extremely grueling, bloody fight against the usual array of Japanese pillboxes, dug-in artillery, and levelled antiaircraft guns. The exploits of Pvt. Manuel Perez, Jr., of the 511th illustrate the kind of fighting that went on during the attack of Fort McKinley. Perez's company, A Company, had been held up along the road from Nichols Field to Fort McKinley by a series of pillboxes. The company had cleaned up eleven of twelve positions blocking its route, but the twelfth proved a troublesome and stubborn obstacle. On the way to the strongpoint, Perez had already killed five Japanese in the open. When the company arrived at the last emplacement, which contained two twin-mounted .50-caliber dual-purpose machine guns, it was held up again. Perez circled around the emplacement and got to within twenty yards of it, killing four more Japanese on the way. Then he lobbed a grenade into the position, and, as the Japanese crew started to withdraw through the tunnel to the rear, shot and killed four more defenders before exhausting the clip in his M1 rifle. He reloaded and killed four more Japanese. Then an enemy soldier javelined his bayonet-tipped rifle at him. The attack tumbled Perez to the ground and knocked his rifle out of his hands. He seized the Japanese rifle and continued firing at the enemy, killing two more. He rushed the remaining defenders, killed three of them with the butt of the rifle, and entered the pillbox, where he bayoneted the surviving soldier. Singlehandedly, he had killed eighteen Japanese who were holding up his company. He was subsequently awarded the Medal of Honor for his courage. Unfortunately, a week later, in a separate action, he was killed before he learned that his heroism had earned him the country's highest award for valor in combat.

Another exploit symbolic of the fighting against the Genko Line was that of Tech. Sgt. Miles T. Lowe, also of the 511th. He commanded a light machine-gun section of twenty-four men of the 511th who were in an isolated position along the shore of Laguna de Bay and some 300 yards from any supporting troops. On the night of 20 February, a force of some 300 Japanese troops made six fanatical banzai attacks against Lowe's position. The crew successfully held off the first four of the attacks, with Lowe personally manning one of the machine guns. After the fourth attack, however, ammunition became dangerously low. Sergeant Lowe led a raiding party outside the perimeter and captured seven Japanese machine guns, two mortars, and an ample supply of ammunition. They raced back into their own position, set up the captured weapons, and broke up the fifth charge. Then the Japanese launched a final banzai assault from both the front and the rear of the position. In that attack Lowe personally killed eight Japanese in hand-to-hand combat. That defense broke the back of the Japanese assault. By 21 February all organized resistance along the Genko Line had ceased. Lowe had personally killed more than fifty of the enemy. He survived to win a battlefield commission to 2d lieutenant and to receive the Distinguished Service Cross for his heroism.

The attack near Fort McKinley was not without its lighter moments. In the field men try to make themselves as comfortable as possible. Some fail miserably, others succeed admirably. Ingenious are the ways the American soldier tries to beat the odds. The height of ingenuity may be exemplified by a private of the 511th who had a young Filipino lad as an aide. He was more than an aide really; he was, in fact, a caddy. During an attack on a pillbox near McKinley, our doughboy sized up the situation from a prone position. Surprisingly, he was unarmed. Our hero checked the area very carefully by raising himself on his elbows. He was no Medal of Honor candidate, but he was no shirker either. After looking around, he beckoned forward his Filipino assistant. That young worthy crawled forward with some difficulty because he was lugging an M1 rifle, a carbine, a submachine gun, and a pistol. Our hero continued to analyze the situation—not unlike a golfer studying a difficult lie—and decided he needed the rifle. The aide dutifully passed it to him. Our hero used it effectively, then handed the weapon back to his aide. (This story is not one of those that are told over and over and made more ludicrous and incredulous at each repetition at division reunions. I first heard the story and recorded it in March 1945.)

By the time Fort McKinley had been overrun, the entire division had been committed to the attack all along the Genko Line. With its neutralization General Swing could begin to give more serious thought to the mission that MacArthur's headquarters had given to him through General Eichelberger's headquarters on 3 February, shortly after he came ashore on Luzon: free the internees held in the Japanese internment camp at Los Baños.

CHAPTER IV: Guerrilla Forces

Despite the enormity of the task confronting him—the attack from the south against the suicidal defenders of Manila and the simultaneous assault against the formidable Genko Line—General Swing instructed his G-2, Lt. Col. "Butch" Muller, to start gathering intelligence about the Los Baños Internment Camp, and told his G-3, Col. Douglass P. Quandt, to start thinking about how to get to the camp, defeat the defenders, and haul back to safety more than 2,000 men, women, and children, many of whom were probably very weak, emaciated, and bedridden. The date was 5 February; the place, division headquarters in Parañaque.

To piece together a complete picture of the then unknown (at least to the 11th planners) Los Baños Camp, its location, its inhabitants, its defenses, and its vulnerabilities, Butch Muller used every information-gathering agency at his disposal: the division reconnaissance platoon, Air Corps photo reconnaissance, organized guerrilla units, and Filipino civilians. In addition to the 11th's assets, Doug Quandt also had to consider what part the several local guerrilla units in and around the Los Baños camp might play. Later, as the raid date approached, one of the most valuable sources of information would prove to be some intrepid internees who had managed to escape.

In reviewing military operations after a battle, there is often much debate about which unit, which person, which commander, or even which service or nation contributed to the success or failure of a given combat operation. And that was the situation following the Los Baños raid with respect to the guerrillas. What part had they played? Were they the unsung heroes or were they actually taking more credit, in later years and in subsequent analyses, than was their due for what they had done?

To determine the extent of the guerrillas' contribution to the enormous success of the Los Baños raid requires an examination of both sides of the issue. One must look at the operation from the perspective of the guerrillas as well as from the perspective of the 11th Airborne commanders and troops who had a part in the raid. To his dying day (9 December 1984) General Swing vehemently described the raid as just another routine mission for his well-trained, battle-tested, and offense-minded troopers. In today's parlance, he might have said, "It was no big deal." Nevertheless, the raid was an overwhelming success, it was not ordinary, and the guerrillas did make a contribution that was undoubtedly significant.

Except for the recon platoon troops, the U.S. 11th Airborne soldiers who actually took part in the raid were, more or less, unaware of any stellar contribution to the Los Baños operation by the guerrillas. This included Maj. Henry A. Burgess, the commander of the 1st Battalion of the 511th, the unit that actually moved by amtrac across Laguna de Bay and into the camp. He said:

> At Los Baños, the guerrillas' greatest contribution was furnishing the intelligence information about the camp, locating guard posts, and guiding Lieutenant Skau's reconnaissance platoon into position against the guard posts and pillboxes in the hours of darkness and participating in the first rush and firefight on the camp. I did not see large numbers of guerrillas in the camp or contributing to the evacuation as related in "Hunters-ROTC Guerrillas," and similar accounts, although a small number assisted Skau. I know Major Vanderpool, ostensibly commander of

the guerrilla movement, had nothing to do with the raid and did not know of the raid in advance.

The other side of the controversy (and it is by now a bit contentious) was expressed by Col. Francisco B. "Kit" Quesada, a member of Hunters-ROTC Guerrillas, who has a somewhat different bias and relegates the 11th Airborne Division almost to a support role. He says that "this daring rescue was staged by the well-known Hunters-ROTC Guerrillas, in coordination with the 11th Airborne Division of the XIV Corps, U.S. Eighth Army." His justifiable pride in his guerrillas may have colored his viewpoint. In point of fact, there is undoubtedly support for both Quesada's and Burgess's perspectives.

The Filipino guerrillas were probably better organized and more effective against the Japanese occupying their homeland than most of the American troops gave them credit for. The U.S. troops were engrossed in their own battles with their own tactics, techniques, weapons, and discipline, for the most part, and gave little thought to the seemingly invisible guerrillas "mucking about the countryside and hiding out in the hills."

Occasionally, guerrilla units would be attached to and integrated rather loosely into U.S. units. At Ternate, on the south shore of Manila Bay, where units of the 11th were fighting to secure that area, my pack-75 battery of parachute artillery had attached to it a company of some eighty guerrillas. I was grateful for them and used them primarily to help secure our battery perimeter and to augment our patrols in the Japanese-infested no-man's-land between infantry units and the supporting artillery. At that time there were a number of such guerrilla units working directly with the other units of the 11th Airborne Division. These attachments were relatively short-lived, and the guerrilla units moved on after a few weeks for reasons obscure to the likes of a captain, battery commander, such as I was.

For most of their operations, the guerrilla units acted semi-independently of the U.S. forces with missions dictated by GHQ-SWPA and coordinated with the U.S. unit in whose zone of responsibility they operated. For example, when the parachute units of the 11th landed on the drop zones atop Tagaytay Ridge south of Manila, they were a bit surprised to find the area generally free of Japanese. And when those same outfits took off the next day to attack Manila from the south, they found the route mostly devoid of Japanese troops. The reason was that the guerrilla leaders had neutralized the Japanese units throughout the area by deploying several thousand guerrillas around the Tagaytay drop zones and along the Main Supply Route (MSR) to Manila.[1]

The 11th soldiers, though, knew nothing about the guerrillas because they rarely saw them. I know that when I landed with my battery on the ridge, I saw few Filipinos. Still, the drop zone was clear of Japanese. The only Filipinos I saw were those I assumed were civilians gathering up our parachutes for the very valuable material they contained. (In short order the Filipino girls were wearing white silk blouses.)

That the guerrillas had not entirely eradicated the Japanese in the area became all too clear to us the next night when they attacked our battalion perimeter. But because the paratroopers landed without much interference from the Japanese and because the 11th made a quick and generally unimpeded run to the outskirts of Manila, one must give the elusive guerrillas credit and the benefit of any doubt.[2]

Equally unknown to most Americans were the guerrilla raids on prison camps where the Japanese had held Filipinos. Another major contribution of the guerrillas was the rescue of downed American pilots. In December 1944 the guerrillas in the southern Luzon area "salvaged" twenty-two assorted U.S. pilots, most of whom were from the U.S. Navy. The guerrillas' efforts in recovering downed pilots did not go unrewarded: they swapped the grateful pilots for medical supplies, weapons, and U.S. food.

Hank Burgess and others in the hierarchy of the division felt that the best use of the guerrillas would have been to form them into company-size units and attach one guerrilla company to each of the line infantry battalions. That way the commander of a

---

1. Vanderpool, Col. Jay D., U.S.A. (Ret.). Letter to the author, 29 May 1984.
2. To reimburse themselves for the assistance, generally unapplauded by the 11th, the guerrillas later stole the 11th's supplies, which they considered a justified gift from their U.S. Allies.

unit with guerrillas attached could properly provide command, control, logistic support, and unity of purpose. He would know where the guerrillas were and what they were doing. The higher command in the Philippines, General MacArthur's headquarters, did not adopt such a scheme, probably because the guerrillas were not well enough organized, disciplined, and equipped.

For the most part the guerrillas fought on their own and usually as individual, autonomous, separate units. Some guerrilla commanders were virtual "shoguns." The U.S. Army supplied the guerrillas with only token amounts of arms, ammunition, and other logistics. One of their main sources of weapons and ammunition was the caches of weapons stashed away for the defense of the islands.

According to Colonel Vanderpool, a guerrilla coordinator:

> Thousands of rifles, pistols, plus ammo, were spirited to the mountains or other safe areas when the Japs overran our Allied forces. Limited supplies came in by submarine or PBY Naval aircraft. U.S. medical supplies were so limited, I personally supervised distribution of ours. Also, the Filipino doctors were not trained in the use of the then new drugs, such as the sulphas.

The United States did, however, supply the guerrillas with an appreciable number of radios and codes for communication to and from the guerrilla command posts, usually remote in the hills and outside U.S. direct areas of combat operations. Via these radios, with guerrilla liaison officers at his headquarters, and with the virtual colocation of Vanderpool's headquarters with the 11th (his was across the street), the commanding general of the 11th Airborne could exercise a fair semblance of coordination and cooperation between the forces and the widespread and necessarily evasive, underground guerrillas. Even so, the system was far from perfect, primarily because of the compartmentalization of the guerrilla bands and the independence of their commanders.

The guerrillas were organized somewhat loosely by area. In the zone in which Los Baños was located, there were a number of units, one of which was the Hunters-ROTC, partially made up of former cadets of the Philippine Military Academy (PMA), the Philippine "West Point," which was, of course, closed in the fall of 1941, even before the start of the Japanese occupation of Luzon in early 1942. The ex-PMA cadets, plus other ROTC students and college undergraduates, formed the Hunters-ROTC and went into the countryside to hunt (hence the name) and to fight the Japanese.

Over the many months of the Japanese occupation of the islands, the U.S. Military Command maintained contact with the guerrillas through two primary sources: (1) officers and men who had escaped capture by the Japanese at the time of the surrender of the islands and who subsequently joined with and helped to organize the guerrillas, and (2) officers and men who were infiltrated clandestinely into the islands and who made their way to specific bands of guerrillas. The mission of these teams of U.S. officers and men was to represent the U.S. High Command (General MacArthur) with the guerrillas, to control and coordinate their activities in order to complement those of the U.S. forces and work toward a common goal, to prevent disasters in which U.S. forces (once they were ashore) and guerrillas might otherwise have unknowingly fought one another, and to arrange for the logistical support of the guerrillas.

The then Maj. Jay D. Vanderpool at the time of the Los Baños Raid was serving as guerrilla coordinator in the Cavite, Batangas, and western Laguna areas. Although he called himself a "coordinator," Major Vanderpool was very much in command of the guerrillas for whom he was responsible. Guerrilla chiefs took orders from him implicitly, if not explicitly. He was the personal representative of General MacArthur and controlled distribution of U.S. military, medical, and communications supplies. He had power to promote guerrilla officers in the Army of the United States through the grade of colonel. He was explicitly prohibited from promoting to general officer rank. "Our 'Generals' were self-annointed," he said. "I really had no occasion to promote—they did their own."

Prior to his arrival in the Philippines, Major Vanderpool had been (and, for a time even after his arrival, was still) the Assistant G-2 of the 25th Division, which in the fall of 1944 was in training in New Caledonia. From there he volunteered to infiltrate into the Philippines. Subsequently, he and his team embarked at a submarine base near Hollandia, New Guinea, on the U.S. submarine CERO (SS-230). After a long, circuitous trip to the Philippines, with many changes in itinerary, necessitated by Japanese army and navy actions, his team landed at night north of the town of Infanta on the east coast of Luzon at the guerrilla camp of Maj. Bernard Anderson, a U.S. officer who had evaded capture by the Japanese after the U.S. surrender. Thereafter, Major Vanderpool made his way cross-country to his assigned area. The U.S. forces had not yet invaded Luzon when Major Vanderpool landed. He was virtually on his own and dependent for his survival on guerrillas. They had to accept him almost on faith.

Major Vanderpool's mission in the Philippines was short, broad, and stringless. After he landed on Luzon, he received the following radio message: "VANDERPOOL from MACARTHUR: DO WHAT WILL BEST FURTHER THE ALLIED CAUSE." (One must wonder, parenthetically, what sort of a message an officer might receive today under similar circumstances.)

The guerrilla organization that Major Vanderpool found when he reached his assigned area caused him a great deal of concern after his service with the organized, disciplined, well-trained, well-supplied, and single-minded U.S. forces. He remembers:

> There were numerous independent quasi-military organizations with military, economic and political goals. Their primary loyalty was to their country, with emotional ties to the United States. There was no central guerrilla control or allegiance. They were, in effect, independent war lords. Some imposed local taxes— some did not. Some were geographically oriented. Some were spread thinly over large areas. No two were alike. Some private citizens supported two or more guerrilla organizations. All had aspirations beyond their current capabilities. I've never seen precise figures, but I estimate they had about 100 or so civilian members for each armed guerrilla. The civilians were their economic base and a source of recruits.

Antonio A. Nieva wrote a firsthand description of the guerrillas, their modus operandi, and their command methods. Nieva gathered his facts from Tabo Ingles, Marcelo Castillo, Honorio Guerrero, and other Hunters-ROTC veterans.

> Until the advent of liberation, there were no concerted plans, cooperation, least of all, coordination among the different guer-

rilla formations. Each organization acted on its own, viewed others with suspicion if not open hostility, gerrymandering spheres of influence for supply and recruitment purposes, not rarely resulting in tragic intrafratricidal warfare. Each guerrilla leader was like a "Datu" in his fief, would not submit to another's orders, nor had sufficient stature and forces to enforce his dominance, bowing only to MacArthur as the recognized Sultan of all the clans.

Once he recognized the extent of his problem, Major Vanderpool did attempt to unify guerrilla efforts by establishing a General Guerrilla Command (GGC) for south Luzon. Terry Adevoso (the Hunters-ROTC overall commander) was its chief of staff; the Hunters-ROTC units its nuclear force. The loose organization and independent fiefdoms of the various guerrilla chiefs, even with the considerable prodding and logistical clout wielded by Major Vanderpool, caused some difficulty when the need arose to coordinate the activities of several bands of guerrillas to a common goal or purpose, for example, a large raid. Major Vanderpool recognized this problem of coordination when he decided to organize an independent guerrilla raid on Los Baños.

By early February Vanderpool was well aware of the plight of the internees at Los Baños through contact with the guerrillas in the area. His command post was located across the street from the command post of the 11th in Parañaque, therefore, he was also cognizant of the dimensions of the 11th's fight against the Genko Line and in the city of Manila, and was well aware that the 11th at that time not only had no troops to spare to attack Los Baños, it had, in fact, no units in reserve for its heavy fighting around Manila. It was totally committed.

On 10 February Major Vanderpool called a conference of his guerrilla staff to discuss the liberation of Los Baños by guerrillas acting on their own. At the conclusion of the conference, during which Vanderpool and his staff decided that the guerrillas, independently, might have some slight chance of freeing the internees, Vanderpool issued a letter order to Lt. Col. Gustavo C. Ingles. The letter directed him to lay the groundwork for a guerrilla-only attack on Los Baños by making a detailed reconnaissance of the area, determining enemy strengths in and around the Los Baños Camp, ascertaining the number and condition of the internees (how many could walk, how many had to be carried), and verifying the number and combat readiness of guerrillas available for the raid. The letter also authorized Ingles "to order an attack with available forces or to await reinforcements." This letter was, in effect, a large order and a veritable "carte blanche" if Ingles were to interpret it literally.

Lt. Col. Gustavo C. Ingles was a member of the Hunters-ROTC but was serving with the headquarters of the GGC as an inspector general. Inspectors general in the guerrilla organization were, unlike their U.S. Army counterparts, operations officers and oriented toward combat operations; they were not staff inspectors or administrators. Colonel Ingles had been a fourth classman (freshman) in the Philippine Military Academy, class of 1945, in the fall of 1941. In the middle of December 1941, his class and the class of 1944 were disbanded. In January 1942 Ingles, Miguel Ver (PMA class of 1943), Eleuterio Adevoso (PMA class of 1944), and members of the Jose Rizal College ROTC Rifle Team formed the nucleus of the Hunters-ROTC Guerrillas.

Major Vanderpool used Colonel Ingles as a "coordinator and troubleshooter with various guerrilla leaders." Other Americans who knew and worked with him considered "Tabo" Ingles to be one of the most respected, hard-working, honorable members of the guerrilla movement.

Ingles, with his 10 February letter of instruction from Major Vanderpool and the GGC in hand, left GGC headquarters in Parañaque on 11 February and proceeded by jeep to Laguna de Bay, by banca (Filipino dugout canoe equipped with outriggers and sails) across Laguna de Bay, and by foot to Nanhaya, Pila, on the southern shore of the lake. Nanhaya was the base camp of the Hunters-ROTC Regiment. Once there, he requested the various guerrilla chiefs in the area to assemble on 12 February in the town hall of Santa Cruz, a town held by the guerrillas.

Most of the chiefs appeared. Present at the meeting were the commanders of the Hunters-ROTC 45th Infantry Regiment, PQOG (President Quezon's Own Guerrillas), the Chinese Guerrillas of Southern Luzon, and the Hukbalahaps. The commander of the Marking Fil-Americans (a guerrilla group organized by

C - O - P - Y

GUERRILLA HEADQUART
Central Luzon

10 February 194~~6~~

Subject: Letter of Instruction, LOS BANOS PATROL

To: Lieutenant Colonel Gustavo Ingles

1.   You will proceed, with a patrol, to work with loyal
Guerrilla Forces in making preparation for the releasing of the
Civilian Internees now at Los Banos, Laguna.

2.   You will coordinate the efforts of the Hunters Guerrii
with those of the President Quezon's Own Guerrillas in order to
perform this mission,

3.   You will take with you an SCR 284 radio and an operate
who will contact this Headquarters between 1800 and 2200 each it
feasable on 5495 kcs. Your call sign will be TWO EIGHT GEORGE
(28G). This Headquarters will be PREP EASY FIVE (PE5). Another
Station EIGHT MIKE ABLE (8MA), located in San Jose, Mindoro will
be in this net.

4.   You will proceed by jeep as far as road conditions and
the enemy situation permits, then banca is recommended across
Laguna de Bay to Southern Laguna.

5.   You will determine and report the enemy strength and
positions by radio, letter and by detailed sketches.

6.   You will report the number of local guerrillas availabl
to assist in the mission and recommend the number of reinforceme
required.

7.   A report of the condition of the road net will be subm
with your opinion as to the feasability of employing tanks or se
propelled guns.

8.   Routes of approach for foot troops and mechanized vehi
will be determined and reported.

9.   A pool of guides will be established who can lea reinforcements into the area.

10.   A report will be submitted immediately as to the numbe
internees and as to their physical condition. Specifically how m
can walk and how many will require transportation.

11.   You are authorized to order an attack with available
forces or to await reinforcements.

JAY J. VANDERPOOL
Major, GSC, DS
Commanding

OFFICAL:
RIGOBERTO J. ATIENZA
Lt. Col.. GSC. Guer.

Colonel Marking), who was also invited to the meeting, did not appear.

Antonio A. Nieva wrote about the meeting:

> The next day [February 12th], for the first time since the Occupation, the different guerrilla area leaders met in peaceful congress to listen to Ingles' proposal. It was not an unfamiliar topic. In the recent weeks, Honorio Guerrero [the Hunters' 45th commander] had discussed similar schemes with some of the same leaders individually. But the scarcity of arms and ammunition, the unavailability of transport and a safe evacuation area for the internees and, above all, the mutual distrust of the guerrilla chieftains, prevented even the preparation of a workable plan. This time, however, previous misgivings as to the venture's feasibility were dispelled by Ingles' authority to call for arms, supplies and reinforcements from the GGC/Airborne headquarters.
>
> The most serious objection was voiced by the PQOG's local commander, Colonel "Price."[3] Though his question—"Who would protect the Los Baños folks from the Japanese retaliation after the raid?"—was undoubtedly valid,[4] the tone and manner of his opposition were so vehement that Ingles and his team misunderstood his motives. Heated words were exchanged and the discussion might have ended in gunplay (not a rare occurrence in guerrilla conferences) had not cooler heads intervened. Only after Ingles assured him that raids on Japanese concentrations after the mission would be integrated in the recommended plan did the "Colonel" agree to participate in the mission.

Despite the fractious and unruly conduct by the guerrilla chiefs, the meeting ended with two major conclusions: (1) all unit commanders present pledged their support, and (2) Ingles promised to requisition necessary ammunition and grenades.

Ingles and his two-man team spent the night of 12 February at Professor Silverio Cendan's cottage on Faculty Hill, just out-

---

3. Romeo Espino, Colonel "Price," was at the time a paroled USAFFE POW. His father had been educated at Johns Hopkins and had been on the prewar faculty of the Los Baños Agricultural College. Before the war, Romeo had been studying biology at the college, and he and his wife, Helen, lived near Los Baños. At the beginning of the war, Romeo joined the guerrillas; Helen stayed in their home in Los Baños.

4. Later events unfortunately proved his misgivings tragically well grounded.

side of and overlooking the Los Baños Camp. The next day he sketched the camp, checked the area, looked for routes of approach, and conferred with the local Filipinos who had knowledge of the area.

That evening, the 13th, he went to the home of Helen Espino. There he met George Gray, the secretary of the camp's administrative committee, who had escaped through a hidden passage along the high-banked creek leading to the villages northeast of the camp. Gray and Ingles talked until dawn about the situation inside the camp, the habits of the guards and their routines, and the general condition of the internees. Colonel Ingles was thus well on his way to accomplishing at least part of the mission that Major Vanderpool assigned him by the letter of instruction of 10 February. In the dark hours of the morning of the 13th, George Gray made his way back to camp.

On 13 February the guerrilla chiefs held another meeting, this time at Dayap, Calauan. There, apparently, amity and brotherhood prevailed because the After Action Report of the GGC headquarters, dated 18 March 1945, states that at that conference it was decided: (1) to appoint a central field command for the operations; (2) that this commander would select a staff for the operations; (3) that all orders issued by the commander were to be obeyed as orders; and (4) that Lt. Col. Honorio Guerrero, commanding officer of the 45th Infantry, was elected to command.

On 14 February Colonel Ingles received another directive from GGC, which ordered him, prior to midnight 16 February, to "send at once a patrol [reconnaissance] to the Los Baños vicinity to dig up the following information: (a) beaches in Los Baños area where soil is hard enough to enable amphibious trucks (DUKW's) to land; (b) roadway from such beaches to the objective; and (c) other pertinent information as covered in your LOI."

The guerrillas were obviously making a major effort to gather all information possible about the area and by now were planning to use amphibious vehicles to evacuate the internees. Where they would come from was yet another matter, which Major Vanderpool must have been coordinating.

As ordered, Colonel Ingles made the necessary reconnais-

GENERAL GUERRILLA HEADQUARTERS
CENTRAL LUZON

C - O - P - Y

14 February 1945

Subject: Directive
To   : Lt. Col. Gustavo Ingles

  1. Acknowledge receipt of ammunition and radio from Major
Gabriel Cruz, Convoy Leader.

  2. This urgent. Send at once a patrol (reconnaisance) to
the Los Banos vicinity to dig up the following info:

     a - Beaches in Los Banos area where soil is hard enough
         to enable smphibious trucks (DUKW's) to land.

     b - Roadway from such beaches to the objective.

     c - Other pertinent info as covered in your letter of
         instructions.

  3. Subject treated Par 2 should be answered on or before
midnight 16th February.

TERRY MAGTANGGOL
Colonel, Infantry
Chief of Staff

sance on 14 February. The After Action Report contains the
substance and consequences of his report:

After a careful estimate of the situation, considering primarily
that the attack on Los Baños was for the purpose of releasing the
internees which he [Ingles] noted were mostly weak and sick,
Lt. Colonel Ingles reported that while he had enough arms and
ammunition to attack the camp and destroy the Japanese garrison, he was not sure that he could hold the camp long enough
to evacuate the internees who were too weak to walk to any point
of safety before the Japanese might be able to reinforce their Los
Baños troops or counter-attack from Lalakay only 6 kilometers
away. Based on this report, Major Vanderpool rescinded his original order of 10 February to attack with only the guerrilla troops
in the area.

Apparently, Major Vanderpool had never believed that the

guerrillas alone could mount the raid, destroy or scatter the Japanese guards, and evacuate the internees to safety without U.S. combat and logistical support. He wrote to David Blackledge in March 1982:

> I considered myself in support of the 11th Airborne Division that landed in my sector of operations. I still had other areas to worry about occupied by the Japanese. . . . Mr. Burgess and I do not agree on prior knowledge and planning for the Los Baños Raid. . . . General Eichelberger . . . then commanding the U.S. Eighth Army . . . and some of his staff, General Swing and some of his staff, and I and some of my guerrilla staff were sharing an officers' mess in southern Manila at the time. . . . Several days before the raid, Lt. General Eichelberger . . . and I had a discussion about the feasibility of conducting an operation to liberate Los Baños [Filipino records indicate this was on 8 February]. General Eichelberger asked me if I could do the job (a) with guerrillas alone, (b) with guerrillas supported by U.S. amphibious tractors. I declined for several reasons. . . . (a) We would need a considerable force to help evacuate 2,000-plus internees reported to be in very poor physical condition. (b) Surprise would be difficult, if not impossible, for a major force going overland or from the beach of Laguna de Bay to the camp. (c) The internees might or might not have sufficient confidence in guerrillas to trust running a gauntlet of Japanese with them. (d) If the raid was not successful, the Japanese 8th Division and other troops in the area would indulge in an orgy of revenge on the surviving internees. . . . I recommended to General Eichelberger that U.S. Forces should be the controlling and most visible elements in the raid, supported by guerrillas in the scouting party and in diversionary attacks to delay counterattacking Japanese elements until the internees could get out.

> The Hunters guerrillas were the primary coordinating elements for U.S. support by guerrillas in that area at that time, as they had a good staff and fair communications systems. When the plan had progressed some, I asked the Hunters to provide all feasible support. Mr. Burgess is correct that I was not involved in the detailed planning for the raid. The guerrilla staff with me worked with the 11th Airborne Division staff to provide forces needed.

In spite of the significance of his discussions with General

Eichelberger, Major Vanderpool had gone ahead with his own plans for a guerrilla raid on and liberation of the camp. Certainly, the letter of instruction to Lieutenant Colonel Ingles supports this thesis. These plans were being worked out while the 11th Airborne staff was gathering information on Los Baños but before the 11th Airborne staff got into the detailed plans for their concept of the raid.

Recently, Colonel Vanderpool wrote that he had not had direct contact with Hank Burgess before the raid.

> After General Eichelberger and I agreed that the raid should include U.S. parachutists, U.S. soldiers and the U.S. Flag, I supported them with guerrilla units and individuals as required. I don't know whether Burgess ever knew we had two plans being developed concurrently—his and an all-guerrilla operation. I don't believe that we met, but we may have.[5]

At that time, through about 10 to 12 February, the GGC headquarters was planning a guerrilla-only raid, and the 11th Airborne staff was beginning to gather intelligence and work up its plan.

It may seem odd and contradictory that Major Vanderpool had a conversation with General Eichelberger on 8 February in which he admitted that the guerrillas could not liberate the camp and rescue the internees by themselves or even with the transport assistance of an amtrac battalion, yet on 10 February he directed Colonel Ingles to make preparations for the release of the prisoners at Los Baños and authorized him to "order an attack with available forces (guerrillas) or to await reinforcements (also guerrillas)."

Vanderpool clarified the reason for his apparent conflict of views and plans. He said recently that it was difficult to:

> reflect our ominous uncertainty of the Jap intentions for the dispositions of the internees. We knew, from our experience at Muntinlupa and New Bilibid prisons, that orders to kill them all could come to the Los Baños Camp Commander to start the executions. We also hoped [to be able to intercept] a massacre sig-

---

5. Vanderpool, Jay D. Letter to author, 29 May 1984.

nal. In previous massacres, the Japanese did not execute all prisoners the same day. For one thing, the logistic problem of disposing of several hundreds or thousands of bodies in a subtropical climate is a challenge, unless you have a lot of bulldozers for mass grave preparation. The ethics would not bother the Japs, but they are very neat and tidy people. Jap combat troops had higher priority missions. The Camp Commander had a limited number of his own men, plus some unenthusiastic internees. Rumors boiled out of the camp with every messenger.

We, therefore, or at least I, thought should the executions start, we would just have to go with what we had available at the time. Hence, the dual planning and preparation for the raid. I did not want to go with all-guerrilla combat forces supported by amtracs, but if the executions started we might have no other choice.[6]

On 14 February GGC issued Field Order No. 2 which mentions the 11th Airborne Division participation in the operation. By that date the guerrilla staff of Major Vanderpool and the staff of the 11th Airborne Division had been working jointly to develop a plan for the raid. (The 11th Airborne units that were to participate in the raid had not yet been notified, however.) Paragraph 1 of Field Order No. 2 states that "one Infantry Battalion (Reinforced) of the American 11th Airborne Division, reinforced by available guerrilla forces, will seize the Los Baños Internment Camp at 1700 hours 18 February and hold the immediate area until internees can be evacuated to American-controlled territory." Paragraph 5c of Field Order No. 2 says that Major Vanderpool plans "to land at Pila, Laguna, on the night of 17/18 February to take command of the Guerrilla Phase of the Operation. A guide will meet command party on the beach."

On 16 February GGC called another conference of the guerrilla chiefs who had pledged to participate in the raid. Pila was the site of the meeting. The purpose of the meeting was (1) to announce that the operation was not, after all, to be a guerrilla-only affair; (2) to notify the guerrillas that they would assist the U.S. troops in the raid; and (3) to assign missions for the raid to the various guerrilla groups.

---

6. Vanderpool, Jay D. Letter to the author, 20 August 1984.

C–O–P–Y

                        Guer 116
                        14 Feb 45

F. O. 2

1. One Infantry Battalion (Rein) of the American 11th Airborne Division, reinforced by available guerrilla forces, will seize the Los Banos Internment Camp at 1700 HOURS 18 February and hold the immediate area until internees can be evacuated to American-controlled territory.

2. The enemy now has:

   a. Approximately 200 troops at the Los Banos internment Camp.

   b. Approximately 1 Company 1,000 yards west of Los Banos Town.

   c. Approximately 300 at Calamba.

3. a. 1 reinforced Company of Paranaque troops will jump into the ricefields Southeast of the objective.

   b. Guerrilla forces will seize and hold the objective when the first Paratrooper jumps.

   c. Guerrilla forces will secure the area of the Parachute Jump site until all Paratroopers are down and organized and then join the American forces as reinforce the Guerrillas at the Internment Camp.

   d. 300 American troops will arrive about 2100 Hour via Laguna de Bay in Amphibious Trucks to reinforce the attack. Guides will be on the beach with lights to indicate that the area is clear and guide this force to the objective.

   e. 300 Guerrillas from Cavite and Laguna will attack and destroy the enemy at CALAMBA.

   f. 1 Artillery Battalion will support the operation from position near Calamba.

   x. Internees will be evacuated by Amphibious Trucks to American occupied positions. Sick and wounded will be given FIRST PRIORITY. Women and children will be given Second Priority. Able-bodied men will be given Third Priority.

4. a. Ammunition and grenades will be shipped to Guerrilla forces as rapidly as BANCAS become available.

   b. Medical supplies will not be shipped to the Internment Camp but patients will be treated behind American lines.

   c. Every BANCA that can be found will be commandeered red and sent to ALABANG, RIZAL to ship arms and ammunitions to SOUTHERN LAGUNA. Lt. Col. Guastavo Ingles, Inspector-General, Guerrilla Forces, Central Luzon, will supervise distribution of supplies.

5. a. Radio Communication will be maintained with HQ 11th Airborne Division.

   b. A site for dropping messages from L-4 Observation plane will be marked with WHITE PANELS in the form of a CROSS in an area SOUTHEAST of the Objective.

   c. I plan to land at PILA, LAGUNA on the night 17 18 FEB to take command of the Guerrilla chase of the Operation. A guide will meet Command Party on the beach.

                                        VANDERPOOL
                                        Major.

GGC assigned missions as follows: Hunters-ROTC, the most important mission, to attack the camp proper; the Huks, to furnish the main reserve; the PQOG, to guide the paratroopers from the drop zone to the camp; Marking's Fil-Americans, (now in the operation), to guard the route to Lalakay and to destroy Japanese reinforcements from that area; the Chinese, to join Hunters-ROTC in the attack on the camp proper. GGC told the guerrilla chiefs that the joint attack was now scheduled for 1700 hours on 18 February. Obviously, the guerrillas and GGC had been and were still making plans seemingly on their own or with some U.S. help—operational and logistical—to liberate the Los Baños internees one way or another.

In actuality, the guerrillas did at least start to deploy their units during the night of 18/19 February. How near they came to surrounding the camp and launching the attack is open to much conjecture. One of the guerrilla After Action Reports states that "the guerrillas were already deployed around Los Baños ready to execute Phase I" on the morning of 19 February. The attack was apparently called off when a runner from the Advanced Guerrilla Headquarters reported to Colonel Adevoso that the assault had to be suspended because "original airborne units and aircraft assigned to the operation were diverted for the liberation assault on Corregidor." This is at least partially false because the attack on Corregidor was made by the 503d Airborne Regimental Combat Team, a separate unit in the Pacific theatre that was wholly independent of the 11th Airborne Division. Nonetheless, "the guerrillas, somewhat disheartened but with high morale, returned to their previous stations," according to the same After Action Report. The guerrilla chiefs now waited for action by the 11th.

There is no question but that the guerrillas provided invaluable information and intelligence on the internee camp, its environs, its daily routines, its defenses, and its morale—both of the internees and the Japanese guards. The guerrillas were generally free to come and go throughout the countryside because the Japanese did not have blanket control and positive domination of the area outside the cities; instead their forces were in pockets. In the southern Luzon area, for example, their military units were generally bunched in areas such as the Genko

Line, Mount Malepunyo, and Calamba. The Japanese 8th, the "Tiger" Division, some 9,000 to 11,000 men, was along Highway 1 from Santo Tomas to San Pablo, about seven miles to the south of Los Baños. The guerrillas wisely did not engage the Japanese forces in head-to-head pitched battles; rather they hit and ran, disrupted the Japanese supply lines, and provided intelligence to the American forces once they had returned to the islands. In short, they fought like guerrillas are supposed to fight.

One difficult and insidious problem the guerrillas faced was the Makapili—a cruel Filipino word for "Japanese sympathizer." The area near the town of Los Baños reputedly held many Makapili, thus making guerrilla movements and operations in that area extremely hazardous because of the difficulty of identifying Filipinos who were collaborators with the Japanese. The Makapili were probably few in number, but the Japanese armed, uniformed, equipped, and organized them into units led by Japanese noncommissioned officers. They did control a few of the towns on the southern shore of Laguna de Bay and caused the guerrillas to be very cautious of their movements, contacts, and communications.

Colonel Vanderpool sheds some light on the operations of the Makapili.

As I recall, Makapili was a generic term for pro-Japanese Filipinos. The Makapili along the southwest corner of Laguna de Bay were locally known as GANAPS when they joined the Japanese military forces. I was told the GANAPS were anti-Spanish and later anti-U.S., and considered the Japanese as liberators. Several rifle companies were trained and used by the Japanese. They were ultranationalists with limited political support, but they may have attained the equivalent of a few battalions of light infantry. They were later deployed east of Manila, and, as I recall, were thrown against a U.S. tank-infantry task force where they were pretty well chewed up. The survivors were hit by Markings guerrillas, who finished what was left of their organized forces. GANAPS were so violently anti-U.S. that our downed pilots were reduced to small pieces by their women, children, and old men.

I went so far as to ride into their barrios with some guerrilla cavalry to post notices in the post office and on telephone poles asking them to mend their ways.

Some of their women served as "magic eyes," that is, masked agents who identified civilians paraded before them as guerrillas or loyal pro-Japanese. The other Filipinos feared and hated them.[7]

In their day-to-day operations, the transmission of intelligence between the guerrillas and the 11th Airborne Division was a two-way action. On the one hand, the GGC (Vanderpool's headquarters) assigned three staff officers who during the planning for the raid lived with the division staff, handled the guerrilla couriers who arrived at the headquarters, debriefed them, and relayed the intelligence to the G-2 Section. They also sent back to the guerrillas in the field specific questions and detailed requests for precise items of information. On the other hand, the 11th Airborne assigned a radio operator to the guerrilla headquarters, to live in the field with the guerrillas in the days before the raid and to receive and transmit messages between the two forces. The man to whom this task fell was Staff Sgt. John Fulton, twenty-four, who was a member of the 511th Airborne Signal Company, the communicators in support of the entire division—not just the 511th Parachute Regiment.

In late January or early February (he is not quite clear on the exact date), Sergeant Fulton, against all the soldierly lore he had ever learned and in violation of all the advice he had received from his first day in the Army, volunteered for a mission. The mission: to sail from the west side of Laguna de Bay with Filipino guides, join the guerrillas behind the Japanese lines (in territory nominally controlled by the Japanese and which had not yet been cleared by the American forces), then establish and maintain radio communications back to the headquarters of the 11th Airborne Division. His call sign was PE5–1. He took with him a radio, a code, an encoder and, rather ominously, orders to destroy his equipment if capture or death seemed imminent. As Sergeant Fulton said:

On that happy note, I prepared myself and my equipment: a small but powerful portable radio, hand generator, code and encoder (I would be my own message center), carbine, plenty of

---

7. Vanderpool, Jay D., Col., U.S.A. (Ret.). Letter to the author, 1984.

extra clips of ammo, as many grenades as I could stuff into jacket pockets, knife and some food.

At the division command post a Filipino guide and an American soldier who had escaped from the Japanese at the time of the fall of the Philippines and who had been living in the field with the guerrillas, met Sergeant Fulton. Under cover of darkness they escorted him to the west shore of Laguna de Bay. There they boarded a Filipino banca for the trip across the bay. Fulton hid himself and his equipment in the false bottom of the boat, a distinct disadvantage not only because the space was small but also because it reeked of the fish that was the normal payload carried in Fulton's cramped hideout. Fulton kept two grenades ready to blow up his equipment—and, as he well knew, half the boat and himself—if they were approached by one of the Japanese patrol boats that frequently checked out suspicious craft on the lake. Fortunately, it was a very dark night and no patrols interrupted their blacked-out trip.

Finally, at dawn on 11 February, Fulton and his guides landed on the east shore of the lake near Nanhaya. Other guerrillas met the party and escorted it inland on foot. During the afternoon of the 11th, Fulton and team arrived at the headquarters of the PQOG, Red Lion's Unit, in Tranca, Los Baños. The unit was commanded by Colonel Price. After arriving at the makeshift camp, he reported to the guerrilla commander—"General" Umali—encoded and sent to the 11th headquarters some messages that were waiting for him, ate, and slept.

Sergeant Fulton spent a couple of weeks at the camp doing precisely what he had been sent there to do: send and receive messages to and from the division headquarters and the guerrillas. He lived, of course, like a guerrilla—eating rice and bananas, rice and bananas, rice and bananas. Occasionally, the diet became epicurean, with chicken fried in coconut oil and candy made from sugarcane for dessert. Sergeant Fulton remembers:

> Considering the situation, these were good times; the camp was carefully guarded but ready to move at a moment's notice, weather was hot but generally good, food okay; and I really enjoyed living with the Filipinos. They were warm, friendly fellows

with a good sense of humor. They had learned long before to "take one day at a time" and enjoy what they could of it. Mañana?? And they really seemed to appreciate my being there.

By 18 February, though, the guerrilla headquarters near Los Baños was becoming more and more involved in the preparations for the raid. On that date, Sergeant Fulton received the following message. (The spelling and punctuation are just as they were in the original message in Sergeant Fulton's scrapbook.)

GUERRILLA HEADQUARTERS
LOS BANOS PATROL CP

18 Feb. 45

12:NOON

Sergeant Fulton, I am sending for the transceiver. The situation is such that that radio is very far from my CP where it should be, delaying the action on my part of important messages. Couriers to the place where you are now and up to this place takes more than three hours hiking and another three boating.

I am sending you a party of armed men with tommy and the rest M-1's. I will be expecting you and the rest of the party to be here tonight or at least before dawn. Major VANDERPOOL will be here by tonight and he might want to use that radio for important last minute communications with hq. of the 11th Airborne Div. It will be just too bad if he asks for that set and it is not around on our part.

GUSTAVO INGLES
Lt-Col., GSC (Guer)
Inspector General

Sergeant Fulton checked with Umali and obtained his approval to report to Ingles at the camp near Nanhaya. The five men promised by Ingles to escort Fulton duly arrived, ate, and were on their way to Ingles's command post with Fulton in about half an hour. The group departed just as it was getting dark and headed north. Ingles's estimate of the time to make the trip was fairly accurate: they arrived at Ingles's camp sometime around four o'clock in the morning.

The trip was not without incident. Once during the night the point man of the group came hustling back to report that a Japanese patrol was on the trail ahead of them. The guerrillas and Fulton quickly faded into the underbrush on either side of the trail and froze on the ground as the enemy patrol passed within a few feet. But Ingles was wrong in one respect, however; the guerrilla group never did go by water but spent the whole night silently edging its way through trails single file and watching and listening with extremely well-tuned senses for other enemy patrols.

Fulton and escorts arrived at Ingles's camp at about 0400 in the morning and were received with open arms. They were fed and bedded down. In just a couple of hours, though, the need for Sergeant Fulton and his radio proved accurate. For the next several days he was busy encoding, transmitting, receiving, and decoding messages.

A few days after Sergeant Fulton's arrival at the Ingles camp, Colonel Price gave him a message for immediate encoding and dispatch. It was ominous:

USPIF

HQS., RED LION DIVISION (25th DIV. PQOG)

In the Field

21 February 1945

To: Sgt. J. Fulton - Please transmit this communication upon receipt:

URGENT

ESPINO TO VANDERPOOL. HAVE RECEIVED RELIABLE INFORMATION THAT JAPS HAVE LOS BANOS SCHEDULED FOR MASSACRE PD SUGGEST THAT ENEMY POSITIONS IN LOS BANOS PROPER AS EXPLAINED MILLER BE BOMBED AS SOON AS POSSIBLE PD.

W. C. PRICE
Col. GSC (Guer)
Chief of Staff

Sergeant Fulton encoded and transmitted the message with haste. During the second and third weeks of February, the 11th

Airborne staff increased the tempo of its preparations and plans for the raid. Butch Muller intensified his efforts to gather all of the data on Los Baños from the guerrilla sources and the Air Corps photos, and was piecing together a picture of the camp, its surroundings and its daily life—particularly the life and habits of the Japanese guards.

Col. Douglass P. Quandt, the brilliant division G-3, made plans for the raid based on Butch Muller's intelligence. The 1st Battalion of the 511th fought along the Genko Line near Fort McKinley completely unaware that they were about to be called off the line to take part in an adventure that they would remember with pleasure and satisfaction for the rest of their lives. Other units in the 11th Airborne went about their combat tasks mindful of the upcoming raid, whose results would not be "x" number of enemy killed but "x" number of people rescued.

CHAPTER V: Internee Efforts

In spite of the increased planning by both the 11th staff and the guerrillas; reconnaissance flights of the Air Corps recce planes; clandestine, nighttime information-gathering excursions by individual or small groups of guerrillas near the perimeters of the camp, the majority of the Los Baños internees were unaware of the extent of the activities designed solely to rescue them.

For the internees, the six weeks prior to the raid was a period filled with emotional highs and lows, with hopes raised and then smashed, with mysterious and illogical comings and goings of the Japanese guards, and with uplifting rumors of imminent rescues mingling darkly with grimly whispered forebodings of their possible massacre.

On the last day of 1944, in particular, the internees reveled at the sight and sound of U.S. Navy aircraft that appeared over Los Baños and bombed and strafed the roads and railroad yards near the camp. In January and February 1945 Navy and Air Corps fighters flew over the camp, high and low, with increasing frequency. While the internees were forbidden to show any signs of happiness at the sights, they could at least begin to feel that all was not hopeless and that they were not a forgotten enclave of unimportant chattels of war. On 6 January, however, there occurred an event over which the internees could and, for a short time, did exult.

On that date the Japanese started to burn their records and sent word to the internees through the administrative committee that the internees would, among other things, turn in all shovels and other tools that had been issued to them. This meant only one thing to the internees, who were now well versed in translating the arcane meanings of various Japanese rituals and actions: collecting their supplies meant that the Japanese were leaving. And that is what they did. At 0300 on Sunday, 7 January, the Japanese prison commandant turned the administration of the camp over to the internee committee effective 0500 that day. The internees were, of course, overjoyed when they heard the news.

After the Japanese left, with no explanation for their sudden departure, of course, the internees erected a pole and hung from it an historic American flag. It was the same flag that had been raised over Fort San Antonio, Abad, Manila, in 1898 by Colonel McCoy, whose widow, May, one of the internees, had preserved and hidden from the Japanese during all the months of her confinement at Los Baños. Not to be outdone, the British internees in the camp raised a British flag that had been given originally to a member of the British community by an officer of the Australian Mercantile Marine, who had rescued it from his ship when it was sunk in Manila Bay. It was then smuggled into Santo Tomas Camp and later into Los Baños.[1]

The inmates celebrated their supposedly genuine deliverance from the custody of the despised Japanese with a moving and emotional religious ceremony presided over by the Episcopal bishop of the islands, Bishop Binstead. The committee also had the children sing "The Star Spangled Banner."

A few hours later, on Sunday evening, a small group of Japanese Military Police arrived to take over the control of the main gate but did nothing to restrict the new-found and jubilant freedom of the internees; the guards simply sat in the guardhouse. They were apparently merely a token force.

The internees immediately took advantage of their new way

---

1. That flag was ultimately presented to B Company, 511th Parachute Infantry.

of life. They contacted the Filipinos outside the camp, bought food with Red Cross credit (a rather bizarre system through which the Filipinos would be repaid later), and put themselves back on three meals a day with doubled rations, the highlight of which was boiled beef, a treat they had not enjoyed in months.

That the Japanese had ample supplies of food in their warehouses at the camp was established when the internees opened the previously off-limits food-storage sheds and found more than adequate stores of rice and corn. The Japanese had told the administrative committee that they had cut down on their rations because they had no assurance of any resupply. When the administrative committee found the cornucopia of food in the storehouse, it issued five kilos of rice to each person. With three meals a day, the internees began to recover their strength and optimism.

Why the internees did not leave the camp during the absence of the Japanese guards and other administrative personnel seems puzzling at first. But Murray B. Heickert, of General Motors and the chairman of the committee at the time, had cautioned them about the dangers of leaving the camp. He told the internees that he had no means to prevent anyone from leaving but suggested that "due to the fact that we were in such an isolated area, it would be good judgment to stand by in case some of our own forces would come in to assist us with our sick and aid in transportation and in getting us to a place for food."

The general consensus of the internees was that Heickert's advice was sound. In addition to that reasoning, there was the area near the camp, infested with Makapili, that was completely pro-Japanese. Wandering inadvertently into that area would probably have been a fatal mistake for the internees. Considering all of the factors bearing upon a decision of whether to leave, the internees almost unanimously decided for themselves that it would be foolhardy to leave the camp, unguarded though it might be.

The absence of the Japanese and the availability of sufficient food were encouraging and hopeful signs. The skies above Los Baños were filled on 9 January with many U.S. aircraft, bombing and strafing on all sides of the camp with little or no opposition from the Japanese. Hopes, optimism, and morale in the camp soared; the internees knew that their day of liberation could not be far off.

But on Sunday, 14 January, at about 0200 in the morning, the week-long hiatus from Japanese control ended; the dream of freedom and eventual release was shattered; dark despair fell on the internees. Major Iwanaka, WO Sadaaki Konishi, and the guards returned to the camp, dirty, disheveled, tired, and stinking "to high heaven." The Japanese claimed unconvincingly to the committee that they had been sent on some sort of an obscure mission, that they had accomplished it, and that they had then dutifully returned to their previous task of guarding Los Baños. The internees thought otherwise. They felt that the Japanese had simply tried to escape to their own forces south of the camp but that they had been somehow frustrated in the attempt. After the war, a Japanese officer who had been at Los Baños explained their week-long absence by saying that "some went to Manila to the headquarters (presumably of General Ko, commanding general of prison camps), and some ran away to the hills."

There is a strong possibility that the Japanese returned to the camp because they felt that it was a secure place for them to be, given the fact that the camp would not be bombed, strafed, or indiscriminately shelled by American forces who knew its location and contents. Some credence to this theory was supplied by a young Japanese clerk who occasionally accompanied the wood-gathering detail outside the camp. The clerk was apparently from a "good" family and because of either his physical difficulties or his attitude toward the war, he had been assigned to menial tasks at the internment camp. On one of the wood-detail trips after the return of the Japanese, the clerk told Ben Edwards that he and the party he had been with outside the camp had been caught on an open road and had been strafed by American planes. Ben Edwards asked him a few days later what he would do when the American forces arrived to liberate the camp. The Japanese replied, "Die." Ben presumes that he did.

Whatever the reason for their return, the Japanese restored the camp forthwith to its previous condition of servitude with severely reduced rations, more frequent roll calls, and unannounced searches for all sorts of real and imagined contraband. In their searches they continued to take whatever valuables the internees still had in exchange for food. The internees recognized it as "the good old Jap system of starving the prisoners and making them give up watches and jewelry."

After the reappearance of the doddering Major Iwanaka and the loathsome Konishi and his guards, the days dragged on monotonously. U.S. air activity, unaccountably and discouragingly, stopped for days. Each day the internees hoped to awaken and find that the Japanese had once more pulled out. But through the long days of January and well into February, these hopes went unfulfilled.

Conditions went from bad to worse. One of the internees reported that by 13 February "the whole camp was starving. People were dying from starvation, pure and simple." By 20 February the grain supply for the camp had run out. To compound the problem of the deaths by starvation, beriberi, malaria, and other diseases, the camp committee was having trouble finding men able-bodied enough to dig the graves and to talking the Japanese out of enough lumber to build coffins. Konishi's lumber embargo was simply another implacable and acrimonious restriction to harass and control the internees.

The internees' committee members were in a melancholy mood. They recognized, from rumors and internees who escaped at night and returned before dawn, that the fighting was heavy near Manila and that the United States was winning. From the camp they could see huge fires around Manila many nights in a row, but then the fires subsided. They concluded too soon that Manila had fallen to the United States.

In spite of the searches, the return of the guards, the continued oppression by the Japanese, the murder of an internee ("for disobeying his orders," according to the camp commandant), the men of the camp were not idle, nor did they cease their constant and tireless search for a way to free themselves and their fellow inmates.

Notwithstanding the Japanese announcement that "any American caught outside the camp grounds would be shot on sight," a number of the stronger men did occasionally slip away through the barbed wire and contact the friendly Filipinos and guerrillas outside the camp.

Freddy Zervoulakos was one of the men who risked death in an attempt to secure food from the Filipinos. Freddy was nineteen years old and was the son of Greek and Filipino parents. He spoke Tagalog fluently. His brother, Tony, was a captain in the Hunters' 44th Division. On the night of 12 February, Freddy slipped under the barbed wire, down the gully, and out of the immediate area. He got as far as the home of Mrs. Helen Espino, wife of Colonel Price. Mrs. Espino's home was about a mile and a half from the camp. There, Freddy met Tabo Ingles who was on the recon mission directed by Major Vanderpool. After some discussion, Tabo gave Freddy a copy of Major Vanderpool's letter of instruction and told him that he wanted to contact a "reputable member of the camp." He also gave Freddy a few packs of American cigarettes, confirming unequivocally that the guerrillas were in contact with the American forces. Freddy made his way back to the camp in the early morning hours of the 13th. Once safely back in the camp, he reported the details of his meeting with Ingles to Ben Edwards and Pete Miles.

Fresh American cigarettes in the camp illustrated a significant situation; the tension among the internees of the camp, heightened by the shortage of food and such common luxury items as cigarettes, was such that in their weakened condition, with their survival instincts sharpened, there was a strong possibility that some of the internees might fight over the cigarettes. Zervoulakos gave some of them to Ben Edwards who said that he could smoke them "only in the middle of the night when others were asleep as the fragrance would have drawn attention, possibly unwanted attention."

Before his internment in various prison camps, Prentice "Pete" Melvin Miles had had a brief but exciting career as a civilian advisor and operational hand with the U.S. Army in the Philippines. By profession he was a mining engineer, and the Army engaged him in December 1941 as a civilian to assist in construction and demolition work. Miles was responsible for mining various installations around Manila and actually blew up the long railroad bridge at Del Gallego as the U.S. Army retreated in front of the advancing Japanese. Because of the loss of that bridge, the Japanese were prevented from operating the railroad from Manila to Legaspi for a period of many months.

Even as a civilian, though, he was wounded and captured in a skirmish with the Japanese on Christmas Eve 1941. Somehow he managed to escape and hid out around Manila for a few months. Unfortunately, he was turned in to the enemy by Filipino collaborators and eventually ended up at Los Baños.

Miles and Edwards immediately contacted the camp committee secretary, George Gray, debriefed him on Freddy's meeting with Ingles, and gave him the copy of the letter that Freddy had brought back with him. Gray considered the contact with Ingles so important that he immediately called a meeting of the camp committee. The committee, somewhat cautiously and apprehensively, decided that further contact with the guerrillas was hazardous to the internees' well-being and should not be pursued. Gray, however, was convinced that a "do-nothing" policy was not the preferred course of action. Therefore, he took it upon himself to set up a rendezvous with Ingles, to assign men who would make the contacts with the guerrillas, and to decide what information and cautions had to be transmitted to the guerrillas before they made any moves, which, if premature and uncoordinated, could only result in disaster for the internees.

On the night of the 14th, Gray and Freddy, acting as guides, left the camp and rendezvoused with Tabo Ingles at Helen Espino's home. George Gray found the discussions with Ingles most revealing but somewhat disturbing. In the first place Ingles suggested, somewhat bravely, that he could smuggle arms into the camp so that the internees could defend themselves. Gray quite properly refused the offer because, as he explained to Colonel Ingles, he believed, correctly, that the camp, a civilian internment facility under international law, was forbidden to take part in hostilities. (Before the war George Gray had been on the legal staff of the U.S. High Commissioner.) Gray also emphasized to Ingles that if the guerrillas made an attack on the Japanese guard posts and their living quarters, the internees would be in grave danger of immediate retaliation by the vindictive Japanese. More important, perhaps, Gray made the point that the guerrillas had no means to transport more than 2,000 people, some sick and feeble, to U.S.-controlled areas, or even to provide security for them in guerrilla territory.

The meeting was extremely important, though, because Gray spent almost until dawn briefing Colonel Ingles on Los Baños, including a detailed description of the layout of the camp; the status of the health of the internees; the exact location of all of the guard posts, the guardhouse, and the guards' living quarters; the approximate strength of the Japanese garrison; and the caliber and number of their arms and equipment.

As the meeting was breaking up, Ingles asked Gray to meet him again on Sunday, 18 February. Gray made no commitment on future meetings at that point, but he did caution Colonel Ingles to remember that the general health of the internees was very poor and that no attempt to release the internees should be undertaken without the consent, approval, and assistance of the U.S. Army authorities in Manila. Gray and Zervoulakos made their perilous night trip back to the camp, through the hidden break in the wire, and into their barracks just before dawn.

That day, 15 February, Gray called a special meeting of the administrative committee and reported to that group the details of his meeting with Ingles. The committee agreed that the release of the internees must be left in the hands of the U.S. Army. The committee felt, moreover, that no further contact should be made with Colonel Ingles or with the guerrillas.

George Gray did not accept that committee restriction either. He discussed the matter in great detail with Ben Edwards, Freddy Zervoulakos, and Pete Miles. That quartet decided that Ben, Freddy, and Pete would keep the rendezvous with Colonel Ingles on Sunday, 18 February. Their mission was to escape, contact the guerrillas, meet if possible with whatever U.S. Army intelligence men were in the area (they had no way of knowing positively at that point that the 11th Airborne was actively plotting their rescue), and give them up-to-date information on the camp and its conditions.

The mission was not without its hazards. On 14 February the Japanese issued a curfew notice that no one was permitted to leave his barracks area after 7:00 P.M. (except on Wednesdays and Sundays, when the curfew was extended to 7:30 P.M.). The restriction prohibited the crossing of roads even between barracks. The iron-clad clincher: anyone caught violating the order was subject to being shot.

Nonetheless, in spite of the increased limitation on their movements, the trio of Edwards, Miles, and Zervoulakos stole out of their barracks at about 2100 on 18 February. Because of the curfew, they took a lantern, Miles feigned illness, and the trio headed for the hospital, which was near the northeastern corner of the camp and very close to the two barbed-wire fences that encircled the camp. They succeeded in reaching the hospital without being challenged.

At the hospital they discarded their lantern, said goodby to the nurses on duty, and crawled under the two fences. Outside the wire, they dropped down into a gully forty to fifty feet deep. Ben Edwards hit a tin can at the bottom of the gully and because they were well within earshot of the main guardhouse, Ben thought that they had torpedoed their mission even before they had gone fifty yards from the camp. They held their collective breaths for what seemed like hours. They detected no unusual reaction at the guardhouse, so they moved on down the gully, slipped under a bridge about 350 yards from the camp, and there met several armed guerrillas, an arrangement that Zervoulakos had set up during his previous meeting with Ingles. The party was now east of the camp and headed south toward Barrio Tranca, about three miles from the camp, to which the guerrillas' chief had ordered his men to lead the internees. The party traveled on paths through coconut plantations and arrived at Tranca about 2300. There they met Colonel Price and his party, among whom was Sgt. John Fulton, the indispensable radio operator and contact between the guerrillas and the 11th Airborne Division headquarters.

The trio gave Price and the group the latest information on the camp. Thereafter, the guerrilla chiefs and the internees discussed at great length what to do with the information and how to proceed to free the internees. For the first time the internees learned that the 11th Airborne was actively engaged in their rescue attempt.

The details of the plan that evolved from the talks with Colonel Price were these: Pete Miles would make his way to the headquarters of the 11th Airborne Division in Parañaque, on the shore of Manila Bay just south of metropolitan Manila. Freddy and Ben Edwards would move to Nanhaya, a guerrilla stronghold on the east side of Laguna de Bay near Pila, Laguna, to await word that Miles had reached the 11th's command post. In the event that he could not get there, then Ben or Freddy would make the attempt. Meanwhile, they would await developments at Nanhaya.

About 0130 on the morning of 19 February, the party left Tranca escorted by six or eight mostly young guerrillas and headed north in the direction of Laguna de Bay. Ben remembers that the night was as "black as the inside of a cow," which, under the circumstances, was undoubtedly fortuitous. They made their way slowly through the rice paddies and plantations and, just before dawn, crossed the national highway that circles Laguna de Bay along its west, south, and eastern shores. Shortly afterwards, they reached the lake and started to find boats for the next leg of their trip. They needed two, of course, one for Miles to go west toward the western shore and one for Ben and Freddy to go east to Nanhaya. The guerrillas leading the party were most adept at finding the boats, and even though they "commandeered" them, the fishermen who loaned them were most agreeable when they saw that there were Americans in the group.

At the beach of Laguna de Bay, the three Americans took a few minutes to wash off the mud and grime that they had accumulated during their long walk through the black hours of the night. During that exhausting trek, before they had crossed the national highway going north to Laguna de Bay, they had to make their way across muddy, water-logged rice paddies. In the darkness the Americans stumbled and slithered off the mud ridges that enclosed the paddies and dammed in the water for rice growing. The fleet, barefooted guerrillas, clad only in shorts and T-shirts and armed with various kinds of nondescript weapons, had no trouble hiking along the paddies. They were, however, quite amused at the Americans' distinct ineptness at "tightwire" walking along the slippery paddy borders. At the water's edge, however, the guerrillas were methodical, businesslike, and effective. The boats were ready in short order for the next, extremely important phase of the trip.

Here the party split up as planned. A few of the guerrillas took Pete Miles northwestward to the headquarters of the 11th Airborne at Parañaque, and the rest of the party accompanied Ben Edwards and Freddy Zervoulakos to the northeast toward Barrio Nanhaya, Pila.

Ben Edwards' party arrived at Nanhaya a little after noon on Monday, the 19th. Representatives of the Marking Fil-American Guerrillas met them and took them immediately to the Nanhaya schoolhouse, which was the headquarters of the commander, Col. Abigado Ortiz (who in later life and, perhaps, safer times, became the chief of palace security for the then president of the Philippines, Carlos Garcia). Edwards and Zervoulakos briefed Colonel Ortiz on their actions the previous night and reported that Miles was on his way to the headquarters of the 11th. Ortiz promised to tell them when he had received a message indicating that Pete Miles had arrived safely at General Swing's headquarters.

Miles and party, meanwhile, made their somewhat tortuous way by sailing banca and by foot to Parañaque, arriving there about 1100 on Monday, the 19th. Miles was immediately escorted to the office of Butch Muller. Miles gave Muller what was probably the greatest single contribution to the intelligence-gathering phase of the operation. Miles had studied closely and intimately the layout of the camp and remembered in great detail the location of the guard posts, the way the guns were sited, and the location of other key defensive installations of the camp.

No aerial photos or guerrilla reports could supply the information that Pete Miles revealed to the G-2 Section of the 11th. Many Japanese machine guns had been camouflaged; Miles knew not only their location but their fields of fire. His most significant pieces of information were the revelations that only the Japanese on guard in the posts around the camp were armed and that the garrison guard off duty rose just before dawn; took calisthenics, unarmed and away from their weapons, in an open area near their barracks; and left their arms, secured and locked in an arms rack, in a short connecting room between two long barracks buildings where they slept. Those two bits of information proved vital to the timing and location of the 11th's raid on the camp.

For a raid of this sort, detailed planning and intimate knowledge of every conceivable part of the objective—the camp— were absolute musts. Pete Miles had an encyclopedic knowledge of the camp's anatomy. The 11th's planners and the commanders of the unit that would make the raid, were concerned about the location and exact fields of fire of the machine guns and pillboxes around the camp perimeter. Miles reported, among many other facts, that many of the guard bunkers contained machine guns sited to cover the wire to shoot escaping prisoners rather than to lay down defensive fires against an attacking force; and that the large, sandbagged, solidly constructed bunker at the main gate had a firing slit about three feet off the ground with a very limited traverse of the gun, was so sited so that it could fire only down the road, could not cover any of the open ground on either side of it, and was placed in front of the wire some distance without any support for it.

With the kind of authentic detail Miles provided, the troop commanders involved in the raid knew that they could blindside that main bunker with little danger to themselves. Hank Burgess said that "the overhead machine-gun infiltration course of training where the machine guns were firing ball ammunition over us was more dangerous than taking out that gun at the main gate." Pete Miles's difficult trip to Parañaque was well worth the effort. Hank Burgess said that "Pete Miles probably contributed more to the success of the raid on Los Baños than any single person insofar as the intelligence is concerned."

Meanwhile, over at Barrio Nanhaya, Ben Edwards and Freddy Zervoulakos, after their briefing session with Colonel Ortiz, were treated to a feast the likes of which they had not seen in months. The guerrillas fed them fried duck eggs, boiled rice that had been heated in a skillet with coconut oil, fried fish, and pork. The guerrillas served the food native style—on banana leaves, without plates. Ben Edwards remembers that "a picnic on the beach had never been and probably never will be more welcome."

During the early morning hours of the 20th, Ben and Freddy and the guerrillas with whom they were encamped, learned from a Filipino boatman who came to Nanhaya that Pete Miles had indeed reached American-controlled territory on the western shore of Laguna de Bay. They assumed correctly that because he was within American territory, he had eventually reached the headquarters of the 11th at Parañaque. Ben thought that they could now relax with the guerrillas "at least as much as one could with only a thin line of guerrillas between you and the Japanese army."

Their period of rest, recuperation, and relaxation was to be short-lived. On the 20th, Lt. George Skau, 11th Airborne Recon Platoon leader, and Lieutenant Haggerty, an engineer officer from the 127th Airborne Engineer Battalion, arrived at Ortiz's guerrilla headquarters in Nanhaya. They had traveled the usual way, by banca and by foot. Edwards was not aware that the plan for rescuing the internees had reached the point where the attack was imminent. But when Lieutenant Skau, with his eye firmly fixed on his own mission and with fairly little regard for the fact that Edwards had just escaped from Los Baños, asked him to lead him back to the camp so he could reconnoiter the area, Edwards knew that the operation was in the final phase of development. Edwards readily agreed to lead Skau back to the camp.

Lieutenants Skau and Haggerty's mission was to reconnoiter the defenses of the camp, to locate a drop zone free from obstacles that might jeopardize the landing of paratroopers on it, to uncover and map out routes from the drop zone to the camp, to plot in detail the location of the Japanese defenses that might impede their march from the drop zone to the camp, and to locate all guard posts, pillboxes, walking guards, and machine-gun pits. Later they also needed to locate and survey a landing area for the amtracs and a route from the landing area to the camp.

Ben Edwards, Freddy Zervoulakos, Skau, Haggerty, and a few guerrillas left Nanhaya in two sailing bancas during the hours of darkness on the evening of 20 February. They followed more or less the same route Ben had used. Once on the beach, they walked to the camp, where they moved very cautiously around its perimeter. They spent a couple of hours in the "lower camp" area because the selected drop zone for the parachute company was adjacent to that general locale.

The tentatively selected drop zone was bordered by a power line and some railroad tracks. Even so, Skau correctly deter-

Los Baños Area

Scale: 1:40,000

mined that B Company could drop in the area with little difficulty. The recon group also reconnoitered the route and the dried streambeds that the paratroopers would take from the drop zone to the camp and the two guard posts that secured that part of the camp. They checked the road and bridges over which the amtracs would travel. They also looked at a possible drop zone in a field to the south of the camp, bordering Vatican City. Skau rejected that area as a possible drop zone because it was separated from the camp by Boot Creek. Ben said they got so close to what he called "Holy City" on their reconnaissance that they could hear sounds from one of the barracks there. After Skau was satisfied that he had all of the information he could gather during the hours of darkness, the party retraced its steps to Laguna de Bay, slipping and falling, as usual, into the rice paddies on the way. They arrived back at the southern shore of the lake about dawn on the 21st.

Unfortunately, only one sailing banca awaited them, and because it was imperative that Skau and Haggerty return to the 11th headquarters with their information, they got the banca, and Ben and his guerrillas had to scrounge up another. The guerrillas quickly found one, and Ben and his party were back at Colonel Ortiz's headquarters by noon. They immediately debriefed Colonel Ortiz on the details of the trip.

For the 11th Airborne Division staff, the intelligence-gathering phase of the raid was about over. Even though the operational planning went on apace with the intelligence-gathering phase, the operational side, of necessity, had to wait for the latest information and intelligence. With the information brought back by Skau, the operational staff could fine-tune the plan, call in selected unit commanders, brief them on the details of the plan, and set a final date and time for execution. The 11th Airborne, internee, and guerrilla paths were converging for the finale.

Maj. Gen. Joseph Swing (later Lt. Gen.), Commanding General, 11th Airborne Division, from February 1943 to August 1948. Courtesy Glenn McGowan

Staff planners for Los Baños Raid. L to R Glenn McGowan, G-1; Roy Stout, G-4; Henry Muller, G-2; Col. Douglass P. Quandt, G-3. Courtesy Glenn McGowan

Gymnasium at Los Baños (Baker Hall)

*Schoolhouse at Barrio Nanhaya. Lieutenant Skau met here with guer-
rillas and planned the February 23rd attack.*

Mamatid Beach and first group of internees, February 23, 1945 Courtesy Art Coleman

Lt. Col. Henry Muller and Lt. Col. Glenn McGowan display a Japanese sabre and flag taken during raid.

Los Baños camp showing burning barracks. Note amtracs in foreground.

Rescued internees being interviewed by members of 11th Airborne Division Intelligence teams. Other rescued internees in background.
Courtesy Glenn McGowan

Frank Smith (left), correspondent for Chicago Sun-Times, *and Lieutenant Colonel McGowan examine Japanese flag seized during raid.*

New Bilibid Prison at Muntinlupa Late February or early March 1945. Food being dropped for internees. National Archive.

CHAPTER VI:
Development of 11th
Airborne Division Plan

By early February General Swing and his staff knew of and understood clearly the 11th's mission at Los Baños: attack the camp, free the internees, and bring them all back to safety. What they did not know at that time was exactly how to do it. After the 11th had set up its command post in a western-style house in Parañaque during the second week of February and Major Vanderpool had established his General Guerrilla Command headquarters in a Filipino house across the street from the 11th's command post, the two staffs could and did coordinate and exchange information quite handily.

Much of the transfer of information took place at mealtimes. Vanderpool's G-2, Col. Marcelo Castillo, was a 1938 graduate of the U.S. Naval Academy; his G-3, Col. Bert Atienza, was fluent in English and had had previous military experience with the U.S. forces before the war. Because of their backgrounds, these two guerrilla officers, plus Vanderpool, could brief Muller and Quandt at least once a day on the guerrilla plans, actions, and results and, in turn, learn of the 11th's plans and operations, not only about Los Baños but about operations throughout the 11th's area of responsibility. Major Vanderpool was very conscious of his mission "to work with and support the 11th, which had landed in his sector of operations." Because they shared a common mess, both General Eichelberger and General Swing were updated frequently on the Los Baños plans and gave guidance when necessary.

With this close coordination, the 11th's staff knew that the guerrillas were planning a guerrilla-only raid on Los Baños and that it was a difficult task coordinating all of the diverse guerrilla units and arranging the necessary logistical support. The 11th staff was cognizant of Tabo Ingles's hazardous trip to the Los Baños area, his chaotic meeting with the guerrilla chiefs, the results of his reconnaissance of the area, and the summary of his talks with the internees. As February wore on, the 11th staff became more and more concerned with two recurring reports about the camp: the near-starvation condition of many of the internees and the rumors of a possible massacre by the Japanese as the war drew closer to the Los Baños area. These two factors gave added impetus to the 11th staff to consummate its plans, to work closely with the guerrillas, and to liberate the camp as soon as tactically possible.

By the middle of February, the staff had methodically collected and put together the various bits and pieces of intelligence and information. With this effort, the picture of Los Baños became clearer. The staff knew, first of all, that the camp was located about 2-1/2 miles from the southern tip of Laguna de Bay and about 42 miles southeast of Manila. A railroad ran through the town of Los Baños, which was on the southern beach of Laguna de Bay, then curved to the southeast less than a mile from the camp on its eastern perimeter. National Highway 1 ran down the western shore of Laguna de Bay, then south to Santo Tomas, east to Alaminos and San Pablo, then north up the east coast of the lake. A national highway also skirted the southern shore of Laguna de Bay.

The camp, some sixty acres in size, was in fairly open terrain on three sides. To the west of the camp, with foothills running almost to the camp's western flank was Mount Maquiling, 3,000 feet in altitude. A fairly well developed network of roads led into the camp from the town of Los Baños; inside the camp also were good roads. On the east of the camp, there was an open field suitable for a drop zone, although a power line and the railroad bordered the field and limited the size of a parachute operation. Barbed-wire fences encircled the camp, and a stream flowed past the camp on the east and north through a fairly heavily wooded area. Six miles to the northwest of the camp the San Juan River ran perpendicular to National Highway 1, providing the Japanese a natural barrier along the southern shore of which they could develop a formidable defensive position. The Lecheria Hills were about half a mile to the south of the San Juan River and dominated the flat terrain for many miles. Those were the physical features of the camp that the planners had to consider carefully.

Another part of the Los Baños portrait that had to be sketched very particularly was the number, physical condition, and mix of the prisoners. The best information that the staff had been able to dig out initially held that there were about 2,130 prisoners, the second largest concentration of Allied internees in the Philippines, all civilian except for 12 U.S. Navy nurses who were captured on Corregidor in 1942. Many internees, the exact number unknown but estimated as high as 50 percent, were in a weakened, debilitated state of health; another number, probably about 240, were enfeebled and bedridden and would have to be carried from the camp. There were also many women and small children among the internees. (One child was born three days before the raid.)

The staff had a relatively clear picture of the defenses of the camp. Ten guard posts punctuated the perimeter. The posts were guarded variously with from one to four men per position. There were also some camouflaged machine-gun positions that aerial photos had not disclosed; Pete Miles, however, with his photographic memory of the details of the camp, accurately located them on the maps that Butch Muller and his G-2 staff had drawn up. Miles also indicated the fields of fire and the areas covered by the machine guns.

The planners did not know, however, precisely how many Japanese were in the guard contingent, but the G-2 estimated, judging from the size of the camp and the number of manned guard posts and from guerrilla reports, that there had to be about 150 to 250 Japanese guards. The G-2 suspected that the guards were combat veterans with considerable battle experience who

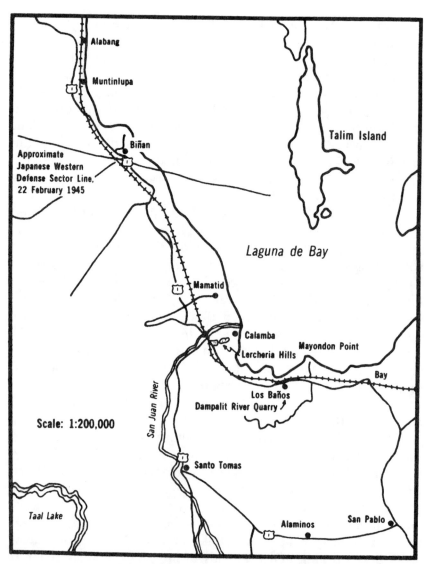

Alabang

Muntinlupa

Biñan

Approximate
Japanese Western
Defense Sector Line,
22 February 1945

Talim Island

Laguna de Bay

Mamatid

Calamba

Lercheria Hills

Mayondon Point

Bay

Los Baños

Dampalit River Quarry

San Juan River

Scale: 1:200,000

Santo Tomas

Taal Lake

Alaminos

San Pablo

had been wounded in action and were no longer fit for front-
line duty. The guards' possible combat experience was a factor
to be considered; combat-experienced soldiers, even after having been wounded, were disciplined, well trained, and resourceful. Their presence in the camp did not make the task
easier. Noncombat, rear echelon troops would have been more
easily cowed, stampeded, and defeated by a sudden attack.

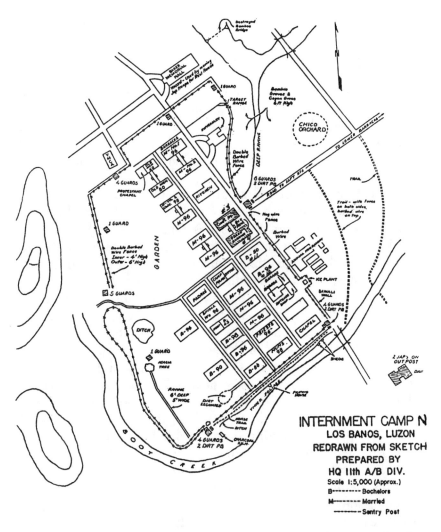

INTERNMENT CAMP
LOS BANOS, LUZON
REDRAWN FROM SKETCH
PREPARED BY
HQ 11th A/B DIV.
Scale 1:5,000 (Approx.)
B-------- Bachelors
M------- Married
--------Sentry Post

Passive physical obstructions around the camp were also factors that went into the Los Baños operational equation. The bar-
riers included double barbed-wire fences completely around the
perimeter; the inner fence was four feet and the outer one six
feet high. Thick foliage boarded the southeastern side of the
camp. A trail wound along the northeastern perimeter; the trail
had a fence topped with barbed wire along its length. Parts of
the fences were also sawali covered. (As the troopers later found
out, sawali looks formidable but is only an optical barrier. The

Japanese, for reasons known only to them, insisted that the fence between Vatican City and Hell's Half-Acre be sawali covered, and until the last six or seven months kept the two areas segregated.) Along the northeastern side of the camp, a deep (forty-to fifty-foot) ravine ran from the camp headquarters and the guard barracks due north to a thick stand of bamboo. Boot Creek meandered from the center of the west side of the camp along the wooded southern edge. Any one of these obstacles might have jeopardized a casual and superficial plan of attack that did not take them into account.

The daily routine of the guards was another important component that the planners had to evaluate and work into the plan. Butch Muller knew from Pete Miles that while off-duty guards were lined up for calisthenics, their weapons were in locked arms racks in the connecting room between the two long barracks buildings, which were directly across the street from the main guard bunker and pillbox. One important but unknown factor was whether at daybreak there might be a guard platoon armed and ready to relieve the guards on post. That possible complication was an additional element of concern.

Also, the staff had to consider painstakingly and very deliberately the numbers and kinds of Japanese units that were within striking distance of the camp, for if they planned and executed a successful raid, eliminated the guards in the camp, and rounded up the internees, the raiding force, behind Japanese lines, was still in a most precarious and vulnerable situation, especially since it was shepherding a slow-moving, excited, disorganized mob of physically debilitated prisoners. At that stage of the operation, the raiding force was most susceptible to being cut off by a larger, combat-ready Japanese force that could attack them and their rescued charges almost with impunity.

To estimate the strength of enemy forces outside the camp, the 11th Airborne staff had to rely on aerial photos, guerrillas, and their own reconnaissance troops. The escaped internees knew little about these outside Japanese elements. Nonetheless, the G-2 had painstakingly assembled a picture of the Japanese who were close enough to the camp to pose a danger to the raiding force. At the Dampalit River Quarry, about two miles to the east of the camp, there was a Japanese infantry company of some

200 men with two 105-mm. guns and four machine guns; at Mayondon Point, a little over two miles to the north on the shore of Laguna de Bay, were 20 soldiers and a machine gun; on the Los Baños wharf on the southern tip of the bay, two 3-inch guns guarded the shoreline and the wharf against illicit banca or other boat traffic; at a roadblock just south of the San Juan River west of Calamba was an understrength company of about 80 soldiers; to the west on Lecheria Hills, there were two 77-mm. guns sighted to the north and an unknown number of enemy troops; most formidable and troubling of all, in a hilly area just south of the Santo Tomas–Alaminos–San Pablo area there were some 8,000 to 10,000 experienced, combat-ready troops of the Japanese 8th Division, the Tiger Division; and from the Alaminos area, one battalion of the 8th Division could march to the camp in about ninety minutes.

By mid-February the pieces of the puzzle began to come together; the image of Los Baños was being brought into focus. At that point in the staff planning, the division G-3 stepped up his level of participation—the development of a scheme of maneuver. This was, of course, where his expertise lay.

The G-3 was Col. Douglass P. Quandt. (In some divisions in World War II, the G-3 slot was upgraded to full colonel, which was true in the 11th, but it was a short-lived promotion. It lasted only until VJ Day.) Doug Quandt was a tall, slender, blond, crew-cut, stoop-shouldered, brilliant, quiet-spoken man, class of 1937 at West Point, thirty-sixth in his class of 298 graduates, thirty years old at the time of the Los Baños raid. He was not particularly athletic, although prior to World War II he played polo. Those of us who knew him always worried about his ability to survive a parachute jump with all bones intact. He had a patrician air—elegant, gentlemanly, and considerate—and a marvelous sense of humor. He was keen minded, sharp witted, articulate, level headed, and with a flair for the dramatic in speaking and writing. He was a planner with great common sense and an encyclopedic knowledge of the division and its capabilities. His subordinates, whether in a battalion or in the G-3 staff section, were devoted to him. Most important of all, he had General Swing's complete trust, confidence, and support. He was, in fact, General Swing's screening board. General Swing moved him from command of the 457th Parachute Artillery Battalion to Division G-3 in New Guinea in 1944. He had such close rapport with General Swing that their relationship was very nearly a father-son intimacy, a bond that had begun when Major Quandt served with Brigadier General Swing in the 82d Division Artillery before the formation of the 11th in February 1943.

With hindsight, more than forty years after the raid, one senses that the contribution of Doug Quandt to the success of the raid was enormous but minimally acknowledged and appreciated. Were he alive today, Doug Quandt would probably say, "Well, what did you think a G-3 was supposed to do?"

Before getting into the specifics, it is important to point out that Colonel Quandt and his G-3 staff planners had to integrate the following facts and considerations into their tactical plan of operations: (1) a large number of the internees could not walk for any distance and would have to be transported in some sort of vehicle; in addition, they would have to be evacuated rapidly and promptly; (2) an all-out, all-guns-blazing assault on the camp would result in needless internee deaths; (3) the assault, instead, would have to be made with stealth, surprise, daring, and speed; (4) the withdrawal of the necessarily small and mobile assault forces and the internees could be by water or overland and would have to be made deliberately but with maximum speed before the Japanese in areas close to the camp could react and attack or set up roadblocks; (5) the attacking units could assault the camp by land (along National Highway 1 and down the west side of Laguna de Bay), by sea (across Laguna de Bay), and by air (a parachute drop); and (6) the raiding force would have to be small enough to get in and out promptly but large enough to defeat the opposition, marshal the internees, block any Japanese forces from moving in to reinforce their Los Baños garrison, and move back to their own lines, fighting along the way if necessary.

With those factors and considerations to guide him, Colonel Quandt developed a scheme of attack utilizing all three elements—land, sea, and air. The most salient components of the raiding force and their missions were the following:

1. The division recon platoon would precede the main body,

Operations Map for Release of Los Baños Internees

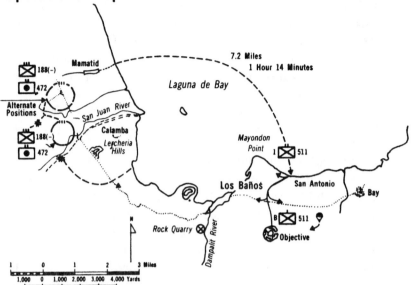

cross Laguna de Bay in bancas shortly before the raid, contact
the local guerrillas, coordinate their participation in the raid,
position themselves and the guerrillas around the camp, and
launch their strike to neutralize the sentries at H-hour; the platoon would also, at H-hour, pop smoke grenades to mark the
drop zone for the parachuting company and mark the landing
site for the amphibious portion of the force. The recon platoon's
and accompanying guerrillas' phase of the operation was obviously a key, if not the most crucial, segment in the entire plan
of attack.

2. An infantry company (reinforced) would parachute next to the
camp, rush immediately to the assistance of the recon platoon
and guerrillas in the event they were not able to eliminate all
of the guards in the immediate camp area, organize the internees for their evacuation, and set up a perimeter defense of the
camp to prevent any Japanese outside the camp from attacking
it.

3. An infantry battalion, minus the company that would make

the parachute assault, but reinforced with an engineer company and two howitzers of an artillery battery, would move across the bay in amphibious tractors. At H-hour the battalion would hit the beach marked by the recon platoon and deploy as rapidly as possible to the camp, still mounted in the tractors if they did not have to fight their way to the camp, on foot if they had to fight. Then it would assist the company that had dropped in and deploy one of its companies to the south of the camp to block any element of the Japanese Tiger Division that might move north and another to the west to block Japanese forces from the Lecheria Hills area. It would set up roadblocks with the help of an engineer platoon that would accompany it and, with their amtracs, provide an alternate means to evacuate the internees.
4. An overland ground attack by a combat team, composed of an infantry battalion reinforced by two artillery battalions and a company of tank destroyers, would move south from Manila along National Highway 1; attack across the San Juan River near Calamba; block any Japanese forces moving up on the west side of the camp from the Santo Tomas vicinity; move to the camp to reinforce the parachute and amphibious elements in the event the enemy tried to attack in force from the south; and bring with it enough trucks to evacuate the internees overland. These trucks were, in the initial plans, the primary means of hauling out the internees. The staff planned that the overland effort would, in fact, be the main effort in holding off any Japanese counterattacks.
5. Air cover would be available for any assistance required.
6. Guerrilla units would fan out to the west and south of the Los Baños area and block any Japanese forces that might move in to prevent the liberation of the camp or interfere with the evacuation of the internees.

The staff had, naturally, kept General Swing fully informed of the developments as they unfolded, and General Swing gave guidance to the staff as it worked on the plan for the raid. But General Swing—tough, direct, unequivocal, personally brave, the epitome of the type of soldier who firmly believes that he cannot and will not be hit by the "miserable, scrawny enemy"—was confident of himself and the division that he had so rigorously trained in the pines and scrub oak of North Carolina, the swamps and bayous of Louisiana, and the heat and jungles of New Guinea. He was a man who believed implicitly in that often-expressed but seldom-observed maxim of leadership: "Give a man a job and let him do it." General Swing's personality had a lot to do with the personality of his division and the manner in which the division attacked such missions as Los Baños.

General Swing was handsome—tall, slender, prematurely white-haired, eagle-eyed, and sharp featured—the casting office's ideal to portray a combat general. He had little tolerance for stupidity and indolence but would countenance a reasonable number of errors from a man during his learning process. The learning process was over, however, shortly after the division got into combat. By then the inept, lazy, and obtuse officers and men had been weeded out of the ranks of the division and sent off to other less-demanding wartime assignments (including those who shot themselves in the foot, literally and figuratively). The rigid, relentless, and totally time-consuming training period of over eighteen months, which General Swing had so closely and personally supervised, was about to produce in combat a finely tuned, well-trained, combat ready division.

General Swing was the type of officer who must inevitably rise to the top and become a general in a wartime environment.[1] He was not too much bound by the letter of any Army regulations or higher command staff orders that he considered defective, shallow, illogical, or just plain stupid. He was used to giving clear orders that he had no doubt would be obeyed to the letter—immediately. One of his favorite aphorisms was clear and to the point: "Do it now. Do you understand?"

During peacetime, General Swing's independence and indifference to "stupid" orders from higher headquarters occasionally caused him minor irritations and, no doubt, apoplectic symptoms in his bosses. During the occupation of Japan, for example, General Swing and his 11th Airborne Division occu-

---

1. General Swing graduated from West Point in 1915 with a class that included such World War II luminaries as Herman Beukema, Omar Bradley, D. D. Eisenhower, James Van Fleet, George Stratemeyer, Joseph McNarney, and Hubert Harmon. He married "Bootsie" March, whose father, Peyton C. March, was Chief of Staff of the Army during World War I.

pied the northern part of Honshu and all of Hokkaido. General Swing was in total command of the area. And, as was his wont, he considered some of the orders and regulations that came out of Eighth Army, one of his superior headquarters in far away Tokyo, to be inimical to the health, welfare, and interests of his division and the people of Japan whom he was ordered to govern. Therefore, he was scrupulously selective in the orders and regulations that he honored. When General Eichelberger, commanding general of Eighth Army, visited Sapporo, the site of the 11th Airborne Division headquarters on Hokkaido, after having been briefed by his staff on General Swing's command techniques, he said to Swing, "Joe, I don't know whether I should court-martial you or commend you." After General Eichelberger realized the good that General Swing had done in his area for his troops, their dependents, and the Japanese, he ended up commending him.

By the time the division was preparing for the raid on Los Baños, General Swing had developed great faith and trust in his subordinate commanders, a trait that had matured during the tough months of hard fighting on Leyte and Luzon. He knew his officers and troops; he knew that they could, would, and did fight. And he backed them up when they needed it.

Thus, the final plan for the raid was no surprise to General Swing (he had been following it and giving guidance as the plan developed), nor was it in his view daring, suicidal, or fraught with any unusual danger. While he did not consider the plan a cakewalk or routine, he knew intuitively that it was well within the range of successful accomplishment by his men. He was very cognizant of the fact that his officers and soldiers were battle-wise, disciplined, aggressive, and totally committed. No man or unit of the 11th Airborne Division ever "bugged out." (As a matter of fact, in World War II we had never heard of the expression.)

The enemy situation had been well explored, and the plan that had been worked up painstakingly by the staff and the commanders who were to participate in the raid included alternative means should any portion of the plan not develop fully. Thus, given the self-confidence of the soldiers and officers of the 11th

and General Swing's penchant for aggressiveness, combative-
ness, thorough planning, and faith in his staff, commanders, and
soldiers, it is not surprising that he approved the plan and ordered it executed. Twenty-three February 1945 was just a few
days away.

CHAPTER VII:
Pre-raid Operations

O n Sunday, 18 February, Maj. Henry A. Burgess and his battalion, the 1st of the 511th Parachute Infantry Regiment, were still totally involved in heavy fighting—infantry versus pillboxes and many, deeply dug-in machine guns, artillery, and mortars—on the eastern end of the Genko Line near Fort McKinley. Sometime during the morning hours that day, Lt. Col. Ed Lahti, the relatively new commander of the 511th Regiment,[1] came up

---

1. Lahti became the commander of the 511th on the death of Col. "Hardrock" Haugen, the original commander of the 511th. Haugen activated and trained the 511th and personally led it through the bloody fighting on Leyte, jumped with it onto Tagaytay Ridge, and guided it through the house-by-house, storefront-to-storefront fighting that marked the slow, treacherous combat involved in retaking Manila. Haugen (West Point, 1930), was nicknamed Hardrock by his troops in recognition of his prowess as a soldier, his superb marksmanship with an M1, his indefatigable ability to run farther and faster than anyone in the regiment, except an officer who had been an intercollegiate cross-country runner, and particularly for his insistence on stern discipline and tough training, factors the troops found abrasive in training but lifesaving in combat.

On 8 February General Swing and the assistant division commander, Gen. Albert Pierson, made their way by jeep and foot to "Hacksaw" Holcombe's 2d Battalion, 511th Parachute Infantry, command post, which Hacksaw had set up in a house

to Major Burgess's command post and told him to withdraw his battalion from the line, to move it to Manila for a "rest," and to report personally to division headquarters at Parañaque. Thus began for Hank Burgess a string of increasingly complex events, which in a total of five days would see him and his battalion in and out of Los Baños—a place he didn't even know existed on Sunday, 18 February 1945. He had no idea why Los Baños was important, he was puzzled as to why he and his battalion should go there, and he could not figure out why General Swing had selected his battalion for what, given the perplexing circumstances of secrecy, a precipitate withdrawal from a hard fight, and orders to report personally to division, must be a unique mission.

In fact, Hank Burgess was far from being an unknown quantity to General Swing. General Swing knew Burgess well and was confident that he could rely on his judgment, initiative, common sense, and cool-headed decisiveness on a mission that General Swing estimated could be tricky and fraught with unusual situations requiring quickfire decisions, one that might have to be executed in a rapidly changing environment, one where the lives of many people were hanging on the quality of those decisions.

---

about 100 yards from the Parañaque River Bridge, across the street from a cathedral. Haugen met the two generals there. General Swing wanted to talk to Haugen about the progress of the 511th through the streets of Manila. Haugen took them to the second story of Hacksaw's command post, where they went across the room to an open window to get a view of the local situation. Using aerial photos, Haugen pointed out the positions of various pillboxes and cleared lines of fire. A Japanese gunner saw them and fired a burst of 22-mm. AA fire. When they used AA fire against troops, the Japanese were in the habit of firing two armor-piercing, two high-explosive, and one tracer round in succession, firing them in bursts of five to ten rounds. One of the high-explosive rounds hit the side of the window, and fragments hit Haugen in the chest. No one else was touched. Haugen was immediately evacuated to the church at Las Piñas (site of the famous bamboo organ), just south of Parañaque, which was used as a collecting station for the wounded; at the church there was a surgical team on duty. The team performed surgery on Haugen but decided that he needed to be evacuated farther to the rear for additional surgery. Unfortunately, he died on the evacuation airplane on the way to the rear. Lahti took over the regiment that day.

Hank Burgess was a twenty-six-year-old major who had been in command of the 1/511th only since January 1945. He had earned General Swing's respect and admiration for his superb military qualities during the training days in Camp Mackall, Camp Polk, New Guinea; and in combat on Leyte.

While the division was in New Guinea, Burgess was transferred from the 187th Glider Infantry Regiment to division headquarters as Assistant G-3, a position that he held through the fighting on Leyte and during which he saw General Swing constantly every day. Haugen contacted him often there because he said "he was the only infantryman in division headquarters." When Haugen brought the 511th out of the Leyte Hills, back to Bito Beach, he relieved the 1st Battalion's commander and requested General Swing to give him Burgess to command the battalion. General Swing agreed. When Burgess reported to Haugen to assume command of the battalion, Haugen told him that he was unhappy with the losses that he had had in the regiment. He also told Burgess that he expected him to be the bravest man in the battalion but that he was not to show it. Thus Major Burgess became the commander of 1/511th. And on Sunday, 18 February, when Lahti directed him to report to division headquarters for a briefing on his battalion's new mission, Burgess had been in command of the battalion in combat for only fifteen days. Burgess would be the first to say that command in combat, particularly of an infantry battalion, ages and matures a man rapidly.

At division headquarters Hank Burgess met first with the G-3, Col. Doug Quandt, who answered his consuming question: "What's going on?" Quandt told him, "You and your battalion are going to help liberate over 2,000 internees from a camp near Los Baños." That statement quite naturally triggered in Burgess's mind a series of other questions. Where is Los Baños? Who is interned there? What are the defenses like? Where are the Japanese? How many? What other troops are available? Do I make the main effort and attack? How do I get the battalion there? How do I bring more than 2,000 civilians out from behind Jap lines? What kind of shape are the internees in? How long do we have to get ready? And, incidentally, why the 1st of the 511th?

For the rest of Sunday, Hank Burgess closeted himself with Butch Muller, Doug Quandt, and their intelligence and operations sections of division headquarters and tried to find the answers to those questions and a host of others that bombarded Burgess's brain the more he thought about the mission. Significantly, he learned that the division staff had not yet decided precisely how to liberate the internees, but he did find out that he and his battalion were to be a major part of the solution.

He studied the aerial photos that the G-2 had gathered; he pored over the maps of the area between Manila and Los Baños, paying careful attention to the road network and the condition of the bridges in the area. He examined and digested particularly the G-2 enemy-situation maps, which depicted as accurately as possible the location and size of the Japanese units in the area. He wanted to know every detail about the Japanese units. How good were they? Did they have tanks? Artillery? How could he keep the Japanese away from Los Baños while he tried to move 2,000 excited civilians out of danger? The more he studied the available information, the more Hank Burgess realized that "there wasn't much" to go on.

As the import of what information there was began to sink in, even to a battle-tested battalion commander, the task seemed at least complicated and certainly unusual. His reaction: "I was shocked to learn that only our battalion of about 412 men and officers (a very small battalion even by parachute infantry standards) was expected to make the raid, and I asked, 'Why us?'" The reply was that "the 1st Battalion, 511th Parachute Infantry, was numerically the strongest one in the division." That statement alone attested to the hard fighting the 11th had weathered: the strength of the 1/511th should have been nearer 650; yet Burgess's battalion was the largest of the seven infantry battalions in the division.

Hank Burgess was undoubtedly being modest in his statement of why he thought his battalion had been chosen. In fact, General Swing selected him for the mission because he had confidence in him and his battalion, and he knew that if anyone could handle the task, Hank Burgess could.

On Monday, 19 February, at division headquarters, Burgess continued to absorb the details of Los Baños and to consider the operational plan that Doug Quandt had sketched out for him. Burgess ordered his executive officer, Capt. Nat "Bud" Ewing, to move the battalion out of its so-called rest area in central Manila and to march it on foot south along the western shore of Laguna de Bay. To maintain the secrecy that such an operation demanded, no word passed to the battalion of what was in store for it. In fact, except for the commander and carefully selected key men, no one in any of the units of the division knew of the intended attack before Wednesday, 21 February.

On 19 February Pete Miles arrived at Parañaque and provided the detailed information that Burgess needed to formulate exactly how he would go about accomplishing his task. And by that late date—late given that D-day for the operation was only four days away—it was imperative that one of the 1st Battalion's companies be selected for the parachute drop next to the camp. Doug Quandt needed to know which company, and he needed that information as soon as possible.

He called in to his office—actually it was just a table set up in a room with other members of his G-3 staff—to Lieutenant William C. Abernathy, the liaison officer from the 511th to division headquarters. Quandt told Abernathy that he needed to know which company of the 1st Battalion would make the jump. Abernathy immediately drove by jeep to the command post of the 511th. There he met Ed Lahti and relayed the question to him, telling him that he had to have an answer in short order. Standing with Lahti in the command post were his S-3, Maj. William Frick; his S-2, Maj. Lyman S. Faulkner; and his S-1, Capt. Robert Foss. There was little discussion. Lahti simply asked his S-1, "Which company in the 1st Battalion is the strongest?" Foss replied, "B Company." Thus, with no staff study and little loss of time, Lahti selected B Company for the parachute phase of the raid. Bill Abernathy returned immediately to the division command post and passed the answer to Doug Quandt. Hank Burgess came to the same conclusion independently of Lahti and also selected B Company for the drop because it was commanded by 1st Lieutenant John M. Ringler, who according to Burgess "was an experienced and excellent troop commander and had the largest company in the battalion, as I recall, about ninety-three men."

On 17 February the 1st Battalion was astride a road leading

to Fort McKinley. A Company was on the left of the road and B Company on the right, on the edge of a wood line overlooking an open field that rose upward slightly. A few days earlier the battalion had knocked out a pair of 3-inch naval guns used by the Japanese as direct artillery. On the night of the 17th, a Japanese battalion hit the 1/511th, pierced its front, and infiltrated as far as the battalion command post. The 1/511th counterattacked and drove the Japanese out of their area. In the morning the 1/511th attacked across the open field and reached the high ground over which ran a railroad track. Behind the embankment, the Japanese had employed 20- and 40-mm. AA guns as ground weapons. The air bursts, ten or fifteen yards in the air, pinned the troops to the ground. Again 1/511th struck through and over the railroad tracks. It was at that point that a runner arrived at Ringler's command post—Ringler and his radio operator—and informed him that Colonel Lahti wanted to see him. Lahti was waiting only a few yards to the rear, and he told Ringler that they were going to the division command post to meet with General Swing. He did not tell Ringler the nature of the meeting or what Ringler's involvement would be. While Lahti may have known of the impending raid on Los Baños, he exercised great caution in not revealing it to Ringler.

When Lahti and Ringler arrived at the division headquarters, the chief of staff, Col. Alex Williams, ushered them into General Swing's office. General Swing, in his direct fashion, got right to the point. According to John Ringler, General Swing "informed me that my mission was to take my company and drop on Los Baños prison camp, release all internees, organize the people so we could start to march them to the point where they were to be evacuated." General Swing also "emphasized to me that unless we were successful, we may have problems getting out of the area and would be engaged in heavy fighting. He asked me if I had any questions, then directed the G-2 and G-3 to give me a complete briefing on the entire mission." Ringler, in his soldierly manner, said, "No questions, sir," and saluted as smartly as he could under the circumstances.

Lieutenant Ringler felt some consternation following the events that had just transpired. First, he had conferred briefly with the division chief of staff, a colonel, a rank that front-line company commanders rarely saw except for their own regimental commander (and in the case of the 511th, the regimental commanding officer, only recently appointed, was still a lieutenant colonel); then he had an "audience" with the division commander himself, a major general. That sequence of meetings, culminating with the briefing of a lieutenant by a two-star division commander, emphasized to Ringler the importance and uniqueness of his portion of the mission.

With concern and great curiosity Ringler reported to the G-2 and G-3 sections for the commanding general's promised rundown on the operation. He remembers that those staff sections

> provided an excellent briefing for me on all aspects of the operation. There were aerial photos available for me to select my drop zone. Intelligence information was available on all weapons emplacements, enemy personnel, and their activities. A Mr. Miles, who had escaped several days earlier and was taken to division headquarters by the Filipino guerrillas, provided all the information. With the information provided me, I was able to prepare my entire plan of attack, even to assignment of platoon areas of responsibilities prior to our jump. This permitted the platoons to assemble on their own and move directly to the target area.[2]

Ringler chose to jump from an altitude of 500 feet so that his troops would be in the air for just three or four oscillations of their parachutes and thus be difficult and fleeting targets for Japanese riflemen on the ground. At that altitude they really needed no reserve parachutes; if their main chute did not open,

---

2. One must recognize at this point the sharp contrast between the manner in which an operation of this moment and consequence was planned in 1945 and the way in which it would have been planned in today's bureaucratic military establishment—microscopically overseen as it is by layer upon layer of a civilian hierarchy in Washington and rigidly overcontrolled by a centralized command of forces and operations in the field. For example, President Carter had constant, direct communications with the force leader, Col. Charles Beckwith, during the aborted mission to free the hostages in Teheran; President Johnson kept detailed track of events in Vietnam with specialized daily briefings. In 1945, however, and particularly in the 11th Airborne Division, General Swing and his staff planners permitted Ringler to plan his own airborne assault and his portion of the attack on the camp without second-guessing him or offering over-the-shoulder suggestions. That faith in the ability of subordinate commanders on the ground was to play a large part later in the success of the Los Baños raid.

there was no time to pull a reserve. But they wore them anyway for confidence. It also permitted the company to land in a tighter pattern than if it had jumped from 1,000 feet or 1,200 feet. Ringler opted for a drop zone that was "fairly small," 1,500 feet by 3,200 feet. The drop zone was bounded by the barbed wire of the compound on one side, by high voltage lines to the south, by a line of trees on the east, and by a railroad track on the north and east. Ringler selected the easily recognizable railroad tracks as the release point—the "go," or jump point—for his drop. He also decided to request Maj. Don Anderson, commanding officer of the Air Corps squadron of nine C-47s that would drop him, to fly Vs in trail—three ships to a V—because of the narrowness of the drop zone and the need for compactness on the ground. For the rest of the day, Ringler conferred closely with the G-2 and G-3 and worked up the detailed plan for his drop, assault, and internee roundup.

Both during training and in combat, Lt. George Skau, leader of the Provisional Division Reconnaissance Platoon, worked directly for the division G-2. Skau, therefore, was conversant with the general planning for the raid and well understood and, most important, appreciated the part that the planners had written into the script for him and his band of intrepid soldiers.

Skau considered, first of all, the most difficult part of his three-pronged mission and the part on which the success of the entire operational plan rested: the absolute need for his platoon, augmented by guerrillas, to wipe out, as simultaneously as possible, with one concerted, coordinated, and precisely timed attack all of the Japanese guard posts, bunkers, and pillboxes surrounding the camp. To accomplish this part of his task, Skau knew that his platoon (thirty-one in number) and the guerrillas who accompanied his men would have to be armed with a carefully selected arsenal of grenades, automatic weapons, rifles, handguns, rocket launchers (to knock out the reinforced pillboxes and machine-gun bunkers thickly covered with dirt and sod), and even the inevitable, basic, direct-assault weapon of the guerrillas, the "bolo," or machete. (The country Filipino uses a "bolo" for everything from opening coconuts to trimming fingernails.) Skau understood well that for this part of his mission to succeed not only did he have to take with him and the platoon the proper assortment of weapons and ammunition, but also he had to organize his men and the guerrillas into teams tailored to attack a specific pillbox or guard post.

In addition to and before he could accomplish that portion of his mission, Skau knew that he had to get his guerrilla-reinforced platoon of heavily armed troops into the area and into their assigned positions by dawn on the 23d without having been seen or heard by the Japanese or detected by the Makapili in and around the camp area. "Stealth" became the key word of the recon platoon's preparation for its part in the raid.

Still, that was only a part, albeit the most important, of his mission. To complete his entire task, Skau had to ferry his platoon and all of its equipment, including extra arms and ammunition for the guerrillas, across Laguna de Bay in bancas without alerting or running into the Japanese patrol boats that mounted a small-scale navy flotilla on the lake to prevent unauthorized Filipino traffic. Once safely across, he had to contact the guerrilla leaders, coordinate with them the employment of guerrillas in the raid and in supporting roles, assign missions to each of the reconnaissance platoon-guerrilla teams, mark the drop zone for Ringler and B Company, mark the landing beach for Burgess and the rest of the battalion, attack the guard posts around the camp at H-hour, and race the Japanese, who would be at calisthenics, to their arms racks. If he considered his menu of tasks extraordinary, Skau typically did not convey his trepidation or concern to his troops. He accepted the mission as just another—admittedly tougher—assignment in a long series of successful behind-the-lines adventures with his men.

The reconnaissance platoon of necessity was made up of enterprising, resourceful, well-trained soldiers—an elite group, even among cocky, self-confident paratroopers. One who exemplified the character of the platoon was Martin Squires. He had joined the 511th Parachute Infantry Regiment while the division was still at Camp Mackall, North Carolina, that World War II cantonment rapidly thrown together by speedy, if not comfort-concerned, contractors.[3]

---

3. Camp Mackall was a collection of militarily aligned black, tar-paper covered, one-story shacks of various sizes and shapes that had been built from the pine trees

Squires had heard of the reconnaissance platoon through a high school and college friend who had volunteered for and been selected for the platoon. With an exuberant group of motivated, high-spirited young paratroopers to choose from, the reconnaissance platoon leader could afford to be particular in his choices. Thus, the platoon took on an aura of elitism and attracted the most energetic, courageous, and doughty of the paratroopers in the division. Squires kept volunteering for the platoon, but it was not until the division was at Dobodura, New Guinea, in June 1944 that he was accepted.

He said:

> We were primarily under Colonel Muller. . . . We were a small group—mostly college men—crazy as h--- and intensely devoted to our leaders, Lieutenant Polka (the recon platoon commander before Lieutenant Skau) and Colonel Muller. We had superior training, I believe—most of us were outdoorsmen to begin with and grew up with a familiarity to hunting, hiking, and camping. Our additional indoctrination to Alamo Scout training while in New Guinea was also very valuable. I came out of a heavy weapons basic at Camp Wolters near Mineral Wells, Texas, so it was natural that after joining the 511th and then the division recon that I was considered somewhat of an "infantry weapons" expert for our patrols.

With soldiers like Martin Squires, Lieutenant Skau had no qualms about his platoon's ability to carry out the multi-faceted mission that the staff planners assigned to it. During the week prior to the raid, Skau studied the terrain maps and photos and worked with the guerrilla liaison officer at division headquarters; then on the night of 21 February he moved his platoon across the bay to join the guerrillas.

---

that until recently had stood where the barracks—so called—were now. Even by World War II military-camp standards, Camp Mackall was grotesquely ugly, particularly because it was located, incongruously, near the beautiful, manicured resort areas of Pinehurst and Southern Pines, North Carolina. (It was so unsightly and had deteriorated so rapidly that, unlike the sturdier World War II camps, some of which are still in use today, Camp Mackall was leveled shortly after the war ended. Today its overgrown acres accommodate a Green Beret field-training area.)

In the week prior to the raid, Lieutenant Skau and Lieutenant Haggerty of the 127th Airborne Engineer Battalion had made their way across Laguna de Bay to reconnoiter the area, contact the guerrillas, brief them on the 11th Airborne plans, survey the area around Mayondon Point to pinpoint the Japanese defenses nearby, and to determine if the soil of the beach would support the weight of amtracs.

On 20 February Skau and Haggerty arrived in Nanhaya, the base camp of the Hunters' 45th Regiment. Not only did the two lieutenants make their reconnaissances, but it was on that trip that Skau announced to the guerrilla commander for the raid, Colonel Guerrero, that the 11th Airborne elements would be ready to make the attack on the morning of the 23d.

By the 21st, however, a disconcerting element entered the problem. The guerrillas had discovered that the Japanese had reoccupied their previously prepared positions at Mayondon Point and had emplaced a number of machine guns in defensive positions around the area that the staff planners of the 11th had selected for the landing of the amphibious element of the force. Haggerty and Skau verified this report, noted that landing there in the face of those defenses would be hazardous, and changed the amphibious landing area to the vicinity of San Antonio, a location on the beach about a mile to the west of Mayondon Point. After making these arrangements and gathering the needed data, Skau sailed back across the lake to report to division headquarters, to brief his troops, and to prepare and equip them for the move across the lake and the attack.

The planners persevered at their tasks at division headquarters during the week of 19 February. Hank Burgess used the time to put the finishing touches on his own plan. On Monday the division headquarters requested amphibious tractors for the movement of the 1/511th (less B Company) across the bay. The request went from General Swing to his boss, Lt. Gen. Oscar Griswold, the XIV Corps commander. This request piqued the curiosity of the XIV Corps staff officers, for, while they knew that the 11th had been assigned the Los Baños mission, it was not until they received the request for the amtracs that they realized that the 11th was deeply involved in planning the raid and perhaps even close to a launch. After some conversation between the staffs and the commanders, General Griswold not only approved the plan but directed the 672d Amphibian Tractor Battalion to provide the 11th with fifty-four of its armored, track-laying, dual-purpose, amphibious, road-running tractors.

"Alligators," as they were occasionally called, were ugly, "coldblooded," and smooth-skinned. They carried a crew of three men, mounted .50-caliber and .30-caliber machine guns on pedestals on the front, were powered by a 9-cylinder aircraft engine mounted forward of the guns, and could carry up to a platoon of fully loaded soldiers with all of their ancillary equipment in the open bay. Officially, and in militarese, they were LVT-4As. They could also carry jeeps or pack howitzers. On land they lumbered along at about fifteen miles per hour, but on water they slowed to a five-mile-per-hour wallow, churning up a wake of white water and making an ear-thumping racket that precluded an undetected arrival. Their only hope for anonymity, secrecy, and privacy was surprise.

Sixth Army, the headquarters under which XIV Corps operated, was likewise in the dark about the raid until the day before the attack. On 22 February Sixth Army became aware of the raid when an alert staff officer inquired of XIV Corps the use to which the tractors of the 672d Amphibian Tractor Battalion were to be put. As Hank Burgess said, gently yet chidingly, "From the result of the raid, it is apparent that the absence of Corps and Army staff planning did not detract from the success of the operation."

Numerically, the largest and most heavily reinforced combat arms element of the Los Baños Task Force was the overland segment. Initially, the mission of the force was not to be principally a diversion. Rather, in the original planning for the raid, General Swing had assigned to Colonel (later Major General) Soule, commander of the 188th Glider Infantry Regiment, the primary mission of attacking down National Highway 1 at H-hour on the 23d, developing and holding a bridgehead over the San Juan River near Calamba, fighting ahead to Los Baños, blocking any Japanese elements moving north from the Santo Tomas–Alaminos area, assisting the 1/511th in evacuating the internees in the trucks that the 188th would have brought with them to the camp, then, with the 1/511th and the rest of the raiding force, moving overland back up Highway 1 to U.S. positions north of Mamatid.

In the initial version of the plan, the amtracs were not to be used to evacuate the released internees because they were slow moving across the water, and the planners thought that they would be susceptible to Japanese fire from the shore and possibly from patrol boats on the lake. The amtracs would have returned empty to Mamatid after having dropped off the 1/511th. The plan called for 1/511th to march out after the raid with the Soule Task Force behind the column of internees, moving north toward Manila.

This plan was scrapped just before the raid because the engineers reported that the roads south of San Juan River were in poor shape and that the Japanese had blown a number of bridges across the streams and arroyos. The trucks would have had great difficulty in reaching Los Baños. Thus, the final version of the plan called for the amtracs to haul out the internees and for the 1/511th to move back north on foot with the Soule Task Force.

Colonel Soule's Task Force consisted of his regimental headquarters and headquarters company, the 1st Battalion of the 188th, the 472d and 675th Field Artillery battalions, Company B of the 637th Tank Destroyer Battalion, and engineers with bridging equipment to span several arroyos north of Los Baños where the Japanese had dropped the bridges. The plan anticipated that this force would make the main attack on the Japanese in the area. And, as a matter of fact, General Swing assigned to Colonel Soule the overall responsibility and command of the Los Baños Task Force, thereby putting him in command not only of his own units but also of Hank Burgess's force, the division recon platoon, and the other units that made up the force.

On Tuesday, 20 February, the several and diverse units within and outside the 11th began to move to their appointed launch points, or got ready to do so. D-day was only three days away.

The 1/511th continued its foot march south from its "rest" area near Manila. And on Tuesday the division staff received word that nine C-47s of the 65th Troop Carrier Group, 54th Troop Carrier Wing, on Mindoro would be available to drop B

Company. On the next day Capt. Donald G. Anderson, the squadron commander, and his operations officer, Capt. H. D. O'Grady, flew one C-47 rather cautiously into cratered, bomb-studded Nichols Field. There they were met by staff officers of the 11th who briefed them on their mission. Following the briefing, Anderson and O'Grady flew a one-ship recon mission at 5,000 feet over Los Baños and returned to Nichols to await D-day. On the 22d eight more C-47s from the 65th Troop Carrier Squadron flew up to Nichols Field from Mindoro to complete the Air Corps contribution to the parachute phase of the raid. Air Corps fighters also made significant contributions as they covered the area during the actual attack.

On Wednesday the 1/511th continued south along the same highway that Colonel Soule's troops would use later in the week, but shortly thereafter, to avoid alerting the Japanese to the raid, left the road and traveled cross-country along the shoreline of Laguna de Bay until they were at a point near Mamatid. There they set up a bivouac in a wooded area and remained as well hidden as the circumstances would permit.

B Company, the unit selected for the parachute attack on the camp, had also backed off the line near Fort McKinley with the rest of 1/511. But B Company was treated differently. Jim Holzem was a member of the company and remembers vividly those days before the jump. After leaving the fight near Fort McKinley, Jim Holzem said:

> Then it seemed that we were put on the shelf for several days. We didn't do much of anything. But something big was brewing for B Company. We could feel it in the air. And the rumors! Something big, something important, was coming up. What was it all about? We were loaded into trucks and driven about twenty miles south of Manila. The trucks drove up to the gates of a large penitentiary called New Bilibid Prison, and we were driven in. Some thanks for all the fighting we had been doing! We were being put in prison. We were assigned cells and that night slept on cots with boards for mattresses.
>
> I guess the reason we were spirited away to the prison was that they wanted to maintain complete secrecy regarding the up-coming operation. Finally, Lieutenant Ringler, our commanding officer, called us together and told us of the operation. There

were over 2,000 American Allied civilian prisoners in a Japanese internment camp about twenty-five miles beyond where our front lines were. Word had come in from Filipino guerrillas that the Japanese were going to execute all the prisoners on the morning of February 23rd, shortly after 7 A.M., right after the guards' morning calisthenics. B Company was to jump on the camp, or very near it, right at 7 A.M., while the Japs were doing their calisthenics. At the same time, the Filipino guerrillas and some of our men from the recon platoon (who would infiltrate into the area earlier) would attack the guards at the various guard posts. Also they were to prevent the guards who were doing calisthenics from reaching the little armory building where their rifles were stacked. Meanwhile the rest of the battalion would be crossing Laguna de Bay in amphibious tanks, called amtracs, or alligators. These alligators would hold about fifty people each.

We in B Company had mixed emotions about the operation. We were very proud that we had been selected for the most exciting part. In all of World War II, I believe, we were the only parachute company to make a rescue jump like this. However, rumors were rampant. This was to be a "suicide jump!" Or "few of us would return." So, you can see why we had mixed emotions. But for no amount of money could you have bought a seat on that plane from a Company B trooper. We had the feeling that this is why we had been training so hard and long, that this was to be the ultimate battle, the highlight of our combat careers.

Jim Holzem had another problem, and he didn't quite know how to solve it. In early February, after the jump on Tagaytay Ridge, B Company had moved up to the vicinity of Manila, in the area around the Parañaque River Bridge. After the fight at the bridge (during which the division chief of staff, Colonel Schimmelpfennig, was killed), the company was pulled back and found itself in a residential area of small Filipino homes set on posts about four or five feet from the ground. Holzem's platoon leader ordered the platoon to dig in, and, in typical GI reaction to that order, Holzem and his assistant gunner, Earl Hooper, were less than enthusiastic about digging another hole in yet another location only to be ordered to move out just as the hole was completed. Shortly, however, the Japanese provided the necessary incentive to make the laggard diggers dig. They fired on Holzem's area with 90-mm. antiaircraft guns with tubes leveled and with shells that exploded just above the company and sent fragments raining down on B Company. Holzem and Hooper started digging with noticeable enthusiasm.

After they had been at the task a few minutes, they paused and looked up. Two Filipino youths, one about fifteen and one about twenty-five, stood watching them. Never one to miss an opportunity to avoid the onus of gouging out earth with a small, folding, entrenching shovel, Holzem offered a T-shirt and a pocketknife to the young men if they would finish digging the holes for them. The Filipinos considered it a deal, and Holzem and Hooper happily sat down to some lunch.

The rations that day contained cans of sweetened condensed milk. When the Filipinos saw the milk, they put down their shovels and asked for a new deal: they would dig for the milk rather than the T-shirt and the knife. Holzem could not understand why they wanted to switch and pressed the younger of the two men for an explanation. The young man, who spoke good English, told Holzem that many Filipinos were suffering from malnutrition, that his sister was married to the older fellow, and that their baby was seriously malnourished and needed milk. Holzem reacted as any red-blooded, hard-charging, intrepid paratrooper trained to kill the enemy would. He made the rounds of both A and B companies, gathering their condensed milk. His score was two full cases. He dutifully presented them to the father and uncle and thought no more about it. A deal's a deal. The Filipinos finished the holes in record time and left.

The next day a Filipino family showed up with mother, baby, father, and uncle. The smiling, grateful family thanked Holzem profusely, and, in a spirit of unbridled generosity, the father told Holzem that the younger man was assigned to him for the rest of the war as hole digger, aide, assistant, or whatever else he wanted him to do. Holzem was dumbfounded and protested, but in vain. From then on Rosendo Castillo was Holzem's shadow, bodyguard, companion, and man Friday. Holzem nicknamed him Oscar, after his grandfather, who had been turned down at the age of 76 for enlistment, much to grandfather's disgust and disappointment.

Oscar and Holzem were inseparable during the succeeding months of combat. Holzem expressed it well:

Oscar and I became very close during the next five months. I was his big brother, advisor, father, friend. And I became his nurse when he had malaria attacks, which occurred about once a month. He, in turn, repaid me amply with his look of adulation and his eagerness to please. He helped us dig foxholes, carry ammo [Holzem was a machine gunner], fill canteens, translate, and he took his "stay awake" turn at night. But what he did best was scrounge for food. My rations were always supplemented with rice, chicken, eggs, and vegetables. He was with me when we stood off 'banzai' attacks; he was at my side when we crossed the machine-gun and mortar-covered approach to Fort McKinley.

After leaving the Parañaque Bridge area, B Company went to the northeast toward the eastern end of the Genko Line. Holzem recalls:

The next nine to ten days we fought around the south side of Manila and Nichols Field. . . . It was during this time that Oscar started accumulating his wardrobe. When he first came with me he was barefooted and wearing only short, tattered pants. Soon he was wearing Japanese army shoes and other articles of clothing. The Jap clothing fit him fairly well, but his ambition was to get GI clothes as soon as possible. The problem was that he was so small he couldn't wear any of our clothes. He did get a helmet from a dead paratrooper, but the steel helmet was too heavy for his thin neck, so he separated the steel helmet from the helmet liner, discarded the helmet, and wore the liner. This at least made him look like he belonged. What he really wanted more than anything was a pair of jump boots. By now he realized that we were more than just plain soldiers; we were paratroopers, and it was the boots that said so. He wanted to be just like us, and he hated those Jap shoes.
Then one day we made a distinct move to the east. We were going to take part in the attack on Fort McKinley. There was a little wooded area about 400 yards west of the high-banked railroad which ran north and south. Once over the RR embankment, we were exposed to enemy fire from Fort McKinley.
As the lead elements of B Company moved into this small

wooded area, a long-range Japanese machine gun fired a burst into the area, killing our radioman, Glen Fox. Glen was the smallest man in the company and not much larger than Oscar. Seeing Glen's body lying there, Oscar asked if he couldn't have his boots. I was shocked and said something like, "No, Glen died with his boots on and should be buried with them on." But our platoon sergeant wasn't as much of a romanticist as I was, and he told Oscar to go ahead and take them. Off went the hated Jap shoes, on went the paratrooper boots, and up stood a ten-foot-tall Filipino.

Over the next few weeks, Oscar and Jim Holzem forged a mutually respectful friendship that was tested in battle. They fought together, stormed a railroad embankment together, held off Japanese night attacks together. The bonds, formed in combat, held tightly, so when B Company was pulled out of the line and moved to Bilibid, what to do with Oscar was Jim's problem. If they were going to jump into the Los Baños area, "what in the hell" was he going to do with a small, fifteen-year-old Filipino with no jump training? Holzem suggested to Oscar that he return to Manila and his family to await B Company's, and Holzem's, return from Los Baños. Oscar adamantly refused; he would have none of that. He was a paratrooper now—didn't he have the boots to prove it?

Oscar pleaded with Holzem to take him along on the jump. And so did the other two Filipinos in the company who had attached themselves to other troopers. Holzem and the other two "big brothers" talked it over and decided to "give it a shot." They dutifully reported to Lieutenant Ringler and presented their case. Holzem and friends told Ringler that the Filipinos were heroic in combat, that they deserved to stay with the great B Company, that they were superb scroungers from the countryside, that the Americans would be lost without them, and that, incidentally, they would be invaluable as interpreters in that unfamiliar environment where surely they would have to talk to the natives to find out any number of things. The latter argument was the clincher for Lieutenant Ringler. He gave the OK for the three Filipinos to make the jump with B Company. The problem of the "big brothers" was partially solved; now it remained to make the three Filipinos real paratroopers overnight, literally. They solved the rest of the problem by giving the three Filipino stalwarts an intensive three-hour course in parachuting back at Bilibid and declared them bona fide paratroopers. It was certainly easier than four weeks in jump school at Fort Benning.

Late on the afternoon of Thursday, 22 February, B Company, reinforced with the Battalion Machine Gun Platoon under Lt. Bill Hettinger, was trucked to Nichols Field, recently taken from the Japanese—so recently, in fact, that there were undoubtedly remnants of the Japanese defense force still holed up along the runways. Nonetheless, when B Company troopers arrived at Nichols, they found nine C-47s already there waiting for them.

After the troops had dismounted and set up a bivouac area near their planes, Lieutenant Ringler proceeded to review with his platoon leaders his final attack order. He had assigned each platoon a different assembly area on the drop zone because he had already assigned each platoon a specific objective at the camp. He did not want to waste time assembling as a company first then having to break down into platoons again. He fully realized the need for speed in getting to the camp and wiping out any guards not eliminated by the recon platoon and guerrillas. Given the radio communications he had with each platoon leader, he knew he would have no trouble in controlling the assembly on the drop zone and the attack.

John Ringler said of his soldiers when he first briefed them back at Bilibid:

> The men of B Company accepted the initial news of the jump in good spirits. I don't believe that they initially understood the full danger of the mission until after our briefings were completed. At that time they became apprehensive of what could happen; however, with the amount of intelligence that we had we were very confident of success. We realized that we might be dropping into a hornet's nest, which could result in considerable casualties. Regardless of our feelings, we knew that the mission was ours to accomplish. This was truly an ideal airborne mission, and that is what we were trained for.

The next important actions for B Company were drawing

parachutes and eating a hot meal.[4] Finally, and by now it was rather late in the evening, B Company's paratroopers bedded down under the wings of the C-47s, lying on parachutes, field gear, or anything else that was handy. No one was particularly comfortable, and, given the next day's mission, no one slept very soundly. And Jim Holzem's problems with the fledgling paratrooper, Oscar, were still not over.

As Jim remembers the situation:

Oscar was unwilling to concede that the large pack on his back (which nearly touched the ground) could conceivably contain a parachute. For some reason this bothered him, and he wouldn't get off the subject. Finally I told him, "Enough, take my word for it."

We slept that night on the runway under the wings of the planes. I doubt that many of us slept very much, as we were all high on excitement. What would it be like? How many of us would be alive twenty-four hours later? We all lay there, each with his own private thoughts: about our loved ones back home; about whether there really was a heaven and a hell; about where we would be tomorrow night—heaven, hell, or still here on Luzon?

On other parts of Luzon, from the headquarters of the 11th at Parañaque to the guerrilla encampment at Nanhaya, from Muntinlupa to Tranca, the various units and elements of the attack force began moving to their pre-H-hour launch sites. The planning and reconnaissance phases were over; the operational phase was about to begin.

---

4. Before our jump on Tagaytay Ridge, our commander had somehow managed to scrounge up steaks and eggs for our last breakfast before we mounted up in the aircraft for the flight from Mindoro to Luzon and the drop on Tagaytay Ridge. Feeding paratroopers such a meal before a combat drop is a tradition of the airborne—and not a few of us cynical types reasoned rather forebodingly that they were feeding the condemned men hearty meals.

CHAPTER VIII: Movement to Launch Positions

By the afternoon of the 21st, Lieutenant Skau had returned to division headquarters at Parañaque after having completed his reconnaissance of the camp and his conferences with the guerrilla chiefs and the escaped internees, Ben Edwards and Fred Zervoulakos. About 1500 that day Skau assembled his thirty-one man recon platoon in its bivouac area near division headquarters. Using the maps that the G-2 had compiled and updated with the latest intelligence from Pete Miles and Skau himself, Skau briefed his platoon on its part in the raid. On the map he pointed out the various pillboxes and guard posts, the routes of the walking guards, the barbed-wire fences, the topographical features such as Boot Creek, the deep ravine near the hospital that pointed directly at the main gate and the guards' quarters, and, most important, the area where the guards would be doing calisthenics in their loincloths at 0700 on the morning of the 23d and the building where the guards' weapons were racked and locked. Pete Miles was also there to answer the platoon's questions and to cite other details that Skau might have missed. Then Skau briefed the platoon on the overall plan involving the dropping of B Company near the camp, the amphibious landing of the rest of 1/511th, the overland route of the 188th Task Force, and the need for haste in helping to organize the internees and move them out of the camp once they had seized it.

After the briefing, Skau directed his platoon to get ready to move out that night. He broke the platoon down into three groups for travel by banca across the lake. He would lead one group, Sergeant Squires would take another small party, and the bulk of the platoon, with most of the platoon's gear, would travel across the lake together in a large banca.

After dark that night, the platoon reassembled and mounted trucks for the first leg of their movement to Los Baños. They traveled about an hour to the barrio of Wulilyos on the shore of Laguna de Bay where they met their guerrilla guides and the three Filipino-manned bancas for their trip across the lake to Nanhaya, the headquarters of the Hunters' 45th Regiment. Two of the bancas were small; the other was a large, "clumsy" one. The Filipino crews promised that the trip across the lake would take about "two or three hours." The platoon would shortly find out how wrong that estimate was.

Lieutenant Skau, Sergeant Andrus, three correspondents, and Skau's small, two-man platoon headquarters group set sail in their banca shortly after dark at about 2000 hours; Sergeant Squires and his group of five men sailed about fifteen minutes after Skau. The bulk of the platoon, some twenty-one men, plus the platoon's weapons, ammunition, rations, supplies, and extra weapons and ammunition for the guerrillas were to have departed in the large banca a few minutes after Skau and Squires. Unfortunately, as they were loading, the Filipino crew chief told them, much to their consternation and disgust, that the rudder was broken; two long hours later the rudder was repaired. They finally boarded the boat and set sail for the south shore of the lake. But, by that time, the favorable winds, light to start with, had died down. The men aboard the large banca were well aware that the platoon would have great difficulty accomplishing its mission without them and the supplies they carried. And as the hours wore on, they became more and more uneasy and apprehensive about their late arrival, the possibility of running into a Japanese patrol boat, and the success of the total mission.

Because of the light winds, it took Skau and his team eight

hours to make the "two-to-three-hour" crossing; Squires and his men made it in ten hours. These two boatloads were able to get ashore during the early morning hours of the 22d. The large banca was nowhere in sight from the south shore near Nanhaya. By dawn of the 22d, it was still almost becalmed in the middle of the lake; the Filipino crew then spent the better part of the day "tacking and other never-before-heard-of maneuvers," according to one of the occupants.

At one point during their nighttime crossing, Sergeant Squires and his team heard a motor launch and assumed, to be on the safe side, that it was a Japanese patrol boat. Squires had a machine gun with him, loaded it, and put it in the bow of his banca, ready to fire if the patrol boat should challenge him. He ordered his men to remain hidden below the gunwales of the boat and if the patrol boat closed in, to "open up with everything they had." Fortunately, the patrol boat lost interest in the banca and did not come close enough to inspect it.

After Skau, Squires, and their men arrived at Nanhaya, most of the recon troops who came with them hid near the Nanhaya schoolhouse and stayed out of sight during the daylight hours. The large banca had still not arrived. Skau knew that his mission would be risky without the men and the contents of the large banca, but he also knew that the other elements of the 11th Airborne raiding force were already in motion toward their launch sites and that the raid could be delayed only at great hazard to the raiding troops and the internees and only in the most serious of emergencies. Therefore, he prepared to execute his part of the raid without the bulk of his platoon and his equipment.

At Nanhaya Lieutenant Skau met once again with the guerrilla leaders, Ben Edwards, and Freddy Zervoulakos in the Barrio Nanhaya schoolhouse. Ben drew a sketch of the camp on the schoolhouse's blackboard, and he and Freddy explained to Skau, Squires, Andrus, and the guerrilla leaders, in more detail than they had heard before, the terrain around the camp, the location and size of the various guard posts, and the location of the fences and barbed wire. Then Skau, in coordination with the guerrilla chiefs, put the finishing touches on his plan for the recon platoon/guerrilla attack on the camp.

During the afternoon of the 22d, Skau held another meeting with the guerrilla chiefs and the escaped internees. Skau had already broken down his platoon into six teams (assuming the arrival of the large banca) and had assigned them their missions; now he attached 8 to 12 guerrillas to each team except Hahn's and Squires's (Squires started out with from 20 to 25 guerrillas but lost a number of them en route). Skau directed one team to mark the drop zone by popping green smoke grenades on the drop zone at 0658 the next morning; to a second team, led by Sergeants Hahn and Bruce, he assigned a guerrilla company and the task of marking and securing the landing beach at San Antonio for the amtracs; he assigned the other four teams, led by Sergeants Town, Call, Angus, and himself, to specific attack positions around the camp (dependent upon the location of the guard posts, cover and concealment, and routes of approach), mainly on the west and north sides. Additionally, he directed one team to break through the fence at the beginning of the attack and to race to the arms rack before the exercising off-duty guards could. Skau picked for himself and his squad perhaps the toughest job of all: knocking out the guardhouse at the main entrance to the camp on Pili Lane. Counting his own men and guerrillas, Skau had a force of 31 recon platoon men and about 190 guerrillas to accomplish all of his missions, including security of the beachhead, guides, and patrols.

Because Ben Edwards was familiar with the details of the camp and its perimeter defenses, Skau tasked him to accompany Sergeant Squires, six recon men, plus about twenty guerrillas and to hit the guard posts on the northwest quarter of the camp. He assigned Sgt. John Fulton (the radio operator), Freddy Zervoulakos, and seven guerrillas to an area south of the camp with the mission of blocking any Japanese guards who might flee in that direction—toward Mount Maquiling, a natural escape route to reach the Japanese 8th Division. The guerrillas working with the recon platoon in the main assault were from the Hunters' 45th Regiment; those helping mark the drop zone were PQOG and Hukbalahaps; and the security force for the amphibious landing site was a company of Marking Fil-Americans.

Finally, during the evening hours of the 22d, the large banca landed on the shore of Laguna de Bay near Nanhaya, and the men in it made their way to the schoolhouse. They were frustrated from their long ride, not only because of its length but also because during daylight hours, they had had to crouch and hide below the sides of the boat. One of them said after the ride, "I was so mad I was ready to take on a whole Jap battalion."

After their arrival, Skau held one final briefing session with the guerrilla chiefs and his own men. Then he gave them their last order:

> On the approach march to the camp, do not give away your positions by returning any Jap fire. Let them think they hear animals in the woods. If the Japs think that a rescue force is near, they will slaughter as many of the internees as they can before we can get there. If any of your men get hit coming up to the camp, carry them with you. Leave no evidence of our troops in the area. Good luck!

After dark on the 22d, the various recon/guerrilla teams began the forced marches to their designated attack locations. The Huks, who would help to guard the drop zone, moved overland to the camp from their assembly area at Dayap; the PQOG, who would serve as guides and secure the evacuation route, moved on foot from nearby Tranca; the Fil-Americans, who would secure the beach, sailed by banca from Nanhaya to San Antonio; and, at midnight, the main assault force of the recon platoon and Hunters' guerrillas sailed in bancas from Nanhaya to the San Antonio beach, where they started a difficult, perilous, time-consuming foot march to their assigned launch positions around the camp. Once they were back on land, these raiders found that the route through the rice paddies was slippery and treacherous in the dark of the night—and the night of 22/23 February 1945 was pitch-black. That condition was advantageous as well since it permitted the raiders to move with less chance of detection by Japanese who patrolled well the area outside the camp wire.

Sgt. Martin Squires and his large team had a particularly hazardous experience. They debarked from their bancas near San Antonio on Mayondon Point about 0100. Sergeant Squires then organized his men for the two-mile march to the camp. His route would take him down the east side of the camp, along Boot Creek, and finally to the west side to attack across the old garden area. He was skeptical of the guerrillas' military discipline, but because he needed their firepower, he organized his column so that a recon trooper was spaced every fifth or sixth place in the column. He reasoned that was the best way to keep control. In his own part of the column, he had one guerrilla, then Ben Edwards, then two recon troopers and four more guerrillas. Throughout the hours of darkness, his system worked well. The guerrillas guided them through the flooded rice paddies accurately and quietly. Two or three times they had to stop when they heard Japanese patrols. All went well until dawn; then he sensed that something was wrong. He went back along the column and found that there was no one following after the fourth guerrilla behind him.

He halted the head of the column and made a fast decision. It was getting close to 0700. He sent Ben Edwards, one recon man, and five guerrillas ahead to get in position for the attack after giving Ben, unarmed up to this point, the .45 Colt automatic that he had carried in a shoulder holster throughout the war. Sergeant Squires then ran back about half a mile along the route they had just traveled to try to find the rest of the column. At a fork in the trail, he found Gene Lynch and Wayne Milton sitting quietly, waiting for him. They knew that he would come back for them, they told him. They also told him that when their part of the column got to the fork in the trail, they found that the column was broken and they didn't know which way to turn and that the guerrillas who had been with them had disappeared. Squires never saw them again.

"The three of us headed for the camp as fast and as quietly as we could go. The firing had started before we could get into position for the attack," Squires recalls. "As we broke over a hill, we came upon a couple of dead Japs."

Ben Edwards and the men with him arrived at their position northwest of the camp on time, but only after one of those unplanned, unrehearsed, unexpected happenings which proved once again that, even in those days, and especially in combat, Murphy knew what he was talking about. It was an event that might have jeopardized at least part of the overall mission.

As Ben, the recon men, and the five or six guerrillas with him were moving as quietly as possible toward their assigned location, they cut through the yard of one of the still-occupied faculty cottages on the west side of the camp. There, one of Ben's guerrillas was attacked by a large dog—obviously one that had stayed away from the kitchen of the internees. In spite of the need for secrecy, stealth, and silence, the guerrilla attacked by the dog instinctively drew his pistol and shot the dog. To Ben and the other men, so conscious of the requirement for surprise, the pistol shot sounded like a pack-75 mm howitzer round fired with charge seven. The time was 0645; Ringler was thirteen minutes from stepping out the door of the lead C-47. Ben Edwards and his men froze, then ducked into the underbrush and held their breath for what seemed like hours. The pistol shot fortunately did not alert the Japanese. Ben and his men continued to steal even more warily into their designated attack positions and ended up being one of the recon teams ready to attack at H-hour.

Other elements of the raiding force also spent the twenty-four hours before H-hour moving to their respective launch positions. On the afternoon of Thursday, the 22d, the Soule Task Force started its move. The 1/188th Glider Infantry Regiment entrucked in its assembly area near Parañaque. The other two major units of the Soule Task Force, the 675th Glider FA Battalion and the 472d FA Battalion, joined the 1/188th on Highway 1 south of Parañaque. The column moved down the highway past Mamatid, where the 1/511th was in bivouac awaiting the arrival of their amtracs for the trip across Laguna de Bay the next morning.

Just before dark on the 22d, the lead elements of the Soule Task Force arrived at the San Juan River. There they were joined by Lieutenant Colonel O'Campo's guerrilla battalion. The infantry men dismounted and took up positions along the north bank of the San Juan. Maj. Jack Kennington, the S-3 and executive officer of the 1/188th, gave four trucks to O'Campo and sent the remainder of the trucks back along Highway 1 to Parañaque. O'Campo loaded his battalion and all of its gear on the four trucks and headed for Calamba to secure the area. Calamba was a known Makapili center, and it had to be neutralized to protect the flank of the Soule Task Force. Kennington recalls that he was "amazed at how the guerrilla battalion got everyone on their vehicles, each man carrying two duffel bags of booty plus weapons, ammo, and so forth. They really towered heavenward."

The artillery battalions wheeled into firing positions behind the 188th along the San Juan, from which they could reach the Japanese across the San Juan and in the twin Lecheria Hills, the key terrain that had to be secured to insure the eventual evacuation after the raid of the other elements of the raiding force, the 1/511th and recon platoon.

While Capt. Leo Crawford, 1/188th Headquarters Company commander, was positioning his machine guns and mortars in the dark, a tank machine gun opened fire, giving the men around it "a good scare and threatening the secrecy of the plan." Where the tank came from is not clear. It was "definitely a friendly tank." Jack Kennington can only surmise that when the battalion was attacking a week before across Nichols Field, it had attached to it some tanks from the 19th Infantry. He assumes that they were still attached for the raid on Los Baños.

During the night, the Task Force dug in, manned its perimeter, and continued preparations for support of the raid the next morning. They were prepared to accomplish four tasks: (1) attack across the San Juan River and clear the area toward the town of Los Baños to permit, after the raid, the evacuation of the raiding force overland, up Highway 1, and through the lines of the Soule Task Force;[1] (2) support the O'Campo battalion's attack on Calamba with mortar and artillery fire; (3) block Japanese forces that might move up from the Santo Tomas–Alaminos area; and (4) move on to the internment camp to assist the 1/511th if necessary.

By the evening of the 22d, the 1/511th had assembled in a bivouac area near Mamatid. A platoon of C Company, 127th Airborne Engineer Battalion, and two pack howitzers from D Battery, 457th Parachute FA Battalion, had joined them in the New Bilibid Prison area and had moved with them to Mamatid.

---

1. Although this was the original plan, it did not work out that way.

During the day, the commanders of the 1/511th held a series of briefings to explain in detail to their troops the upcoming raid. The battalion commanding officer briefed his company commanders; they, in turn, briefed their platoon leaders. Then the platoon leaders assembled their men and went over their part in the operation from start to finish. Each man had the opportunity to examine the maps and aerial photos of the camp that the division staff had so carefully prepared. They studied the sketches supplied by Pete Miles and memorized the location of guard posts, pillboxes, and perimeter defenses.

By nightfall of the 22d, the men of the 1/511th knew precisely what was expected of them. Capt. Tom Mesereau and his men of C Company knew, for example, that C Company would dismount from the amtracs at the camp and would move out to establish a roadblock to prevent the Japanese troops of the 8th Division from reaching the camp. Mesereau was under strict orders from Major Burgess to "move off toward the 8th Division to await its advance guard [which would take at least an hour], then to fall back, buying time, but not to become attached to any real estate and to avoid casualties if possible." Lieutenant Fraker and his men of A Company, reduced by the heavy fighting around Fort McKinley and Manila to less than fifty men, knew that their mission was to dismount as soon as the amtracs landed at the camp and to deploy around and secure the area. Another platoon and the two howitzers from D Battery, 457th Parachute Field Artillery Battalion, were tasked to dismount from the amtracs at San Antonio and set up a perimeter to defend the beachhead.

B Company, 1/511th, had moved by truck to Nichols Field and dismounted near its aircraft. There, Ringler and his platoon leaders briefed the troops on their separate mission and gave each soldier in the company a small map showing the layout of the camp, the machine guns, their fields of fire, the pillboxes, guard posts, and walking patrol routes. They pointed out on the maps the ditches and arroyos where a man could lie without being hit by Japanese machine guns. They also gave them specific locations for their weapons so that they could protect the camp as necessary. This was especially important to Lieutenant Hettinger and his Battalion Machine Gun Platoon, which Burgess had attached to B Company for the drop. The briefing of the men was detailed and complete. Burgess says that their route from the drop zone to the camp "could have been traversed in the dark had the timing of the drop been off."

At dusk on Thursday, the 22d, the amtracs that were to carry the amphibious element of the attack force waddled out of the water of Laguna de Bay and churned across the sand at Mamatid. To the paratroopers of the 1/511th in hiding there, the arrival of those vehicles, fifty-four amphibious tractors of the 672d Amphibian Tractor Battalion, with which the paratroopers were thankfully unfamiliar, was a silence-shattering experience. One amtrac is noisy—its motor roars, its tracks clank—fifty-four LVTs made enough noise to alert the entire Japanese army anywhere on Luzon, or so it seemed to the security-conscious paratroopers. Burgess, in particular, knew that the Japanese had three patrol-boat outposts nearby: on Talim, on an island in Laguna de Bay, and on Punta, at the tip of a peninsula that jutted into the center of the lake. He did not relish the possibility of alerting the patrol boats.

The curious paratroopers inspected their means of transportation once the amtracs had moved off the beaches and had ground their way a few hundred yards inland, churning and blowing sand as they moved. Each amtrac had a ramp at the rear for loading and unloading troops, vehicles, and bulk equipment. Each one was about fifteen feet long, eight feet high, and eight feet wide, and weighed eighteen tons. It could carry an infantry platoon of about thirty-three men. The amtracs looked formidable and impressive, but their steel sides were thick enough to stop only small-arms bullets. Nonetheless, they gave a sense of security, false though it was.

After a quick look at their transportation for the morrow, many—if not all—of Burgess's men decided that they would have preferred to jump into combat from a C-47 rather than ride across a large body of water encased in a slow-moving, clangorous, floating, iron pillbox. But theirs was not to decide or elect; they were committed to riding in the dark in the lumbering amtracs (which a number of skeptical paratroopers reasoned could not possibly float—even unloaded) across an alien lake to a remote, never-before-seen beach, twenty-five miles behind Japanese lines.

The prospects of such a cruise probably caused even some of the most intrepid troopers a few anxious moments as they tried to settle down before boarding their implausible transportation. Paratroopers, many of whom had taken off in aircraft but had never landed in one and whose idea of the proper way to enter combat was vertically, were intuitively suspicious of moving to combat noisily, horizontally, on water, at a top speed of five miles per hour.

Units of the 127th Airborne Engineer Battalion, the organic engineer battalion of the 11th, were in the parachute element of the attack force, the amphibious portion, and the overland component. They had contributed significantly to the preparation for the raid by their preliminary engineer reconnaissance work. For example, on the morning of 20 February, an engineer patrol from the 127th made a route reconnaissance of the road south of Muntinlupa to determine the condition of the road and the bridges and whether the route would be able to support the trucks and artillery of the Soule Task Force. They found that Highway 1 was in fairly good condition but that the bridges were in very bad shape. The bridges over the Binan River would require reinforcement, and the bridges over both forks of the San Cristobal River and the San Juan River had been dropped into the riverbed by the Japanese. The engineers had to halt their reconnaissance at the north bank of the San Juan River to avoid alerting the Japanese to the impending attack. But on their way back toward Manila, the engineers reconnoitered the beaches near Mamatid and selected sites suitable for the embarkation of the amphibious force.

C Company of the 127th Airborne Engineer Battalion, in keeping with the standard airborne organization of the 11th Airborne Division (one-third paratrooper and two-thirds glider-rider) was the only jump-qualified company in the battalion and consequently worked normally in support of the 511th Parachute Infantry Regiment.

In mid-February 1945 most of the 127th Airborne Engineer Battalion was repairing and improving Nichols Field and adjacent areas, terrain that had only recently been wrested from Japanese control by the 11th Airborne. Several days before the Los Baños operation, Lt. Alan H. Chenevert, a platoon leader in C Company, received an order to report to Col. Robert Soule, the overall commander of the Soule Task Force. Colonel Soule and his staff gave Chenevert a briefing on the impending operation around Los Baños and tasked him and his men to install two roadblocks at the internment camp to impede any possible effort by the Japanese to come to the relief of their Los Baños garrison. Chenevert decided that a reinforced squad could accomplish the mission. In his original plan all members of his platoon were to jump in with B Company, but because of the weight and bulk of the demolition equipment, some of his men and equipment were assigned to move with the amphibious portion of 1/511th. After receiving his mission from Colonel Soule, Lieutenant Chenevert returned to his platoon on Nichols Field.

Early on the morning of 22 February, he sent his platoon sergeant, Johnson, from Nichols Field to New Bilibid Prison with the bulk of his platoon and with the demolition equipment. He told Sergeant Johnson to report to Major Burgess and to join the 1/511th moving by amtrac. Chenevert remained behind at Nichols Field with a detail of eight men. They continued to work on the airfield while awaiting an additional shipment of C-3, a plastic explosive material. When he received the C-3, Chenevert intended to rejoin his platoon either at New Bilibid or Mamatid. However, the C-3 never did arrive. As the night wore on, it became evident to Chenevert that he would not have time to rendezvous with the rest of his platoon. Capt. Walter Brugh, C Company commander, then made arrangements for Chenevert and his men to join Ringler's company for the jump.[2]

Since Lieutenant Chenevert and his men were already at Nichols Field, they needed very little time to move to B Company's C-47s. Once there, Chenevert briefed his men on their

2. In recent correspondence Col. John Ringler (U.S. Army, Ret.) states that he does not recall that Chenevert and his men jumped with his company at Los Baños. His lack of memory on this point is entirely understandable: Chenevert and squad did not join B Company until long after dark, when they were assigned probably by the executive officer of B Company to various aircraft whose sticks were not complete, and they could very easily have passed notice by Ringler, who was far more concerned with organizing his men, checking their gear, handling last minute details, and jumping his company into Los Baños precisely on time. After all, the timing of the entire operation was geared to the opening of his parachute the next morning.

mission: Set up the two roadblocks near the camp to block any Japanese units that might try to reinforce their garrison. The most important roadblock was slated for the main road, Pili Lane, leading into the camp. After reviewing the details with his men, Chenevert and his squad drew their parachutes, located and moved to the several aircraft from which they would jump, arranged and checked their considerable amount of gear (weapons, packs, demolition equipment, rations, ammunition) with which they would have to jump the next morning, and settled down for whatever sleep they were capable of conjuring up. In their minds this operation was by no means a "piece of cake."

On the evening of the 22d, the staff and company commanders of the rest of the 1/511th at Mamatid put the finishing touches on their plans for the raid. They assigned men to specific amtracs, briefed the company commanders of the 672d Amphibian Tractor Battalion on their role in the operation, then supervised the loading of crew-served weapons, ammunition, medical supplies, extra rations, water, and communications gear on the various amtracs in readiness for a predawn, black-out launch into the water of Laguna de Bay the next morning.

The 672d Amphibian Tractor Battalion was in an anomalous situation. In the first place the battalion commander was a lieutenant colonel, Joseph W. Gibbs, Field Artillery; and he was, for the Los Baños operation, working under the command and control of a major, Hank Burgess. In the second place an amphibian tractor battalion was normally employed to ferry assault waves of troops from large ships (LSTs or LSDs) to shore because the shallow-draft LVTs (amtracs) could carry the infantry over underwater obstacles that might stop the larger ships. The battalion's mission was usually completed when they hit the beach and dropped off their cargo of men and equipment. In the current operation the battalion was expected to move inland a couple of miles with the paratroopers and assist in evacuating the internees. And in the third place the battalion was being called upon to navigate in the black of night across 7.2 miles of open water; to make two minor and one major directional change, navigating only by hand-held compasses; to keep the amtracs closed up and in formation; then to land undetected at a remote target area behind Japanese lines at H-hour, 0700, on the 23d, at the same time that Lieutenant Ringler's parachute opened over the drop zone adjacent to the camp.

Cpl. Jasper Bryan Smith was a forward observer with C Company of the 672d. His job was to land on the beach ahead of the amtracs and use semaphore flags to direct the amtracs to their landing sites. He and his fellow forward observers were known to the 672d troops as the "wigwag" boys.

On the afternoon of the 22d, after the 672d had landed at Mamatid, Smith and some of the other forward observers were practicing their signals. Smith noticed his company commander talking to two Filipinos. Shortly, the company commander motioned Smith to join them and told him that he was to go with the two Filipinos. One was a Filipino third lieutenant, according to the commander, and would lead the patrol. The company commander told Smith that his was a secret mission, that they had to travel quietly and keep their voices down at all times during the trip. As he recalls it now, Smith was not too clear about his mission; he thought maybe they were "trying to capture a barrio town from the Japs," but he dutifully gathered up his two flags, a carbine, some ammunition, and a canteen of water and went with the Filipinos. After dark, they got into a banca and set sail. Before daylight Smith and his two companions landed on the south shore of Laguna de Bay and started inland through what Smith said "looked like a jungle." They walked very slowly and cautiously and came unexpectedly upon a Japanese sentry with "rifle raised and ready to fire at any noise." Smith "flipped a carbine round at the guard," temporarily distracting him. Then one of the Filipinos grabbed his weapon and the other "got a choke hold around his neck." The Japanese died quietly.

Smith and his two friends moved ahead through the dark woods. Shortly, they came to a fence with a barbed wire on the top. Smith remembers:

I could see buildings ahead. There were people, white-looking, in the windows. It may have been around 6:00 A.M., maybe a little later. Not too sure. We could see Japs taking their morning exercises. We poked our gun barrels through the fence. One Filipino was carrying a loaded machine gun.

Smith didn't seem to know it, but he was at the Los Baños Internment Camp ready to help liberate it.

All was not calm, serene, and orderly at division headquarters on the night of the 22d. Colonel Muller reported to General Swing that he had received some information which indicated that the secrecy of the raid might have been compromised. First, a radio report, supposedly from an Alamo Scout in the area, stated that the Japanese had reinforced their garrison at Los Baños with 3,000 more men. Second, at midnight on the 22d, an Air Corps night fighter, a P-61, reported spotting the headlights of many Japanese vehicles moving in the vicinity of Los Baños.[3] General Swing mulled over this information but did not consider the reports reliable enough to pass on to the raiding force. He did, however, alert the 2d Battalion of the 511th Parachute Infantry Regiment to be prepared to join the Soule Task Force along Highway 1 if that unit found itself with more enemy opposition than it could handle.

At Mamatid Hank Burgess also had an anxious moment on the 22d. About midnight a Filipino wandered into the outskirts of the bivouac area of the 1/511th and was halted by two guards. They asked him what he was doing and what he wanted. He replied, innocently enough, that he was a native of the area out for a walk and just wanted to know "when you soldiers are going to raid Los Baños." When word was passed to Burgess about this encounter, he was somewhat concerned. Was this true? he asked himself. Elaborate measures had been taken to keep all

---

3. After the raid, the G-2 learned that the movement of the Japanese forces detected by the P-61 recce aircraft was, in fact, part of a planned reinforcement of the Japanese troops in the Mount Bijiang–Mount Maquiling area by Lt. Gen. Masatoshi Fujishige, who was commander of a group called the "Fuji Heiden," composed of the 8th Infantry Division, Gyoro (suicide boat) battalions, and airfield and separate artillery units. Fujishige was the overall commander of the part of southern Luzon that included Los Baños, Mamatid, and south to Batangas and Lucena. He was aware of the movement of the amtracs from Manila to Muntinlupa, but, fortunately, he made the erroneous assumption that they were tanks and were moving into position for a thrust down Highway 1. The Japanese troops he moved to the area were part of the 17th Infantry Regiment and the 116th Gyoro Battalion. In any case, at midnight on the 22d, General Swing could hardly call off an operation that was already under way. Militarily, he did the correct thing: He prepared to reinforce where the enemy might concentrate.

planning and movements secret. He could be a spy. If he were turned loose, would he get word to the Japanese? Some suggested that he not leave the area alive. Burgess finally resolved the problem by telling him he was going to ride in the tractor with him. He went the whole way in a state of fear and panic and was released when they got to Los Baños.

Hank Burgess attempted to sleep after that incident, but by 0400 he and his men were up, buckling on their equipment, checking weapons and communications, and making their way to their assigned amtracs for boarding. By 0500 they were loaded and ready to move out. By 0515 on the 23d, all fifty-four of the amtracs had crawled into the water in the darkest of nights and were moving out across Laguna de Bay in a column of threes, guided by their compasses. About forty minutes into their trip, the lead tractor did a 90-degree turn to the right and the column dutifully followed the lead. Thirty minutes later, the column made another slight turn. At dawn the lead amtrac was within sight of the beach at San Antonio on the west side of Mayondon Point. The waterborne paratroopers looked up and could see nine C-47s in a column of Vs overhead, flying south. They were so low that Tech. Five Arthur Coleman, an amtrac driver of the 672d, "couldn't believe that they could jump at so low an altitude." The amtrac column of threes swung into a column of nines ready to hit the beach in six waves. At 0658 hours Burgess and Gibbs in the lead tractor could see the colored smoke on the beach, a signal from the recon men that the amtracs were indeed at the right place at the right time in spite of the primitive nature of their navigational system.

Back at Nichols Field, by 0530 hours on the 23d, the troopers of B Company, with the attachments of battalion machine-gun platoon and engineers, were getting ready for the jump. First, they put on their pack harnesses and slung their packs from the front of the harnesses. From their web belts hung canteens, bayonets, first-aid kits, and pistols. A poncho doubled over their web belts in the rear. Once they had pulled on and fastened their webbing and harnesses, they helped one another put on their main parachutes. Then they buckled the leg straps of the parachute harness and snapped the third strap of the parachute across their chests. Next they attached their reserve parachutes to their chest-strap buckles. Finally they threaded one wide strap (the bellyband) of the main parachute through the reserve chute across their chests. They slid their M1 rifles, muzzle first, down across their chests and through the belly-band. Finally, before boarding, each aircraft stick lined up in reverse order of their exit from the planes. Each man checked the man in front of him, pulled his static lines from the outside of the main parachute where it had been fastened with retaining bands (rubber bands), and handed the snap-fastener of the static line to the man whose equipment he was checking. The man behind made certain that the static line was free and not looped under the shoulder straps of any other piece of equipment.[4]

After the ground check, the order came down the line of aircraft to mount up. The sticks of jumpers climbed clumsily into the aircraft, loaded down as they were with about fifty pounds of personal gear, their weapons, M1s or carbines, grenades, am-munition, and their main parachutes. The sticks moved to the front of the aircraft, and the troopers took seats in the canvas bucket seats along the bulkheads of the C-47s. There were about fifteen men per plane.

At 0600 hours the nine C-47 crews started their engines af-ter they had performed their preflight inspections. Then the pilot went through his pretakeoff checklist. The C-47s then lined up and started taxiing to their takeoff positions. By 0630 the last aircraft broke ground from the runway of Nichols Field, and all nine planes were airborne. The engineers had done their job: the bomb craters on the runway were filled in satisfactorily enough to permit the takeoffs. The column of nine aircraft cir-cled over the field and made one orbit until they were in their proper flight formation, Vs in trail, three planes to a V, for the run to Los Baños. At 0640 the C-47s left the airspace above Nichols Field and headed on course south for Los Baños, pre-

---

4. If the static line were not free, the jumper, after exiting the aircraft, would almost certainly be killed because the static line would try to pull the nylon canopy through his equipment. Obviously, the parachute would not open and he might still be at-tached to the anchor cable in the plane by his static line, which could not break free. In some cases a jumper might cut himself loose and pull his reserve, but it's almost impossible to cut oneself loose while banging along the underside of a plane at ninety or more knots.

cisely on schedule for their twenty minute run to the drop zone just to the northeast of the Los Baños Internment Camp. The jumpmasters, standing in the doors of the C-47s, could see the amtracs churning across the lake beneath them.

At 0655 the red light to the right of the jump door in each of the nine C-47s came on. Each jumpmaster, standing in the door of his plane, with his hands holding the sides of the exit door, yelled above the noise of the engines, "Stand up and hook up." At that command each trooper unfastened his safety belt and stood up facing to the rear of the plane. With his left hand he hooked his static line snap fastener to the anchor cable that ran the length of the plane's interior and held onto his snap fastener. Then the jumpmaster yelled, "Check your equipment." Each man checked his own equipment and the parachute of the man in front of him, making certain again that the static line was free and clear. Then the jumpmaster called out, "Sound off for equipment check." The last man in the stick yelled, "Fifteen OK" and slapped the rear of the man in front of him. In turn, he yelled, "Fourteen OK." Down the sticks the checks and the confirmations of readiness progressed. Next the jumpmaster yelled, "Close in the door." Each man shuffled forward, left foot leading, as close as possible to the man in front of him. By this time the aircraft column had slowed to ninety knots, the jump speed of the planes. The aircraft were echeloned slightly higher to the rear so that the following planes would not run through jumpers of the first V.

In the lead aircraft Lieutenant Ringler had his face out the jump door of the C-47 checking the ground, approximating the altitude of the plane (his was at 400 feet), looking to make certain that there were no aircraft under his, and searching for the green smoke on the rapidly approaching drop zone. The slipstream wrinkled his face and neck and tugged at his jump helmet, a steel pot with a paratrooper's chin strap holding it securely on his head. He spotted the railroad just ahead, the camp to the right in the near distance, and the drop zone that he had scrutinized so carefully from aerial photos. At 0658 Ringler spotted what he was looking for—green smoke slowly wafting upward from the grenades popped by Sgt. Robert Turner of the recon platoon. Ringler stuck his head back in the plane and saw that Maj. Don Anderson, pilot of his aircraft, had switched on the green jump light, indicating that Major Anderson had also seen the smoke and that the planes were in safe jump altitude and attitude and over the "Go Point." Ringler shouted, "Go" and stepped out the door into the slipstream. He was followed by his men as fast as they could shuffle down the aisle to the rear of the aircraft to make their exits. All of them had been cautioned, needlessly, to make exits as rapidly as possible so that the sticks would be close together on the ground.

The people of Los Baños were ecstatic at the sight and sound of the aircraft. Sister Miriam Louise Kroeger said that on 22 February, Bishop Jurgens had directed the priests and nuns to have exposition of the Blessed Sacrament and public recitation of the Rosary throughout the day. Sister Kroeger remembers:

> On the second day of exposition, Bishop Jurgens had just approached the altar when the heavy drone of planes was heard overhead. I happened to be seated in sight of the Japanese guardhouse so I dared not look out. Meanwhile, there were the stifled cries of people in back of me. I couldn't even imagine what was happening. The suspense became too much, so I got up slowly and started on my way out of the building. What a vision! Our own American men dangling in midair from their parachutes, which had opened a few moments earlier. Simultaneous with the sight of such a dream come true was the machine-gun fire of the Japanese. We dropped to the floor and prayed.

The stage was set. The cast was in position. Ringler had raised the curtain on schedule. All hell broke loose.

CHAPTER IX: The Raid

When John Ringler's parachute snapped open over the dried rice paddy drop zone some 900 yards from the camp's eastern perimeter, not all of the recon platoon and guerrilla teams were in their assigned attack locations; but when those troops who were out of position saw B Company's parachutes over the drop zone, they forgot stealth and secrecy and started to race to their designated areas. Some had to run across open fields; others were struggling through the deep ravine at the northeast corner of the camp; and one team raced down the main road, Pili Lane, leading to the largest guard post in front of the camp headquarters.

Some teams were ready. The group that had gone to the drop zone had popped its smoke grenades precisely on time, and the guerrillas with that team had fanned out around the drop zone and secured it. The team that had gone to San Antonio to mark the beach area for the amtracs and to set up a perimeter around the beachhead had also been on time; the guerrillas there were deployed in an arc around the landing site when the amtracs landed. Two of the five teams that Skau had assigned to attack the camp's defenses, Sergeant Town's and part of Sergeant Squires's, were in place at 0700.

Three of the teams that were to make the direct assault on the perimeter, however, had lost their way on the trail during the night and were not in position at H-hour. Sergeant Call and his squad were just entering the ravine on the outside of the camp near the hospital when the attack started. Sergeant Angus and his men were still running across an open field, by now in broad daylight, to attack the rear gate. Lieutenant Skau's group, which carried the only machine gun in the platoon, was still two hundred yards from the main gate, its target.

Sergeant Town and his team approached the camp from the southwest corner. As his team was moving up to the camp perimeter, Carroll, Sergeant Towns's BAR man, spotted four guards streaking across an open field. Carroll emptied a full BAR clip into the fleeing Japanese and killed all four. Shortly afterwards Sergeant Town spotted a guard trying to escape through a ditch and killed him with a rifle shot.

Sergeant Call and his squad, still scrambling out of the deep ravine on the northeast side of the camp near the hospital after the attack had begun, came under heavy fire from a previously unreported machine gun somewhere to the north of the main gate. Sergeant Call was hit in the shoulder, and Botkin, one of the recon men with him, had his nose bloodied from a grenade fragment.

Sergeant Angus and his team approached the camp from the rear gate area near the southeast corner of the camp close to the dairy. The pillbox guarding that gate was deserted. Angus and his men made their way into the camp without drawing fire and killed two Japanese who were hiding just inside the gate.

By 0715, when the first troops of Ringler's company arrived at the perimeter of the camp from the east, the men and the guerrillas from the teams of Squires, Angus, and Town were attacking the camp from three sides. By that time a number of the guards had fled and some had been killed. Three or four Japanese were bottled up in the pillbox near the front gate, which had fired upon Sergeant Call and his team. Sergeant Call contacted B Company, and a 60-mm. mortar team responded with four or five rounds on the pillbox. Sergeant Call and his men then threw grenades into the bunker and killed the remaining Japanese.

The recon men and the guerrillas continued their attacks on the perimeter, the pillboxes, and the bunkers along the fence line for the next fifteen or twenty minutes with bursts of small-arms fire, staccato clips from their BARs, and a fusillade of hand grenades. In addition to their rifles and pistols, some of ancient vintage, a number of the guerrillas were armed with bolos—long, heavy, single-edged machetes. Once they had eliminated as many of the guards on the perimeter as they could find, the recon men and the guerrillas stormed the fences of the camp.

Inside the camp the internees were lined up for the morning roll call. The off-duty Japanese guards were, as expected, taking their morning setting-up exercises in the open area just outside the camp commander's cottage next to the camp headquarters. (The camp commander could thus keep an eye on his soldiers' performance of the exercises; the internees took great delight in seeing the guards harassed "brutally" by their officers for improper performance of their calisthenics.) The new guard relief soldiers were fastening on their cartridge belts before going out to replace the guard relief that had been on duty during the night.

As the new guard relief began to leave its barracks, the nine C-47s roared overhead, just to the east of the camp. When the Japanese saw the paratroopers in the air, they halted abruptly whatever it was they had been doing. The guard relief rushed back into its barracks; the loincloth clad guards at calisthenics milled about for a time, then ran back to their barracks to dress and head for the arms racks.

When the internees heard the firing of the weapons and the grenades around the perimeter, listened to the bullets zipping through the straw walls of their barracks and cubicles, they fell to the floor if they were inside or to the ground if they were outside. Those who could, headed for ditches or other folds in the ground. Father McCarthy says that "they tried to make themselves as small a target as possible."

Patty Kelly, a young internee, said when the bullets started flying, "my mother and I ran back into a barracks and hid under the bed. There were a lot of nuns in that barracks, and they were saying their Rosaries."

Margaret Whitaker remembered that "as soon as the parachutes opened, we dashed back into the barracks because we knew we were going to be leaving. We had to get our belongings ready." A young friend of hers made the mistake of standing up while bullets were still flying through the building and was wounded slightly in the stomach. Margaret's mother, not willing to sit around doing nothing while waiting to be rescued, spotted some recon men and guerrillas trying to break through the barbed wire. Mrs. Whitaker found a wire clipper somewhere and helped them cut through the fence. Cpl. Jasper Bryan Smith (he was the "wigwag" boy of the 672d Amphibian Tractor Battalion) and his three-man unit were on the perimeter when the attack began. He saw several guards hiding in some nearby foliage. He and his two Filipino friends started firing when everyone else did. "Several Japs quickly fell to the ground, freshly killed by our weapons' fire," he recalls. "I saw a person [probably Mrs. Whitaker] hand a tool that looked like a cutter. The GI cut the chain around the gate of the fence." Smith's job then was to await the arrival of the amtracs and direct them into the camp.

After about twenty minutes of intensive fire, most of the guard posts had been neutralized, the recon platoon and guerrillas and the paratroopers of B Company had swarmed into the camp, and Skau and his men had beaten the Japanese in the race for the arms rack in the connecting passageway between the two guard barracks just inside the main gate. The Japanese who had been exercising tried to hide in barracks or in ditches and were killed, or they stampeded for the hills south of the camp.

Two of Skau's men rushed the camp headquarters. They saw a Japanese officer leap through the glass window behind his desk and head for some trees outside the camp fence in a futile attempt to escape. Skau's men killed him before he reached the trees. The survivors of the guard detail that had been getting ready to relieve the on-duty guards scattered inside and outside the camp. Still, the camp was not totally secure. B Company had to fight a few defenders to get into the compound and then some guards who had hidden in various internee barracks, in culverts, and in shrubbery around the camp.

B Company's parachute jump had gone almost perfectly. Lieutenant Ringler, who had stepped out of his aircraft at 400 feet altitude, said that while he was in the air, "I wasn't aware of any shooting at us from the ground. My time in the air consisted of only a couple of oscillations and I was on the ground. If there was any firing, it was very light or the enemy was off target."

Each of the succeeding aircraft[1] flew in over the drop zone at a slightly higher altitude. Air Corps fighters flew cover over and around them. Just as soon as each jump plane passed over the railroad track—the "Go Point"—its jumpmaster standing in the open door at the head of his sticks gave the command "Go" and stepped out into the slipstream. He was followed in rapid order by the rest of his men. As each paratrooper made his exit from the jump door, he turned slightly to his left (aided by a twisting push from the slipstream) and toward the rear of the plane. When he jumped, he locked his feet and legs tightly together so that if his chute opened while he was upside down, he would have less chance of getting his parachute lines tangled between his legs. Immediately on jumping, each paratrooper clamped his hands on the ends of the reserve on his chest, ready to pull the ripcord on the right-hand side of his reserve if necessary, counted to three (one thousand, two thousand, three thousand), put his chin down as far on his chest as possible to prevent his three-pound steel helmet from whiplashing his head and neck, and waited three seconds for the opening shock of his T-5 parachute with its twenty-eight-foot-diameter canopy. (If he hadn't had an opening shock in three seconds, he was taught to pull his reserve.) If his body position was as prescribed in jump school, the static line pulled his canopy open fairly smoothly and popped open with only a medium-size jolt. If he failed to keep his chin tucked in, his legs together, and his body bent over his reserve, or if the plane had not slowed to about ninety

---

1. One of the planes was a C-47 with the word RESCUE painted in large yellow letters on its side. The Air Corps had obviously gone to great lengths to provide the paratroopers with the required nine C-47s.

knots, at the maximum, the opening shock of the parachute rattled his teeth, neck, and back. A bad body position when the parachute snapped open induced stargazing in broad daylight.[2]

Jim Holzem and Oscar were in one of the planes behind Ringler's. When the green jump light went on, Holzem said:

> We went out of the plane almost as one man. The only hesitancy—and it was a brief one—was caused by Oscar. As he got to the open door, he balked for an instant. But I was right behind him, and I was used to riding an equipment bundle out the door. So out Oscar went. Someone else in the squad took care of getting the machine-gun bundle out. Again, we carried John Blansit's BAR.
>
> The jump went perfectly. All our chutes were close together. But that darn Oscar. He was walking on the top of Ed Siemer's chute. I yelled to him to get off before he deflated Ed's chute. Ed was yelling up at him to get off. Finally, he slid off, but he was having the time of his life.
>
> We all landed close together in the field. I got out of my harness and ran over to Oscar to help unbuckle him from his parachute harness. Then I said, "Let's go" as I headed toward where the equipment bundle had come down. Looking back, I saw Oscar wasn't with me. He was still back by his parachute. Figuring he must have problems, I ran back to him. When I got to him, I understood. After he had gotten out of his chute harness, he pulled the rip cord on the reserve chute. When I got there, he had pulled it out the full length and spread it out. "By God, Jim," he said, "you were right. There is a parachute in here."

Holzem and his men found their machine-gun bundle, and John Blansit recovered his BAR. Together they took off toward the camp. In a few minutes they were stopped by firing from the camp. The squad leader called for John Blansit and his BAR. He double-timed ahead. Holzem heard the BAR fire; the firing from the pillbox stopped; Blansit had knocked it out. The B Company men in that area then ran into the camp through a hole in the perimeter's barbed wire.

---

2. Great improvements have been made in today's military parachutes: the World War II T-5 parachute is to today's 32-foot, delayed-opening, steerable, camouflaged T-10 parachute as a model-T Ford is to a Rolls-Royce.

After Lt. Alan Chenevert landed on the drop zone, he began to round up his demolition squad. Since they had jumped from various aircraft, it took him about ten minutes to find all of them. As soon as they were together, they moved out to set up the assigned roadblocks. The most important one, the one on the main road leading into the camp, was a combination of mines, abatis, and satchel charges. After the infantry paratroopers arrived at the site, they covered the roadblocks with interlocking machine-gun fire.

Fred Brooks, one of Chenevert's engineer demolition experts who jumped in with him, said:

> Our mission was to booby-trap the main road, 200 yards from the gate leading in and out of the prison. The 511th had two machine gunners, two tripod carriers, and two ammo carriers. One was on the left flank of the road, and the other on the right flank. This would give them a crisscross fire on the main road and gate leading in or out of the compound. It would also protect us while we were placing our charges. We also ran primer cord along the road and up to the 511th machine-gun placements. We then connected the charges to our hand detonators. Looking from my position on the right flank, I had an excellent view of the main gate and prison. I also noticed a very well-worn path outside of the prison. I thought it was very peculiar at the time. Later I found out they had a twenty-four-hour patrol every day.

The internees reacted in a variety of ways to the sound of the firing all around them. Fr. George J. Williams, S.J., had celebrated an early morning mass that morning. After mass, at 0700, he and his barracks mates lined up for the daily roll call. As he was moving to the lineup area on "shaky legs," he turned and saw some planes coming across the lake from the north. He paid little attention because "planes had been a common sight in recent days. Only the previous afternoon the Japanese battery two miles west had been savagely strafed." But as the planes came abreast of the camp, he noted little objects dropping out of them and immediately deduced that the Americans were dropping leaflets to give them some encouragement. But then he and his friends saw the small objects blossom into parachutes. "They're paratroopers," they yelled and headed for their barracks as the firing around the perimeter started.

Bill Rivers and his close friend, Freddie Lambert, were standing in roll-call formation as usual with the rest of their barracks mates at 0700. Their barracks was two buildings away from camp headquarters and next to the camp fence on the east side. Thus, they could easily see the flight of nine C-47s to the east when they flew over the drop zone. When the first chute opened, Rivers heard almost simultaneously the beginning of the small-arms fire and grenade explosions. At that moment he recalled Ben Edwards's advice to him when Ben had left the camp a few days earlier. Ben Edwards had told him that if he heard more than two shots in a row, he should get in a ditch and stay there. When they heard the prolonged firing, Rivers and Lambert proceeded to take Edwards's advice. Rivers immediately dived into a muddy ditch, but Lambert, more fastidious and, as it turned out, more fortunate, had gone into the barracks to get a petati mat to lie on so that he would not have to sprawl directly in the mud. About the time Rivers got in the ditch, a Japanese guard came around the corner of the barracks and aimed his rifle at him. At just that moment, Lambert, inside the barracks, knocked something over and made a noise that startled the guard. He fired at Rivers, but the round went wild. Seconds later, with Rivers burrowing into the mud, a guerrilla ran around the corner of the barracks and killed the guard with a burst from his "grease gun."

Even so, Rivers and Lambert were undaunted. They decided to go down to the guards' barracks, just two buildings away, to help themselves to what must be, by now, the guards' abandoned breakfast. They found tubs of cooked rice in the guards' kitchen and a number of other internees helping themselves to the unexpected feast, in spite of the gruesome sight of several dead Japanese lying nearby. Lambert grabbed a sack of brown sugar and headed back to the barracks. Rivers stopped long enough to strip the epaulets from the blouse of a Japanese subofficer (he still has them among his souvenirs). Twelve or thirteen dead Japanese lay in front of their headquarters.

In their barracks Rivers and Lambert stuffed themselves with the brown sugar and rice from the Japanese kitchen. The firing of small arms and grenades was increasing. Rivers and Lambert went to the end of their barracks and saw some U.S. soldiers moving toward the camp headquarters. They decided to follow them. As they got near the headquarters, they saw the fence of barbed wire covered with bamboo mats suddenly fold inward, and "a whole herd of the damnedest vehicles I'd ever seen, roared into the camp," recalls Rivers. "When I saw the white star with the two bars on each side, I feared that the Russians had somehow rescued us, as I'd never seen that insignia before. But when I heard one soldier profanely order 'Red' to give him the field phone, I believe I heaved a sigh of relief."

By 0715 John Ringler had assembled his company and was leading it toward the camp from the northeast. A dry riverbed in the area of the drop zone, oriented toward the camp, gave cover and concealment to some of the paratroopers converging on the camp. Even though the original outburst of fire by the recon platoon–guerrilla teams had wiped out or sent most of the guards scurrying toward some measure of safety–some of the guards were still roaming about the camp or were hiding in culverts or ditches inside and outside the camp. Ringler's men killed some of them who were attempting to escape to the south and east outside the fence. By the time B Company reached the fences of the camp and had broken through, only a few Japanese were still at large, and they posed only a minor problem to the raiders. Ringler's men hunted them down individually and killed them. Hank Burgess wrote that "for some time after we secured the area, our troops continued to find Japs hiding in the area for several hundred yards around the camp, which resulted in isolated sharp clashes and bullets passing over everyone."

George Skau had assigned to Ben Edwards, Martin Squires, and their guerrillas the guard post that was just inside the fence opposite the YMCA building on the northwest corner of the camp. The barbed-wire fence on that side of the camp was in two rows, the outer one was covered with sawali, which prevented Ben and his team from seeing inside the camp. Ben recalls:

When the first parachute opened, we threw grenades over the fences toward the spot I had told everyone was the location of the guard post. Unknowingly, I threw a phosphorous instead of a fragmentation grenade, but it landed in the guard post. We cautiously climbed the sawali-covered fence then jumped down and crawled under the inner fence. At that point there was only one Japanese in sight, and he was running toward a culvert under a camp road. He got to the culvert before any of us could get him, but we pointed out his position to one of the other recon men who was nearby, and he very calmly walked down the road to the culvert and flipped a grenade into it. Several guerrillas who were also nearby dragged the body from the culvert and administered the coup de grâce with a bolo. I told them to knock it off and find live Japs.

There was considerable firing for a few minutes, and I vividly remember thinking that the tracer ammunition someone was firing looked like tennis balls floating through the air. Sometime during the attack, a bullet hit the ground just in front of me, and either fragments of the bullet or rock splinters hit my shins, causing small wounds on both shins. (I was wearing the khaki shorts that I had worn during the escape.)

The amtracs carrying Hank Burgess and the remainder of the 1/511th waddled out of the lake and crawled across the beach at San Antonio on schedule. Hank Burgess's amtrac, in the lead, hauled in Sergeants Hahn and Bruce, the two men from the recon platoon who had marked the landing beaches with smoke grenades. The guerrilla company, which had accompanied Hahn and Bruce to San Antonio, stayed there to help secure the beachhead.

The Japanese unit that had reestablished a position on Mayondon Point two days earlier and had caused the shift of the landing to San Antonio fired a few rounds at the amtracs as they swam ashore, but Burgess ignored the sporadic firing. He dropped off the two pack-75s from D Battery of the 457th Parachute FA Battalion and one of his infantry platoons to secure the beachhead on which they had just landed and to block enemy movement on the national highway that skirted Laguna de Bay's southern shore in that area. Then he and his battalion proceeded the two and one-half miles down the road toward Los Baños.

As the amtrac column neared the camp, a Japanese officer darted from a Filipino house along the road. He was trying to pull on his trousers over his otherwise nude body, giving the more ribald American soldiers an idea of what he had been up to, and he was carrying his ever-present Samurai saber. The lead amtrac cut him down with a burst of machine-gun fire.

Hank Burgess described his first view of Los Baños:

> There was a high barbed-wire fence enclosing the camp, with a gate ajar about two feet. A stone pillbox at the gate was staring at us with guns in firing slits; several guerrillas were shooting wildly at the structure from a distance of 100 yards or more. As we continued to drive toward the pillbox, two Filipinos, armed with old Lee-Enfield rifles, told us that the Japs were still alive. They were wrong, for the guards had been grenaded at daylight by two men of the reconnaissance platoon. . . . Our driver simply drove through the gate, knocking it to the ground, and into a large area on the edge of the camp inside the barbed-wire fence. Everyone quickly dismounted, and C Company, under Lt. Tom Mesereau, moved off toward the 8th Division to await its advance guard. . . . A Company, less than fifty men under Lieutenant Fraker deployed around the loading areas. "I was appalled at the condition of the internees. None of us was prepared for what we found. The prisoners were hysterical and euphoric, most of the larger men weighed no more than 110 pounds, and the women resembled sticks.

Tech. Five Arthur J. Coleman was a driver of one of the amtracs in the 672d. After they came ashore, he recalls:

> We followed a track or trail to the camp. No resistance encountered. We turned around and dropped our tailgates. People were milling around, the barracks began to burn, some asked why. Someone said, "Oh, there is Pete Miles,[3] he went over the wall the other night."
>
> One man said to me, "Son, come to Chicago after the war and I will give you a good job with International Harvester." I didn't realize the emotional extent or significance of the situation at that time. I wanted to smoke but had very few to share. I lit one and tried to hide it but to no avail. A small fellow, a Merchant Marine, I think, said, "Don't throw that butt away." I gave him and others all I had.

---

3. Pete Miles volunteered to return with the Burgess force to help liberate his friends.

At that time a guerrilla looked into a drain tile under us and said, "There is a Jap in there." He promptly threw in a grenade and ran to the other side to see the results.

The internees looked very thin and were dressed in worn and tattered clothing. They were very hungry and ate our rations without asking for them. We had boxes of 10-in-one rations partially emptied of the better items, with crackers and less desirable items remaining. They ate everything but the boxes. They were showing us how thin they were. I tried to make them feel better by showing my own ribs.

After the amtracs arrived and stopped on the road leading to the camp, there was a bit of "mopping up" to be done. Just outside the camp, a Filipino told a 672d sergeant that a Japanese soldier was hiding in a nearby house. The sergeant dutifully entered the house. Some other Filipinos inside pointed to a closet, indicating where the Japanese was hiding. The sergeant opened the closet door, found that the Filipinos were correct, took no chances, killed the Japanese with his carbine, and strolled off—mission accomplished.

Hank Burgess led the amtrac column down an asphalt road past Baker Memorial Hall, through a perimeter gate, and down the road past the hospital. Once inside the camp, he realized that the area was congested and that he could not bring all fifty-four amtracs inside the wire, let alone load them, turn them around, and head back out the way he had come in. He stopped the column after only six or seven amtracs had entered the camp and directed the remaining amtracs to pull off onto the baseball diamond and the open fields opposite Baker Memorial Hall just outside the camp's perimeter wire.

Riding unobtrusively in one of the amtracs as a passenger with no command or control over the operation, was Maj. Gen. Courtney Whitney, General MacArthur's staff officer charged with overseeing the entire guerrilla organization on Luzon. (MacArthur, in *Reminiscences*, writes: "I detailed Gen. Courtney Whitney to coordinate and direct the entire [guerrilla] organization. He was ideal for such an assignment. A prominent Manila lawyer, his thirteen years there had made him thoroughly familiar with Philippine conditions and personnel. Rugged and aggressive, fearless and experienced in military affairs, his driving force found full play in charge of a guerrilla army.")

Hank Burgess had been astounded to have Whitney appear at Muntinlupa just before the amtracs took off for Los Baños and present him with an order authorizing Whitney and another man in civilian clothes to go with them to Los Baños. Whitney also requested two enlisted men to accompany him "to carry some documents" out of the internment camp. After the amtracs arrived at Los Baños, Whitney and his civilian companion left the area where the amtracs had parked and entered the camp itself. They returned shortly carrying "several boxes well tied together containing documents which he [Whitney] deemed to be of considerable military significance." Burgess remembers that "I didn't really believe it at first, but he [Whitney] was really sincere about keeping those boxes together and was with them all of the time. He was also one of the early people to leave Los Baños."

The contents of the boxes has never been identified but may have contained documents from the Japanese headquarters.

Burgess went back into the camp, where he had a very hard time getting the internees to listen to instructions. Organizing them for movement out of the camp and making them realize that time was of the essence were nearly impossible. He also realized, when he saw them, that many of the internees could not walk the two and a half miles to San Antonio, where they would be picked up by the amtracs and taken back to Mamatid. At this point, Burgess did not have a clear picture of the condition of Ringler's and Skau's soldiers and guerrillas, nor of the military situation in and around the camp, nor of the fate of the guards, nor whether the Los Baños commander had been able to communicate with the Japanese 8th Division commanding general and inform him of the raid.

For their part, the internees felt that once the huge, well-armed Americans had arrived, all was under control and their deliverance was assured. They wandered about happily or returned to their barracks, either to await orders or to gather up all of their scanty, but highly prized, possessions.

At about 0745 Lieutenant Skau reported to Burgess that all of his men were all right. Lieutenant Ringler also reported that none of his men had been killed or wounded on the jump or during the break-in of the camp. That information eased Burgess's mind. Ringler also reported, however, that he was having an almost impossible time getting the bulk of the internees to move out of their barracks toward the amtrac loading area. Burgess was in a difficult, chaotic situation: he had no loudspeaker system with which to control the internees; his communications network with his own commanders was minimal; he could not reach the 188th Infantry,[4] even though he could hear faintly the artillery that accompanied and supported the Soule Task Force. He had noted rather shrewdly, and a bit anxiously, that the sound of the firing was not getting any closer. He concluded that the Soule Task Force could not possibly reach the camp for at least three more hours. By this time, an hour had already elapsed, and the clock was ticking away toward the two-hour deadline: the time when he thought elements of the Japanese 8th Division might be arriving near Los Baños from their bivouacs in the San Pablo–Alaminos area.

To add to Burgess's pressure, he recalls:

> Colonel Gibbs, commander of the amphibious tractors, wanted permission to leave us and return to Mamatid while we waited for contact and evacuation by the 188th Infantry. Several of his machines had quit along the route, and their safety was a matter of concern to him. In previous operations his vehicles had rarely been so far inland or remained with troops in such vulnerable positions. He was a lieutenant colonel. I was a major, and technically he was under my command; it bothered both of us, but we "unilaterally agreed" he would stay.

Burgess had two other major worries: (1) a disorganized mob of more than 2,000 milling, excited, almost-hysterical men, women, and children who did not appreciate the need for haste and scores of whom could not walk; and (2) the camp's location, which made it extremely difficult to defend.

The camp was in a flatland dominated by high ground to the south (the direction of the 8th Division) and surrounded by

---

4. A liaison officer with communications frequencies and codes for the Soule Task Force was supposed to have joined Burgess at Mamatid. He didn't show up.

heavy foliage that would provide cover and concealment for an attacking infantry force. Most of his troops were busy rounding up the internees and searching for hiding Japanese or were with Mesereau and Fraker in blocking positions outside and around the camp. The only artillery he had in his task force were the two pack-75s that were at San Antonio preparing to defend that beachhead, if necessary. Hank Burgess made a very quick estimate of the situation and decided that he could not establish an effective perimeter around the camp given the terrain and the troops he had at his disposal. He said that he could not even "defend it against snipers, let alone Japanese infantry."

Taking all of those factors into consideration, adding the continual ticking away of precious minutes and the fact that there was no sign that the Soule Task Force would arrive within a short time (each passing minute at this point must have seemed like an hour to the commander on the ground who had the full responsibility for the lives and safety of the prisoners and his own men), Hank Burgess made the decision that would insure the success of the raid: he decided not to wait for the arrival of the Soule Task Force and ordered Colonel Gibbs "to load the internees, deliver them to Mamatid, and return to the landing beach [San Antonio] until all the internees and troops were evacuated."

Once the decision was made, his problem was how to assemble the internees, move them to the amtracs that were lined up on the main road leading into the camp and on the ball field, give them instructions, and move them to Mamatid.

When Ringler had reported to Major Burgess at about 0745, Burgess had not yet made his decision to move the internees by amtrac (he was still of the opinion that the Soule Force might arrive with some trucks). Ringler told him that he was having a very frustrating time rounding up the internees, moving them out of their barracks, carrying only a minimum of baggage toward the area where the amtracs had assembled.

Ringler made an observation that provided a key to solving the roundup problem. He had noticed that the guards' barracks, where the recon platoon had had a firefight with the guards near the arms racks, were burning, that the fire was moving toward the six amtracs that had driven into the camp past the hospital and were now parked near the guards' barracks and the camp headquarters. Ringler also noticed that the internees in that specific area were moving ahead of the fire toward the amtracs. Burgess seized on the burning barracks as the answer to the question of how to move the internees. He told Ringler to go to the south side of the camp, up wind, and torch the other barracks.

"The results were spectacular," Burgess remembers. "Internees poured out and into the loading area. Troops started clearing the barracks in advance of the fire and carried out to the loading area over 130 people who were too weak or too sick to walk."

David Hogenboom, now a professor of physics at Lafayette College in Pennsylvania, was about eight years old at the time of the Los Baños raid. He was the second son of a Presbyterian minister whose family was moved by the Japanese in 1942 from their home in Tacloban, Leyte. Eventually, they were transferred first to the internment camp at Santo Tomas then to Los Baños.

Because he was so young at the time of his family's incarceration, David was more accustomed to Japanese and Filipinos than he was to Americans. When he saw the first U.S. soldiers at Los Baños, he thought they looked "huge and yellow," colored as they were by Atabrine, the drug all soldiers in the Philippines took daily to prevent malaria.[5]

That the amtracs coming across the lake were noisy was attested to by a number of the internees. David remembers that early on the morning of the 23d, his father, Leonard, now retired and living in Florida, awoke at dawn and imagined that he heard the sound of many engines. He sat up in bed rather startled, but in a few minutes he realized that the sound had faded away, and he thought nothing more of it.

As they were lining up for roll call, Bunny Chambers, another internee, pointed to planes in the sky to the east. Leonard

---

5. The disease was merely suppressed by the Atabrine, a fact many soldiers (the author included) found out when they returned to the United States and stopped taking the daily dose of Atabrine. It was a foul-tasting pill. One pill could easily dye yellow a full load of laundry.

Hogenboom told her, "Those planes are not bombers; they're transports." When he saw the paratroopers jumping from the aircraft, Leonard was ecstatic and felt that soon they would be liberated. He immediately gathered his family and pulled them into a drainage ditch while the fighting erupted about and above them. Then the amtracs arrived, and Leonard Hogenboom began moving his family to the amtrac loading area. He was far more systematic about his rescue than were most of the internees.

Another of the internees told Art Coleman, who had driven one of the clanking tractors into the camp, that he and his buddy had heard the amtracs coming across the lake for hours. The internee had told his friend that "today we're going to be rescued." The doubting buddy had told him that "what you're hearing is airplanes."

"No," the first internee had insisted, "I'll bet you the biggest steak we can find in San Francisco that today we'll be outta here."

Sister Louise Kroeger, a Maryknoll nun, remembers her rescue:

> We thought each soldier an angel, and a giant one at that. They were massive compared to our malnourished men in the camp. We were told to pack what we could carry, the soldiers would come back to pick up what things we left behind. The crowd of more than 2,100 starved and emaciated people filing out between the burning buildings to the amphibious tractors was a pathetic one. But there was no joy in the world to equal that of those same war-spent victims. One priest stopped to kneel on the ground and raise his hands to heaven, thanking God for our rescue. An American soldier, realizing that any delay could mean the death of us, went over to the priest and said, "Come on, Father; let's get the hell out of here."

Another nun, Sister Maria del Rey Danforth, had risen at her usual hour of 0545, somewhat earlier than the other nuns in her barracks. She used the time to go to the chapel to "guarantee herself a few quiet moments of prayer . . . before the day's scramble of rice hulling and wood gathering, and news-from-rumor sifting began." Then she went to mass at 0600. All during the mass, she heard a low rumble at some distance. She decided that the noise came from planes above the clouds. After mass, she went to roll call at a little before 0700 and waited stoically to be counted by the "officials." The Japanese official for her barracks was Ito, who according to Sister Maria was "rather nice. . . . I think he liked the Sisters."

Just as the roll call began, Sister Maria looked to the east, as she often did, to delight in the sunrise. She saw the nine C-47s begin to drop Ringler's paratroopers. She had always thought that their rescue would come from the direction of the lake, that the battle would rage for a few days, then the Americans would come in and overrun the camp. When she saw the paratroopers, she knew that the American forces had devised a different and much more efficient solution to their rescue. She and the other nuns who had lined up for roll call ran for their barracks. She recalls:

> I hadn't reached the cubicle when hell began popping and I ducked under the beds—pushing Sister Maura Shaun over a bit to make room for Sister de Chantal to squeeze alongside.
>
> Several times we peeked over the windowsill. Bullets flew past the window like rain, really. There was a lull, and Sister Antoinette said, pointing to our tin can of rice that she had been cooking outside, "That rice is burning. Battle or no battle, we can't afford to lose it." We pushed my bed back to share space, and Sister ran out and brought in the tin can and native stove, complete. She was just inside the door when the battle broke out afresh and down we went again under the beds. In the middle of it, the swinging doors on the front of the barracks swung open and there was a huge American. He was so big you couldn't see the gang of Filipino guerrillas behind him. And the expression on his face when he saw the place full of nuns!
>
> "Won't my mother be proud when I tell her that I rescued the Sisters," he said. "Now, where are the Japs?"
>
> "Welcome," we shouted. He ran down the center aisle toward the next barracks, with his ragamuffin, armed-to-the-teeth guerrillas behind him.

The fighting moved on to the row of barracks on the southwest side of the camp, next to the row in which Sister Maria's barracks was located. Sister Antoinette continued to stir the rice and stoke the fire in their cubicle. They had intended to eat the rice sparingly throughout the day, but on this occasion they squandered it all on breakfast. Another nun, Sister Frederica, did not escape the consequences of the battle being fought around her. The cup she was holding in her hand was hit by a bullet that burned her wrist, took the skin off her thumb joint, and shattered the cup.

Shortly afterwards, a soldier came through the barracks and told the nuns to pack only what they could carry and to go to the baseball field immediately. Sister Maria had always imagined that she would be forced to leave Los Baños in a hurry. As a consequence, she had put away in her tampipi (a Filipino box of woven busipalm, shaped like a suitcase) her habits, her good shoes, and all the decent underwear she owned. Her preparation to get out of the barracks was minimal. She hoisted the tampipi on her shoulder, stuffed into her pocket the few toilet articles she had, and started toward the baseball field.

On the way she stopped to find and to help Mother Ethelburga, an Assumption Sister who was seventy-seven and who had become a charge of hers. By that time all of the nuns were pouring out of their barracks, clutching their few possessions, heading down the street between the rows of burning barracks. The soldiers were "like ushers at a Sunday school picnic, helping people along, calling good-natured replies to witticisms, but wasting no time for all their easy good nature."

When they got near the area where the amtracs were loading, Sister Maria transferred Mother Ethelburga to Sister Marie Bernard and went to help Sister Mary Andrew, who seemed exhausted. Sister Maria could see the amtracs, but they were on the other side of a ditch about eight feet deep and ten feet wide. She and the other nuns were undaunted. They threw their bags down into the ditch, sat down on the side of the incline, and slid to the bottom. Then they threw their baggage from the bottom to some soldiers at the top, who then pulled the nuns out of the ditch. "How kind and courteous they were. Circumstances could easily have pardoned gruffness or severity, but no, every soldier was as good humored, even suave, as a department store floorman." The soldiers then helped the nuns climb into the amtracs.

One of the recon men, racing through a women's barracks, was stopped by a woman who asked him, "Are you a Marine?" The soldier admitted that he was not, that he was just one of your "everyday GI paratroopers." "All my days in Los Baños I've dreamed of being rescued by a Marine," she said smiling warmly but a little sadly. "And you're not a Marine." For once, the paratrooper was speechless.

In one of the men's barracks, Clyde DeWitt, who had practiced law in prewar Manila, was trying to make his bed just before the morning roll call. He lived in barracks 26, which was in the southwest corner of the camp adjacent to the barbed-wire perimeter fence. When the firing started, he and his barracks' mates threw themselves to the floor. While they were lying there, a rumor passed along that the Japanese guards were coming through the barracks. DeWitt and his friends regarded that as an ominous development, but they realized there was nothing they could do. After a few minutes, the firing died down, and DeWitt raised himself from the floor and looked out the window. He recalls:

> We saw a little brown man with a handkerchief around his head and a carbine in his hands passing by, crouching so as not to draw fire. We were not sure who or what he was until he looked at us, his face wreathed in smiles. Here are his never-to-be-forgotten words: "Howdy, folks." It was so friendly, such an anticlimax to what we expected, that we got up and paid little attention to the firing. . . . He was the first Hunters' guerrilla I have ever seen.

After Ben Edwards and the recon men and guerrillas with him broke into the camp through the wire on the northwest corner, Ben hurried into the barracks area and attempted to urge the internees to move toward the amtrac loading areas or, if they were sufficiently able bodied, to start the walk down the road toward San Antonio. As he moved from barracks to barracks, Ben unexpectedly met some resistance and anger from the internees.

In one barracks, he said of his experience:

> I encountered almost complete noncooperation in that a group of older men refused to leave without their trunks, boxes, and other belongings, a good portion of which was probably just junk but was considered treasure by the fact that it was all they had. Some did have canned goods they refused to leave, and others were just so confused that they didn't want to leave.

A woman in one of the barracks grabbed his arm and, pointing to a well-known internee black marketer, screamed, "Shoot him, he's a traitor!" Ben admits that at the time he gave some thought to the request as he recalled stories about the alleged traitor's cat eating well and gaining weight on canned salmon while internees starved to death. He decided, however, that at the moment of liberation, he would show compassion for the scoundrel.

He was somewhat shaken when next he saw his friend Pete Miles. As he moved from barracks to barracks, Ben saw two soldiers carrying Pete Miles on a stretcher. He feared that Pete had been wounded in the attack, but realized after talking to him that the events of the past few days—his escape, his long trip to the headquarters of the 11th, his return to the camp with Hank Burgess in an amtrac—had finally "done in Pete Miles." Even as he lay on the stretcher, Pete clutched a Garand rifle, which he finally gave to Ben to keep for him. The soldiers carried the exhausted Miles to an amtrac, which carried him safely to Mamatid.

A few correspondents had come in with the 511th. Frank Smith of the *Chicago Times* jumped in with Ringler's B Company. Francis McCarthy, a United Press war correspondent, came in with Burgess and the amphibious element. McCarthy's trip to the camp was more than routinely reportorial. His sister, Marian, and his brother, Floyd, were internees in the camp, and he had not seen them since the Japanese captured Manila in 1942. "I found them almost immediately, and Floyd embarrassed me by running up and down the corridor of his barracks, shouting, 'I told you my kid brother would come in to rescue me. Whoopee!'"

By 0830 Burgess saw some progress, although the situation in the camp and around the loading areas was still chaotic. "Little seemed to have been accomplished," he recalls. "Troops, internees, and amtracs were jammed into a small area, and there was great confusion."

Actually, however, a great deal was being accomplished. Chaos had been reduced to slightly disorganized confusion. The internees were finally beginning to arrive at the ball field in increasing numbers. The women, children, and elderly and the 130 or so internees who were too sick to walk were beginning to load onto the amtracs first. Those who could walk started the two-plus-mile trek to the beach at San Antonio, guided and guarded by Burgess's men. In spite of the soldiers' pleas for haste and a minimum of baggage, though, the internees felt that the U.S. Army paratroopers could accomplish anything. The internees came to the loading areas laden with every suitcase, parcel, and box that they could possibly carry. One old man even brought his carpenter tools. The soldiers hustled the internees as forcibly, yet as gently, as they could. The original plan, to load and move by amtrac the women, children, and the lame first, soon broke down as fathers wanted to stay with their families, men wanted to stay with their girlfriends, and others, fearful of being left behind, swarmed aboard. Burgess gave up and loaded the amtracs as rapidly as possible.

Those who did start out on foot were supposedly the strongest of the prisoners. They were, nonetheless, having a hard time of it as they stumbled along the roads carrying what was supposed to be only a minimum of baggage. Some of the priests carried their sacred chalices and ciboria. Some of the walking internees had become ill as a result of having eaten the rich American combat rations that the troops had given them in the camp. Fortunately, a couple of the amtracs that had broken down on the march into the camp had been repaired, and Burgess used those vehicles to shuttle to the beach as many of the walking internees as possible.

Fr. William R. McCarthy, MM, reminisced about the movement of the internees from the camp:

> The dazed prisoners, stunned by the long months in prison and the climax of that morning's events, stumbled toward the trucks [amtracs]. Patients on hospital cots, some bloated from beriberi, others too weak from starvation to walk, were carried to the trucks. Men, women, and children followed, bundles under their arms or dangling from sticks, carrying their scant possessions with them.
>
> I remember one group walking out of Los Baños toward Lake Laguna. Cocamo, the Panamanian, who came among us brown-skinned and plump, was now streamlined; Red, the nightclub girl; Gypsy, the man of many parts; Big Louis, the gambler; Alex Calhoun, the banker; Les Yard, the Hollywood reporter; Clarence Cumming, the leather merchant; Clyde DeWitt, the lawyer; Bill Spencer, of Pan Am; Mike O'Brien, an export brewer with the former San Miguel Brewery in Manila; Fr. Russ Hughes of the wood-chopping gang that did such noble work to keep fires under the stew pots; Darley Downes, the Presbyterian minister who had been in Japan before the war and could speak fluently with the guards; Floyd McCarthy, a businessman from Manila; his sister, Tumble [Marian]; and their brother, Francis, of United Press, who came by amtrac with the brave young men of the 11th Airborne. With many others we walked over the highway of freedom against a background of flames, as one straw barracks quickly followed another in an all-consuming fire fanned by the morning breeze.

As was the custom with pilots in World War II who named their planes after voluptuous real or imagined girlfriends, amtrac drivers gave names to their vehicles. One of the shuttle vehicles picked up a load of nuns and priests. As that amtrac drove through the internees and troops marching back along the road, it caused a few laughs. The name painted on the side was "Impatient Virgin."

In the camp Burgess and the 1/511th now spent their time making certain that all of the barracks had been evacuated, that all of the internees had been transported by amtrac or were moving on foot toward the beach, and that all of the men of the 1/511th and the recon platoon were accounted for.

Burgess said that "the personnel of B Company did a fantastic job, and several of the soldiers even went back to the so-called sick house and brought out the corpses. I remember one soldier came out with a corpse under each arm."

Burgess had no control over the guerrillas, and after the initial assault the guerrillas, for the most part, had faded back into the areas surrounding the camp, back to their bases in the barrios. Both Burgess and Ringler report having seen only very few guerrillas in the camp itself after their arrival. This does not diminish the guerrillas' contributions. John Fulton and Bill Rivers, in particular, praised highly the bravery and accomplishments of the guerrillas in the initial attack at 0700.

By approximately 1130 hours, the evacuation of the camp was complete, and most of the barracks were in flames. Then Burgess and a rear guard, made up mostly of Ringler and his B Company and the recon platoon, left the camp and followed the tail of the marching column of internees and paratroopers.

Burgess marched with his operations sergeant, Sergeant Muntz, a huge man who had been a football player in Pennsylvania. He was strong, tough, and highly intelligent, according to Burgess. As they marched along at the rear of the column, Burgess and Muntz found a woman who was struggling along, carrying a small baby in addition to other gear. Burgess persuaded the hulking Muntz to carry the baby for her. As he carried the baby down the road toward the beach, Muntz's fellow paratroopers heckled him with catcalls and other remarks that questioned Muntz's virility and combat worthiness. Muntz simply replied that he would see them on the beach. The heckling stopped.

Along the road evidence of the raid was obvious. Several Japanese bodies lay by the roadside. One had been "boloed" and lay on a pile of coconut husks near the intersection of National Highway and College Junction.

Burgess's problems were far from over. Even though he knew that the camp had been cleared of internees, that the Japanese garrison had been killed or dispersed, that his troops and the recon platoon had suffered no fatalities and only two wounded, that there had been only two guerrillas killed and four wounded in the initial onslaught, that all of the internees had been rescued with no loss of life so far, that only a few of the 2,122 internees had suffered minor injuries, and that the amtracs up ahead were moving on Laguna de Bay to shuttle the internees to the safety of Mamatid, he still did not know what had happened to the Soule Task Force.

Early on the morning of the 23d, the soldiers of the Soule Task Force, which was deployed along the north bank of the San Juan River, watched the C-47s, carrying the paratroopers of B Company, fly overhead. They could see the amtracs carrying the rest of the 1/511th, "parading down the lake," to San Antonio. At 0700, on schedule, the glidermen of the 1/188th attacked across the San Juan and toward the Lecheria Hills. The opposition in the hills was light, but the commanding officer of the task force realized that the twin hills were the key terrain that had to be secured to guarantee the safe evacuation of the 1/511th. For, at that point, Shorty Soule still believed he would have to assist the 1/511th both in the evacuation of the internees and in its withdrawal up Highway 1.

In addition to moving east across the San Juan, the 1/188th was also supporting the guerrilla attack near Calamba with mortar and machine-gun fire and was moving to secure the Santo Tomas–Batangas approach to the Los Baños area. With these missions, it took the task force a little longer than anticipated to move toward Los Baños.

In the San Juan area the 1/188th found several bodies of Filipino civilians with hands tied behind their backs, and the battalion aid station was busy treating civilians with wounds. The Makapili in the area were probably responsible for those atrocities.

The Japanese opposition in the area was light but caused fatalities nonetheless in the Soule Task Force. While the 1/188th was clearing the area near the Lecheria Hills, two enlisted men from B Company were killed by Japanese fire. The commander of B Company of the 637th Tank Destroyer Battalion, which was attached to the Soule Task Force, was killed when he attempted to inspect a gun emplacement at a road junction and found that it was still manned by a Japanese soldier. It took the battalion until midmorning to clear the area just across the San Juan River and below and around the Lecheria Hills.

After moving through the area and mopping up whatever enemy it could find, the battalion started down the road to Los Baños. The men could see the amtracs making their way back up the lake, and they could see smoke grenades, artillery-shell bursts, and mortar detonations in the Los Baños area. By noon the infantrymen of the 1/188th had reached the Rock Quarry at the Dampalit River near the town of Los Baños. Colonel Soule, apparently basing his decision to go no farther on what he could see was happening on the lake, ordered his task force to withdraw to the San Juan and maintain a bridgehead across the river. It was not until he ordered the 1/188th to withdraw that Jack Kennington, the executive officer of the 1/188th, realized that the 1/511th would return to Mamatid via the amtracs rather than by an overland move up Highway 1 with the units of the Soule Task Force.

During the withdrawal and the reestablishment of the bridgehead at the San Juan River, the 1/188th suffered one more KIA and some heavier fighting. Cpl. Mike Bonfiglio of the battalion's communication section was patrolling the wire line to A Company and was fatally wounded in an exchange of fire with a Japanese patrol. He died in the field hospital the next day. Jim Adamson's platoon of A company came under heavy attack from a forty- or fifty-man Japanese unit that came down the Santo Tomas–Batangas approach. The platoon repulsed the attack with no further losses. Thereafter, the task force found few of the enemy.

In retrospect, John Ringler credits the Soule Task Force with a great contribution to the success of the raid by virtue of its having engaged and distracted the enemy along the San Juan River and in the Lecheria Hills–Rock Quarry area and by blocking the highway from Santo Tomas to the internment camp.

As Hank Burgess continued his trek down the road from the camp to the beachhead, he worried about the problems that still confronted him. He had to move the remainder of the internees along the road to San Antonio and then to Mamatid; in addition, he still believed that afterwards he had to move his battalion overland to join the Soule Task Force and march back up the highway to his own lines. He still had to consider the possibility of a very disruptive attack by the Japanese 8th Division or by Japanese units from the vicinity of the Rock Quarry or Mayondon Point against his forces and the totally defenseless civilians in his charge, all of whom were in a very vulnerable position. He was far from being home free.

CHAPTER X: The Evacuation

The column of amtracs and people moving down the narrow, dusty, palm-tree-lined road to the embarkation point at San Antonio was a military commander's nightmare. To a man used to organization, precision, and immediate responsiveness to orders and commands, the ragtag, chattering, stumbling mob of men, women, and children walking along the road amid the rumbling, dust-raising amtracs that were loaded to their "gunnels" with cheering, scrawny people and piles of boxes and suitcases made Burgess wonder if he could control this rabble long enough and move them fast enough to evacuate all of them to safety.

Along the line of march, here and there, were Japanese bodies, some mutilated by bolos, to remind the evacuees of their previous condition of captivity and the fight that had taken place to release them. Filipinos from the small barrios along the route stood beside the road, waving and cheering and throwing bananas and coconuts into the amtracs. Part of Burgess's battalion walked with the column at various points to guard it and to guide and assist the walking internees; another part of the 1/511th formed a rear guard that followed the column out of the camp by some fifteen minutes.

The 2d platoon of B Company was the rear guard, with the mission of covering the withdrawal to the beach. Before he left the area, Lieutenant Miller, the platoon leader, had his men check the camp carefully for stragglers. When he was assured that all internees had cleared the camp, he ordered his platoon to move out and follow the column.

Jim Holzem and his machine-gun crew were part of the 2d platoon. The machine gunners and the 2d platoon had been assigned initially to cover the main road, Pili Lane, leading into the camp. The last troops out of the camp at the rear of the 2d platoon were Lieutenant Miller, the platoon leaders, Holzem and his crew, including Oscar, and Frank Smith, the Chicago newspaperman who had made the jump with B Company. In spite of the long walk in front of him, Frank Smith insisted on carrying a large Catholic altar missal that he had rescued from the burning chapel. It was so large, according to Jim Holzem, that "he had to use both hands to carry it as he would an armload of firewood."

The column wound its way to San Antonio; the head of the column arrived there about 1000 hours. The walking internees moved into the perimeter formed by the soldiers of the 1/511th and piled their luggage and boxes in a huge, jumbled stack near the shore. Then they settled down to await the return of the amtracs. The soldiers who had been accompanying them moved out to the perimeter and helped to strengthen it.

The amtracs, after assembling on the shore, turned up in columns of threes, slid into the lake, and began their two-hour trip across Laguna de Bay to Mamatid. In the amtrac in which Sister Maria Del Rey Danforth was riding, the soldiers manning the craft prepared for the eventuality that the amtracs might be fired on from the shoreline. They loaded their machine guns, told the internees to stay hidden below the sides of the amtrac, and swung their guns around to train them on the shoreline. The soldiers, "businesslike but nonchalant," according to Sister Maria, did not "even crouch down behind the guarding iron sides."

Once the amtracs were waterborne and underway, the Japanese along the shore did in fact fire on them. Sister Maria recalls that "our guns answered often but the soldiers were so bored with it all. They swung the guns here and there, pulled the trigger now and then, put in more ammunition as casually as if they were doing it on a stage."

The Japanese continued to fire for about twenty minutes then stopped as the amtracs moved out of range. Sister Maria recalls:

> Then we stood up on the luggage again and looked over the lake. What a sight! The amtracs stretched in triple lines behind us, each with a double swirl of churning water on either side. The flags flew so proudly, one behind the other. So far as I could see, the Japs did absolutely nothing in their attack. On the south shore a column of smoke arose from the trees; it was the camp in flames, the soldiers said.
>
> Both of the boys I could see wore rosaries and scapulars around their necks. The woman crouching beside me, a very hearty, loose type, remarked that probably the boys' mothers and wives had put them on.

The Japanese fire from the shore near Mayondon Point was neither heavy nor accurate, but it did cause some trouble for a couple of the amtracs. One of them was hit by small-arms fire from the shore shortly after it entered the lake. Bullets punctured the pontoon section—actually the sides—of the amtrac and caused it to settle low in the water. The driver quickly off-loaded the internees into another amtrac, which tied up alongside for the transfer of the passengers and their baggage. The damaged amtrac did not sink, but it was so low that water almost topped over the sides; another amtrac pulled it carefully to Mamatid.

In order to try to suppress the fire from the shore, one officer of the 672d, rather brazenly and perhaps dangerously, led a contingent of six amtracs close to and along the shoreline, firing their machine guns as they moved slowly along the tree-lined shore. When they received answering small-arms fire from the Japanese, the drivers turned their amtrac tailgates (the tailgate was much thicker than the sides) to the bullets and churned out in the middle of the lake without suffering any casualties to passengers or vehicles.

Fr. Leo A. Cullum, SJ, presently of St. Thomas More Chapel in Manila, had a ride across Laguna de Bay that, even in the context of the stirring events of the day, was something less than routine. He had walked from the camp to San Antonio and had found sitting space on the forward edge of one of the amtracs in the first lift to head for Mamatid. He sat next to Albert Jones, a paratrooper from B Company who had injured his leg on the jump. Father Cullum and Jones were sitting on cushions on the top front of the amtrac. When the amtrac went into the lake and had gone only a few hundred yards from the beach, it hit a sandbar. The forward edge of the amtrac climbed up over the bar then splashed down the other side, forming a huge wave that swept across the front of the amtrac, washing Father Cullum and Jones off their perches and into the water. Some loose valises were also dunked. Father Cullum popped to the surface and grabbed one of the valises that was floating nearby. Jones, however, because of his injured leg, was in trouble. He yelled to Paul Schramm, another B Company man in the Amtrac, for help. Schramm dived into the water and held Jones up until the amtrac made a 180-degree turn and returned to pluck the three men out of the lake.

Father Cullum related:

> That is more or less the way I remember it. There was some irregular shooting by the Japs from the shore. I seem to remember that one spent bullet landed in the amtrac. For some years I communicated with Paul Schramm. We probably rescued the valises. I remember using some water stained books that were in mine. The valises were naturally full of air and buoyant. The joke among my students was that my teaching notes fell overboard and I dived in after them.

Sometime before noon and after the first wave of amtracs had departed for Mamatid, B Company, the rear guard, the recon platoon troops, a very few guerrillas, and the remainder of the walking internees reached the beachhead at San Antonio. The troops of the 511th who had arrived before Burgess and his command section had expanded the perimeter around the beachhead. By that time Mesereau and his C Company and Fraker and his A Company had also pulled back from their blocking positions and helped to enlarge and thicken the perimeter defenses around San Antonio. The two pack-75s of D/457th were in firing positions some distance away. Burgess awaited the return of the amtracs with some anxiety.

Even on the beachhead, Burgess was still without radio contact with Shorty Soule and his 188th Glider Infantry Task Force, which, if the operation had gone according to the original scenario, was fighting its way down Highway 1 past the Lecheria Hills and on toward Los Baños. Nor did Burgess have any radio contact with the headquarters of the 11th Airborne Division. Rather ominously, when C Company moved back to the beachhead perimeter, Tom Mesereau told Burgess that he had had some contact with Japanese forces, but that he did not know if the Japanese were headed toward the Lecheria Hills or toward San Antonio.

In the midst of the confusion and disorganization surrounding Burgess on the beachhead, he was forced to face one more disconcerting predicament, one that resulted, illogically, from the fact that he did finally achieve one radio link with the outside world. D Battery of the 457th had a forward observer along the San Antonio perimeter to direct the fire of the two pack-75s. About noon a small Cub liaison aircraft (in Army parlance, an L-4), a two-seater, normally used for adjusting artillery fire from the air, appeared over the beachhead. The forward observer on the ground saw the plane, recognized it as an artillery aircraft, and moved his radio to an opening among some coconut trees near the beach in order better to communicate with the Cub overhead.

The passenger in the airplane was not, however, another artillery forward observer; it was General Swing. He wanted to speak to Burgess, he radioed to the forward observer on the ground. The young lieutenant promptly got word to Burgess that the commanding general was overhead and wanted to talk to him. Burgess went to the radio, took the mike, and when the commanding general gave him the go-ahead, he outlined the situation on the ground: all internees had been evacuated from Los Baños; the amtracs had deposited the first load of internees on the beach at Mamatid and were presently on their way back to San Antonio; in about two and a half to three hours he would be able to bring out the rest of the internees as well as his whole battalion and the recon platoon, in one more lift of the amtracs; his troops had suffered only four wounded. Burgess then said, "End of message. Over."

General Swing came back on the air and calmly acknowledged that he was very pleased and relieved at the results. From his coolheaded and composed manner, thought Hank Burgess, one would never know that the Los Baños mission and its potential hazards had been uppermost in General Swing's mind for the past week. Then in a typical Swing reaction to the situation as Burgess had described it, and because he was not a commander to give up terrain and a tactical advantage gained with so few casualties, General Swing dropped a bombshell on Burgess. The commanding general asked his commander on the ground if after he had arranged the evacuation of the remainder of the internees it might not be prudent, possible, and tactically feasible for Burgess and his battalion to stay where they were, capture the town of Los Baños, then move west to contact the 188th Infantry. "Could you do this," asked the commanding general, "without heavy casualties?"

Burgess remembers that "I was so startled at the inquiry that, rather than reply, I turned off our radio and commenced examining the situation in which we found ourselves."

Burgess performed a mental staff study and examined his situation in record-breaking time: the Los Baños Camp was empty of both internees and his troops; the first shuttle run of the amtracs, each carrying 30 to 35 internees and their baggage, left San Antonio at about 1000 hours with about 1,500 internees and a number of his men who had ridden along to guard them on the trip; the amtracs would be back about 1300 hours; about 720 internees and the rest of his battalion and the recon platoon were on the beachhead awaiting the return of the amtracs; his battalion was in a good defensive perimeter, covering the beachhead in a wide arc; he did not know where the Japanese 8th Division was but felt that, logically, given the raid and the tumultuous activities connected therewith, some word of the attack must have reached the Japanese 8th Division commanding general, and Japanese infantry units should be either approaching San Antonio or moving to block the road over which he would have to fight to connect up with the 188th; and, finally, he had no knowledge of the location or the situation of the 188th because of his lack of communications with Shorty Soule. He had to assume the worst: that the 188th was being held up near the Lecheria Hills at an arroyo where the bridge had been destroyed because that general area, he suspected, was strongly fortified by the Japanese. He balanced his forces, about 460 soldiers, some of whom had already departed for Mamatid to shepherd the first wave of the internees, against the Japanese 8th Division and concluded, without fear of being far wrong, that he was vastly outnumbered. He realized that if he couldn't get through to the 188th some six miles away, that he would be isolated beyond the front lines of the division with artillery support consisting only of 75-mm. pack howitzers. He would not even have the relatively limited firepower of the amtracs and their men because the commanding general of XIV Corps had ordered the 672d to withdraw upon the completion of the evacuation of the internees.

Next he considered the condition of his troops. He realized that they were still exhilarated and in good condition. But some of his men had been marching all night or most of the night, and the other troops had been able to get little sleep or rest. He figured that if they had to march another six or seven hours in unfamiliar terrain with the possibility of a heavy fight against increasing numbers of good Japanese infantry supported by artillery, they might take some heavy losses. Besides that, the battalion had few rations because he had issued almost all they had to the internees.

He also considered the tactical situation. During the raid, every man knew what he was supposed to do and when he had to do it. Each man knew that if the 188th Infantry did not reach the camp, that the 1/511th would withdraw to the beach, as they had done. Burgess judged that if he had to leave the beach at 1400 or 1500 hours with the remainder of the battalion and move over ground for which he had no maps or photos, he would have difficulty in maintaining control.

He felt that if he had to gather in the company commanders and inform them of a new mission and have them go back to their companies, brief their platoon and squad leaders, and then move either into the town of Los Baños, with the prospect of street fighting, or across strange country where visibility was limited and the terrain unknown, he would be taking on a formidable task.

In addition, and this loomed large in his litany of factors, Burgess had no medical detachment, no doctors, no ambulances, and no litters; all that support was with the 188th. Any wounded would have to be hand-carried until he linked up with Shorty Soule.

So Burgess, balancing the pros and cons, made his decision in short order. "I decided against the 'suggestion' and ordered the artillery radio to remain silent. To communicate further [with the commanding general] about the subject might have led him to order me to make contact with the 188th. Accordingly, we continued the evacuation of the beach by the amtracs." He reasoned that General Swing would just have to assume that he had lost radio contact with him.

In "losing" radio contact with the commanding general, Burgess violated one of the fundamental laws of the military: a subordinate does not knowingly and deliberately cut off contact with his superior officer in any situation. It is particularly hazardous to one's future in a combat situation. But Burgess got away with it for two reasons: (1) he was right; (2) in this particular case, the commanding general was a very understanding man. Burgess continued the evacuation.

Sgt. Harold "The Moose" Mason was one of the artillerymen in D/457th who went into the Los Baños area by amtrac in support of the 1/511th. The two howitzers in his section had been firing off and on all morning at an area near Mayondon Point, from which the amtracs in the first lift had received small-arms fire. By midafternoon the howitzers and crews were still in their firing positions awaiting further missions. An artillery crewman noticed that they could no longer hear firing from an infantry mortar platoon that had been in the next rice paddy. The artillery crew chief checked the area and found, to his consternation, that the mortar platoon had already moved out. Somehow, no one had notified the artillerymen that they, too, should leave and head for San Antonio. Like a good soldier, the crew chief first checked with his observation post, received no response, then made the decision to "March Order." In their haste the sections hooked up their guns, still in the firing positions, to the jeeps and took off. (Hooking up pack-75s in firing positions to a jeep is a mortal sin among artillerymen; the howitzers are "out of balance" and can be easily damaged on rough terrain.)

The soldiers in D Battery took turns running beside the jeeps and riding on the tails of the howitzers all the way back to the beach. When they arrived there, only the last elements of the infantry units were still in position waiting for additional amtracs to return. The infantrymen gave the artillerymen a loud welcome. And because the Japanese fire was getting heavier and more accurate, the artillerymen dug in next to the infantry.

When the amtracs finally arrived at San Antonio to lift off the last of the soldiers there, one of Burgess's officers ordered the troops first to load as many as they could of the internees' bags, valises, and packages, a great pile of which still cluttered the beachhead. The artillerymen then lifted their pack-75s onto the top of the luggage piles that filled the wells of the amtracs. Then the amtracs moved into the lake. The Moose remembers:

> We were a pretty good distance away on the water when the bullets started to sing and whiz over both sides of us. Richocheting off the water gave them an eerier sound yet. The howitzer was high enough on the pile of baggage for us to contemplate firing a round back at the hill, which was the only place we thought the firing might be coming from. So we loaded and fired at the hill with a charge one, I believe. The machine gun stopped firing but the "track" was dipping from side to side and taking on water with each dip. The amtrac driver pointed a .45 pistol back at us and said, "Anyone loading that thing again gets a bullet in the head."

The cannoneers from Dog Battery decided right then that their one round had knocked out the Japanese riflemen on the hill and that they really did not need to fire another round. The section chief, looking down the barrel of the .45 pistol, is reputed to have said with nonchalance and some haste, "Cease firing. End of mission."

Ben Edwards and Freddy Zervoulakos, after walking with the last of the infantrymen leaving the camp, loaded on one of the last amtracs to leave San Antonio. By the time they dipped into the water and headed for Mamatid, at approximately 1430 hours, the Japanese had closed in and were dropping mortar and artillery rounds near the amtracs. One round landed in the rear of the amtrac in front of them, and Ben recalls that "for a split second the vehicle looked like it was riding a wave; the stern was high and the bow low, as if surfing. There was also some small-arms fire directed at the last group of amtracs, and one internee, Ned Parrish of Liggett & Meyers, received a minor wound to his forehead." To escape getting hit by Japanese artillery fire, the amtracs changed course wildly after each incoming round.

By the time the last amtracs were preparing to leave San Antonio, the Japanese in the area surrounding the beachhead had moved closer and had found the range. Initially, the fire was light, scattered, and relatively harmless, but later the Japanese were able to cover the beach with increasingly heavier fire. As the afternoon wore on and more and more of the American troops departed, the perimeter shrank in size as the covering forces pulled back in to be evacuated. As the number of U.S. troops decreased, the Japanese became bolder and stronger.

Hank Burgess was in a contingent that was the last to leave on a flotilla of about six amtracs. By that time the Japanese were dropping artillery on the beachhead and on the departing amtracs, firing from their positions in and around the Rock Quarry. The Japanese gunners managed to "bracket" the departing and the zigzagging tractors, but they failed to hit any of them when they "fired for effect."

By 1500 hours, with the departure of Burgess and the last six amtracs, the beachhead at San Antonio was empty of internees and troops. Some guerrillas of the Marking Fil-Americans, who had had the mission of guarding the beachhead, remained there to guard the piles of internee baggage that had not fitted into the amtracs.

At Mamatid the internees were under better control than they had been on the march from Los Baños and in the embarkation area at San Antonio—where, Burgess realized, even if the internees did not, that they were still behind the Japanese lines. Mamatid was a different story: it was within our own lines; the internees were in one large group in a small, constricted area; and they carried a minimum of baggage. When they got off the amtracs, the internees wandered happily about, looking for close friends, hugging one another, and embarrassing the

511th soldiers with the warmth and feeling of their gratitude and congratulations.

The internees, who had been imprisoned for more than three years and were almost totally unaware of the prodigious war effort of the United States, were astounded, awed, and overwhelmed by what they were beginning to see. The Reverend George J. Willmann, S.J., remembers:

Throughout this epochal day, we were constantly surprised by the magnificent mechanical equipment of our liberators. Hidden away as we had been for over three years from the modern developments of the war, the new rifles and machine guns, the tanks, planes, trucks, and jeeps filled us with wonder and amazement.

But even more striking, I think, to most of us were the gentleness and courtesy of the soldiers. They distributed their own small rations with lavish prodigality. They tumbled over each other to carry the stretcher cases. They offered helping hands to all with such kindness and sympathy that we could hardly believe these were tough, courageous troops in the midst of an operation that one veteran told me he considered the most hazardous in his experience.

Fortunately for us the magnificent planning had prevented a massacre. The Japanese had been all around us, ready for the kill. But the diversionary attacks and roadblocks, with the lightning tactics of the attackers, had prevented them from getting through to us. We were free. The long-hoped-for event had occurred and had been consummated in incredibly bizarre fashion with a magnificently planned and executed three-pronged attack.

Sister Maria was with the first group that landed at Mamatid, about noon. She was impressed more with the logistical plenty of the Army than with its modern gear. She recalls:

Here we began to see something of the magnitude of Uncle Sam's war effort. Drums and drums of gasoline, trucks and ambulances and jeeps and amtracs. Cans and cans of food, loaves and loaves of bread, great tanks of coffee. Thousands of Filipinos running here and there, bands of us standing in groups near our stacks of baggage, newspapermen grinding cameras and taking notes. The smells of spilt gasoline, butter squashed into the sandy beach, sweaty men. And over it all a terrific sun burning your eyes and crisping your skin.

In the last amtrac to leave San Antonio was the second platoon of B Company, Lieutenant Ringler, the correspondent, Frank Smith, Holzem and his faithful Oscar, and a taciturn Filipino guerrilla leader who "stayed aloof in a corner of the alligator," according to Holzem. The amtrac reached the shore at Mamatid with little difficulty, and when it left the water it started to travel along the road that was built up on a levee. The roadway was about eight feet above the rice paddies on either side. The road was very narrow, and the driver could not keep the amtrac on the road. The amtrac slid sideways down the embankment, and when it hit the rice paddy, it turned over on its side. Holzem and Oscar were on the downed side, and they felt the weight of a lot of soldiers, weapons, and ammo on top of them. Fortunately, no one was seriously hurt.

Holzem recalls that the first time he ever saw Lieutenant Ringler mad was during that incident. "Here we had made that spectacular parachute jump in the morning; effected a successful rescue of 2,122 people—all without the loss of life or limb— and now, after it was all over, we were almost killed by a careless driver."

The first group of internees waited about an hour at Mamatid before they loaded up on the twenty-one trucks and eighteen ambulances assembled by the 11th Airborne Division G-4. Their route took them along Highway 1, the national road, for the fifteen-mile trip to Muntinlupa, the site of the New Bilibid Prison, the place they were to call home for the next few weeks, until they could be evacuated to the States.

The road to Bilibid was lined with cheering groups of Filipinos under bamboo arches that bore the words "Welcome Victorious Americans and Guerrillas." The internees unloaded inside the walls of Bilibid, now cleared of its former occupants: the Filipino political prisoners of the Japanese who were either freed by the Americans or executed by the Japanese before the arrival of U.S. forces. The internees moved into the prison's big cell blocks, which were furnished with double-decker beds, fully supplied with "well fed and happy bedbugs," according to Sister

Maria. The second group of internees arrived at New Bilibid at about 1600 hours. "When we landed here," Sister Maria remembers, "they took our names and checked us off as 'released' from the Los Baños Internment Camp. Then, a smiling soldier boy handed us each four Hershey bars. How good they were! We went to the kitchen and got bean soup. Oy, bean soup, real bean soup!"

At New Bilibid the XIV Corps, under the command of General Griswold, took over the care and feeding of the rescued internees from the 11th Airborne Division. General Griswold had designated his corps surgeon, Col. Robert E. Allen, to establish a facility for the internees' reception, registration, medical attention, feeding, and clothing. The corps selected New Bilibid because it was large enough to accommodate all of the internees and because it was empty.

The corps troops had done a great deal of work to make the prison habitable for the internees. They had cleaned it thoroughly of everything, apparently, except for Sister Maria's bedbugs. The mess personnel had set up a dining room and kitchen for 750 people in the Catholic chapel. Two corps clearing companies and a Sixth Army field hospital detachment provided the medical support for the internees. The corps special service officer, not to be outdone, set up a movie room and a public-address system for record playing. (Cassettes and Walkmen were, of course, not yet in vogue.)

After registration,[1] the internees went straight to the mess lines. They needed no pushing, organizing, or second calls. The evening meal the first day lasted from 1600 until after midnight. Many internees reported that they were not above going through the line at least four times. And no one cared.

Initially, intelligence from the camp had indicated that as

---

1. By a very odd coincidence one of the released prisoners was the ex-fiancé of Hank Burgess's wife, Mary. Mary's father, Professor Hayden, had been a professor of political science at the University of the Philippines and a correspondent for the *Christian Science Monitor* before the war. From 1933 to 1935, he was the vice governor general of the Philippines and later was acting governor during the absence of Frank Murphy, the governor general. During the war, Professor Hayden served on General MacArthur's staff as the civilian advisor for Philippine affairs. Mary Hayden had attended the University of Michigan before the war and there met a

many as 600 of the prisoners might be litter cases. In fact, after the internees were registered and the sick sorted out from the reasonably healthy, only 107 people needed hospitalization. Their difficulties ranged from malnutrition and beriberi to pregnancy (three).

The internees lived at New Bilibid until they could be processed and sent on their way, either to their homes in various countries or to their Philippine missions in the case of a number of the ministers, priests, and nuns. By 8 March 1945 most of the internees had left New Bilibid.

The war, suffering, and privation were over for the men, women, and children formerly incarcerated in the internment camp at Los Baños; but the war was far from over for the men of the 11th. Immediately, they went back into combat; the Los Baños raid was a brief but highly successful and uplifting episode in their lives. They were, after all, trained primarily in the art of defeating and killing the enemy, even though their considerable military skills had just been put to a very humane use: rescuing helpless civilians.

For the unfortunate people of the barrio of Los Baños and the area around the empty, charred remains of the internment camp at Los Baños, the suffering was about to begin. The Japanese who dominated the area simply refused to accept the Los Baños rescue without a bloody, sadistic reprisal.

---

young man who took a great interest in her, so much so that after his graduation, he went to the Philippines to seek his fortune. He became a banker in Manila. Mary met Hank Burgess in the summer of 1941 when Hank was stationed at Fort Lewis, Washington, with the 115th Cavalry of the Wyoming National Guard. After Mary met Hank Burgess, she knew that she could not marry her fiancé, the banker in Manila. She wrote and informed him. According to Mary, her friend called her (an almost unheard of event in those days) on 11 November 1941 to verify the letter and to ask if there was someone else. "As I was not committed to Hank in any way," says Mary (I was a senior at Michigan and he was soldiering), I said 'No'— a big fat lie as it turned out." Mary's friend stayed on in Manila and was eventually imprisoned in Los Baños. Neither Burgess nor the young man in question was aware at the time of his release of their mutual regard and admiration for Mary Hayden. After the war, Mary attended the wedding of her former fiancé to a woman whom he had met and courted in the Los Baños lockup. (As Mary says now, "Thank goodness he got my message before the war.") Mary and Hank were married in the spring of 1946.

CHAPTER XI: The Aftermath and the Reprisal

I t should have been appropriate, and proper, to end the story of Los Baños simply with a fadeout of a scene picturing ecstatic ex-internees smiling, talking, hugging and patting each other, and eating Army chow ravenously in the dark, cavernous, un-locked cells and open areas of the New Bilibid Prison at Mun-tinlupa.

That is, in fact, a partially correct tableau of the end of the Los Baños saga.

The released internees were overcome with joy when they realized that they and their families had survived months of deprivation and harassment at the hands of their captors. They congratulated one another on their mutual good fortune.

The ex-internees were awed by the U.S. war machine, its equipment, its men, its seeming invulnerability and invincibil-ity. Those who had gone into prison three years earlier remem-bered, especially since they had been living in the Philippines prior to Pearl Harbor, the dark days of the Pacific War; the defeat of the U.S. Army on Bataan; the siege and capture of the "Rock" (Corregidor), previously considered impregnable and unconquerable; the stupefying surrender of U.S. forces to the "hordes of little yellow men" who thereafter captured them, humiliated them, and subjected them to years of captivity under primitive and inhumane conditions. The internees felt that those conditions were inhumane: after all, the internees were neither criminals nor prisoners of war.

Now, after only a short trip and a few hours of freedom, the internees were able to catch a glimpse of the massive military organization that had marched, flown, and sailed back from the bitterness of defeat from as far away as the southernmost tip of New Guinea to the triumphant reentry into and recapture of Manila, their beloved "Pearl of the Orient." That is the good news of the Los Baños epic.

The bad news had two facets for the internees: (1) the almost total destruction of the once magnificent Manila, demolished and ravaged by a defeated, vengeful, vindictive enemy bent on smashing and ruining that which it could not hold; and (2) the Japanese barbarities near Los Baños Camp.

The explicit fact of Japanese revenge, retaliation, and simple spite is nowhere more directly authenticated than in the carnage the Japanese visited upon the hapless, defenseless, totally innocent Filipinos of the barrios around Los Baños and the people living near the college. Those Filipinos deserved no such ruthless brutality. Their fate is the shameful, dismal side of the Los Baños story, a grim chapter that stains an otherwise seemingly fantastic, fictitious tale.

Coincidentally, the liberators of Los Baños, the 1/511th under Hank Burgess, were the first American troops to discover the slaughter of the Filipino civilians in and around the charred remains of the Los Baños Internment Camp. That discovery was made eight days after the Los Baños raid.

If the troops of the 1/511th had harbored any ideas that they were going to have a period of R and R after their eminently successful foray into Los Baños, they were quickly disabused of those notions the morning after the raid. The paratroopers had spent the night of the 23d at New Bilibid Prison,[1] and about an hour after breakfast the next morning, Hank Burgess's regimental commander ordered him to "saddle up"

---

1. Sister Rose Maria said, "When the parachutists arrived at Muntinlupa about 5:00 P.M., we, who had arrived earlier in the day, cheered and clapped until our throats were hoarse and our palms were red."

immediately and to prepare to move south. Burgess's new mission: replace Ernie LaFlamme's battalion, 1/188th, along the San Juan River, the area to which 1/188th had withdrawn during the afternoon of the 23d. LaFlamme, in turn, was ordered to move his battalion back to rejoin his regiment in the fight for Manila, which had not yet fallen completely into American hands.

By midmorning of the 24th, Hank Burgess was marching his battalion in a column of twos along the sides of Highway 1 south from Bilibid past Binan and Mamatid to the positions on the San Juan River just vacated by LaFlamme's 1/188th. The ostensible reason for holding this terrain and putting a battalion there even though all of Manila had not yet fallen to the Americans was, according to Hank Burgess, "to keep the Japanese in the Lecheria Hills away from the internees."

As Burgess and his command group were walking down the road with the rest of the battalion, a jeep came racing up from the rear of the column. The driver was looking for Burgess and told him that there was a press conference at division headquarters that General Swing wanted him to attend. Burgess turned the battalion over to his executive officer, Bud Ewing, got into the jeep, and returned to division headquarters at Parañaque.

At headquarters it was apparent that the raid and its success had raised some interest among members of the press. On the day before, the 23d, there had not been much Stateside coverage of the raid in newspapers because the fall of Iwo Jima, after a bloody battle, and the historic raising of the U.S. flag on Mount Suribachi by the Marines, occurred the same day and dominated the news.

Burgess had never before attended a press conference, nor had he been exposed to newspapermen during his combat days with the 11th. For some reason, reporters were relatively scarce in the 11th Airborne Division areas. At the press conference, it was obvious to Burgess that "higher headquarters," in the aftermath of the raid and because of its overwhelming success, seemed to be claiming some credit for the intelligence gathering, the planning, and the splendid results achieved by the 11th Airborne and the Filipino guerrillas. It also became clear to Burgess that the reporters had no idea who had done the planning, the intelligence gathering, or who had actually executed the raid. Burgess recognized the need for caution under the circumstances, surrounded as he was by glib staffers from "higher headquarters" who seemed to be answering smoothly a lot of the reporters' questions. As far as Burgess was concerned, he had been given a mission, he had accomplished it; now he was confronted with the inevitable result of success: Who gets the credit? He decided to keep quiet and stay out of the conversation.

After the conference, Burgess stopped Doug Quandt, the division G-3, and asked him what the press conference was all about and just what was the "plan" the reporters referred to constantly. Quandt, who had been in the conference room before Burgess's arrival, said that they were talking about the 11th Airborne Division's operations order for the raid. Both he and Burgess knew full well that such an order had never been committed to paper.

Doug Quandt, with the wisdom and experience of the seasoned G-3, told Burgess to come with him to his office and together they would write the operations order for the raid. With Quandt's facile command of military English, knowledge of proper formats, and 20-20 hindsight, and with Burgess's real life, indelibly engraved experience not yet twenty-four hours old, they produced a model operations order for the Los Baños raid that would have earned an A+ in any service school. Immediately, Quandt sent copies of the written order to Corps and Army headquarters. As Burgess said:

> Both of them [the higher headquarters] then wrote and back-dated their orders and plan for the raid. That sequence of events explains why the raid is taught in so many military classes as how the 11th Airborne Division executed the orders and plan perfectly, just as General Swing had been ordered by those higher echelons of command.

Burgess went on to say about General Swing:

> He was always in command of the raid as to troops, time for execution, and method of operations; he didn't, and we didn't,

need a lot of written orders to liberate Los Baños. For months we had fought with coordination of units on oral orders.

Don't get the idea there was no plan. General Swing had a plan with alternatives for execution and gave the unit troop leaders freedom to chose the alternative of execution within the plan.

After Burgess finished helping Doug Quandt write the operations order for the raid, he jeeped back to his battalion, which by midafternoon had walked down Highway 1 about ten miles from New Bilibid and moved into the area where LaFlamme and the 1/188th had been dug in. Burgess was not happy with what he had found. The location may have suited LaFlamme's mission, but it did not suit Burgess's.

It was apparent to Burgess that the Japanese, holed up in the Lecheria Hills, even if only few in number, were in a position to dominate the entire area around Calamba, the San Juan River, and southeast toward the town of Los Baños. It was also apparent that from the hills the Japanese could see LaFlamme's battalion move out and Burgess's battalion move in. What made Burgess dissatisfied with LaFlamme's position was that it had been dug in along some relatively open terrain directly under the eye of the Japanese in the hills. Burgess was determined not to expose his battalion to that kind of a position. Nonetheless, he had to devise a ruse to fool the Japanese.

During the afternoon, he had his battalion make an obvious occupation of the same positions that LaFlamme and his battalion had just left. Then he had his company commanders send men in small groups at odd intervals 600 yards to the rear, where the terrain was more favorable for a defensive position. There he had the companies dig individual firing holes and machine-gun pits. After dark, and the night of the 24th was very dark, Burgess had his companies booby-trap their forward positions with hand grenades and move back to the newly dug positions 600 yards to the rear. Previously, he had had the artillery calculate firing data for shelling the abandoned positions.

As Burgess had expected, the Japanese came down from the Lecheria Hills and elsewhere after dark on the evening of the 24th, and "banzaied" the old position. When the troops of 1/511th heard the grenades explode in front of them, they called for the previously registered artillery fires and swept the area with machine guns and mortars that had also been laid on the old position. The next morning they counted forty-odd Japanese bodies in the old position; the battalion's loss, according to Burgess, was "a couple of hours of sleep."

The troops of the 1/511th battalion practiced the same tactics the entire time they fought in the area near the Lecheria Hills. They never stayed in the same position two nights in a row. They dug new foxholes and machine-gun pits every day and occupied them after dark each night. Thus, their casualties were extremely low throughout that part of the campaign. Finally, early in March, the Japanese withdrew from the area back toward Los Baños. The 1/511th followed them and only then discovered the heinous massacre of the Filipino civilians around Los Baños and the college, a war crime of the most sinister and immoral proportions.

In the barrios around Los Baños, Burgess and his men found the Japanese had "tied families beneath their homes, [most of which were built on stilts with the floors about six feet above the ground] with their arms behind their backs around the stilts, or posts, supporting the house," recalls Burgess. "Men, women, and children were all tied, block after block, then the area was set afire." When the men of the 1/511th found the area, they were overcome by the stench of the dead bodies, which were so decomposed that their identification was impossible. Burgess estimates that about 1,500 Filipinos had died in the massacre throughout the area. Burgess is of the opinion that the Japanese 8th Division assumed the Filipinos around Los Baños had assisted in the raid. "Its elements arrived in the afternoon [of the raid] and proceeded to wreak vengeance on the civilian population."

Since there was mass murder of helpless and innocent noncombatant Filipino men, women, and children, which happened shortly after the raid on the internment camp, and because it was confined to a small area around the camp, one must agree with Burgess that the Japanese instigated the attacks out of revenge, vindictiveness, and sheer retribution for the supposed assistance that the neighboring Filipinos had given to the internees both before their release and in support of it. If the reprisal raids were only to punish the guerrillas in the area, there would not have been the bloody and excruciating torture of uninvolved Filipino bystanders.[2]

In recent years Gustavo Ingles has tried to piece together an accurate picture of what happened during the reprisal raids of the Japanese 8th Division in the specific area near the college. He interviewed Jose Esguerra, Jr., who was an officer of the PQOG and who participated in the raid on the camp, and Prof. Andres Aglibut, who resided behind the chapel on the grounds of the camp. Professor Aglibut suffered the loss of a daughter during the Japanese massacre.

Colonel Ingles found:

> The reprisal raids of the Japanese Army were concentrated in the houses near the college gate. There was also an attempted raid at Faculty Hill; however, when the Japanese raiding party noted the presence of the PQOG in the area, they proceeded to the coffee plantation.
>
> The Japanese units were reinforced by YOIN. The YOIN was a semimilitary unit composed of Filipinos who were rabid pro-Japanese. The members wore military uniforms similar to those worn by Japanese army personnel, and their unit commanders were Japanese noncoms.
>
> Raids were usually conducted after midnight and terminated before daylight. Except for the raid at the college gate, minimum utilization of gunfire was employed, and the victims were usually killed by bayonets and/or decapitated with samurai swords. During the daytime, the raiding parties returned to their base.
>
> The raids began past midnight on February 25th at the houses in the vicinity of the college gate. Since the residents evacuated earlier to Faculty Hill, the raiding party found all the houses empty. In their disappointment the raiding party raked the houses with automatic rifle fire and burned all houses.
>
> The chapel area is about half a kilometer away from the gate. The residents were awakened by the sound of the automatic rifle fire, and most of them took refuge inside the chapel. Among the evacuees were the Banzon, Diaz, and Intengan families. There

---

2. Two nights before the Japanese reprisal raids started, Helen Espino, Colonel Price's wife, tried desperately to make the Filipino civilians in the barrios hide in the hills. Few of them responded to her pleadings.

were around a hundred of them—mostly women and children.
Prof. Andres Aglibut, whose house was just behind the chapel,
did not evacuate his residence. Late in the afternoon he visited
the people inside the chapel. He was requested to go to Maquiling School where the headquarters of PQOG were supposed
to be stationed to request food and protection. Professor Aglibut
found the Maquiling School empty. It turned out that Colonel
Espino had evacuated his headquarters to Faculty Hill to protect
the bulk of the residents who had evacuated to that place. Professor Aglibut returned to the chapel emptyhanded with the sad
news that the PQOG had left. The occupants decided to evacuate the chapel early the next morning.

Past midnight that evening, the Japanese raiding party arrived. Some occupants of the chapel fled through the rear door.
Those left behind were able to close the front doors and barri-
cade themselves inside. Those who fled by the rear door were
chased by the Japanese and YOIN and were bayoneted.

The commotion awakened Professor Aglibut, who saw Japa-
nese soldiers trying to break down the rear door of the chapel.
In the darkness he saw outlines of soldiers bayoneting civilians.
He fled with his family through the back door of his house.

The Japanese, having failed to break down the doors of the
chapel, set it and the neighboring houses on fire. The stillness
of the night was punctuated by the cries for help of women and
children and groans of agony of the dying as they suffocated or
were crushed by burning roof trusses.

The patrol of PQOG arrived at daybreak, and what they saw
shocked them: around seventy people inside the chapel burned
to death. In the surrounding area were a number of victims bayoneted to death.

Sadaaki Konishi, the supply warrant officer, despised by the
Los Baños internees, and the man who dominated the senile
and enfeebled camp commander, Major Iwanaka, was very much
a part of the outrageous attack on the Filipinos in the environs
of Los Baños. Konishi had managed to escape unharmed during
the raid on the camp.

Early on the morning of the 23d of February, Konishi was
still in bed in his room in the headquarters building near the
main gate of Los Baños Camp. Shouts and the noise of the guards
running about and the scurrying of the off-duty relief from their

calisthenics area to their barracks awakened Konishi. He ran to the door of his room. One of the guards yelled to him that American paratroopers were dropping from the sky near the camp. At about that same moment, Konishi heard "rifle fire directed to the camp from all directions."

In the midst of all the confusion, Major Iwanaka gave the order for the Japanese guard force to evacuate the camp. Konishi and about seven guards ran to the ravine outside the wire near the camp hospital, the same gully through which Ben Edwards and his party escaped on the night of the 18th. Konishi and his group hid in the bushes of the ravine and planned to escape immediately to the hills to the west of the camp, but in a very short time they saw the amtracs on the road coming into the camp and decided to stay concealed in the ravine until it was safe to move. Konishi and his party stayed hidden there until midnight. Some of the guerrillas and recon platoon actually passed within a few yards of them, but the ravine was thick with foliage and undergrowth and provided good cover for the Japanese. About midnight Konishi and his men made their way to Mount Maquiling and joined Major Iwanaka and the other surviving Japanese who had managed to escape to that area. Iwanaka ordered Konishi and ten of the Japanese soldiers who had been guards at Los Baños to join the Saito Battalion, which was located in Mount Maquiling.

The Saito Battalion, commanded by Capt. Ginsaku Saito, was a battalion in the 17th Infantry Regiment commanded by Colonel Fujishige; his regiment was part of the 8th Division whose commanding general was Lieutenant General Yokohama. The Saito Battalion had two companies: one commanded by Lieutenant Kudo and one commanded by Lieutenant Fujii. Major Iwanaka and a group of the men who escaped from the camp left the Mount Maquiling area about 27 February.

Sometime after the raid on Los Baños, probably about 24 or 25 February, Fujishige gathered together his battalion commanders and company commanders and ordered them "to kill all guerrillas, men, women, and children, in Los Baños" and "to prepare to kill 100,000 men, or 70 men for each of us. Also, each man must destroy one tank before he dies."

On numerous occasions during the period from 24 to 28

February, in order to carry out Fujishige's and Saito's orders, Konishi came down from the Saito Battalion's hideout and bivouac area on Mount Maquiling with various raiding parties. Not all of the raids were specifically to kill Filipinos. On one of his trips to Los Baños, Konishi met with the mayor, a man named Almasan, and told him that he was the supply officer of the Saito Battalion and that all foodstuff confiscated by the Japanese Military Police should be delivered to him. In particular, Konishi said he wanted sweet potatoes ("the battalion commander liked potatoes very much"), green coconuts, and meat.

Most of the raids, however, did have vengeful killing as their purpose. On 28 February, Konishi, Captain Sato of the Kempei Tai located in Los Baños, and two other Japanese met with the mayor and told him that they were going to investigate the Gardner family that night because they had seen lights burning in the house; they wanted the mayor to accompany them. The Gardners were an American family who still lived on the west side of Los Baños on National Highway 1. For some reason they had not been interned previously, nor had they availed themselves of the opportunity to move out of the area with the liberated internees of Los Baños. The Japanese also asked the mayor to select four people to work with them in the "investigation." One can only assume that the four would be Makapili. The mayor selected four men and sent them with Sato and Konishi but did not accompany them to the Gardner house himself.

The next day Konishi appeared on the street of Los Baños and met the local chief of police. Konishi told him that he wanted him to round up five additional men "to bury a certain body that was also dead."

One of the men selected by the chief of police was Fernando Bernardo, a resident of Los Baños. Konishi told Bernardo and the others to find shovels and to come with him to the home of the Gardners. About 100 yards from the Gardner home, the party found the bodies of Mr. and Mrs. Gardner. Tied to the arm of Mrs. Gardner was their four-year-old son, Jimmy, who was alive. He tried to get up from the ground and called out, "Mama, I'm hungry." Konishi called a guard who was inside the Gardner home. Two minutes later the guard came out with a fixed bayonet on his rifle. Konishi then went into the Gardner home. Another Japanese told the Filipinos in the party to back off ten yards and to turn their backs. When they turned around again, they saw that the Gardner child had been bayoneted to death. Then the Filipinos buried the three bodies.

During another raid into the area, on 6 March, thirty members of the Chinese Ang Kai household were assembled by Japanese soldiers at the Ang Kai home. The Japanese had separated the men from the women and had tied the hands of the men behind their backs. Konishi was present and wrote down the names of the Chinese. Mathilde Chu, saved from the eventual massacre by Mayor Almasan to live at his house, said that Konishi told them, "Most of the Chinese are pro-American and we are going to kill them. . . . I am in charge of gathering and killing Chinese under Captain Saito's orders and in charge of the internment camp, but do not be afraid, there will be no more killing." Later she modified what she remembered his saying to, "Saito's orders are to kill all Chinese and Filipinos, but from now on, no more killings."

Regardless of what Konishi actually said or who was in charge of the killings (he did spare members of the Chu Kam family), the Japanese took the thirty Chinese to the outskirts of town and butchered twenty-eight of them. There were two survivors: Ang Kim Ling, eleven years old, and Ang Elisa, nine. Kim survived four bayonet thrusts and Elisa sixteen.

In other parts of Los Baños, the Japanese murdered thirty or forty additional Chinese on the same day, 6 March. By then the Japanese had massacred hundreds of Filipinos and Chinese, and it was probably only the arrival of Burgess and his battalion that prevented the continuing rape of Los Baños.

That there was a massacre of unarmed, nonmilitary civilian men, women, and children in and around the former Los Baños Internment Camp is beyond question. Whether the murders were in retribution for the successful release of the internees is a somewhat debatable point, although the bulk of the evidence seems to support the contention that the killings were indeed a reprisal against the local Filipinos for their supposed assistance to the internees before, during, and after the raid.

Ben Edwards, however, pointed out:

The Japanese and the Makapilis demonstrated their sadistic

tendencies at Calamba, Canlubang, and other Laguna towns and barrios days before the Los Baños liberation.

I do not believe the atrocities in and around the college were the direct result of the liberation! I have always been of the opinion that the taste of defeat drove the Japs into a frenzy that set off sprees of killing. I seem to recall being told, or reading, that over 185,000 civilians were killed in Manila alone during the liberation. I personally know a family that lost the mother and two daughters when the Japs set the Ermita District of Manila afire and then butchered people as they ran from their houses.

There is a good deal of controversy about what went wrong in the days immediately following the raid on Los Baños and who was at fault in failing to protect the civilian population of the area. Days before the raid there was a meeting of the guerrilla chiefs, during which they wrangled about who was to do what to whom and with whom; and at that time Colonel Price, who was the commanding officer of the Red Lions unit of the PQOG, expressed in strong terms his need for assurance that if the internees were liberated, there would be ample protection provided for the Filipinos in the Los Baños area, particularly for those still living in faculty housing and barrios in and around the college itself. (His wife, of course, still lived in the area near the internment camp.)

Col. Gustavo Ingles, who had represented Major Vanderpool and Col. Terry Adevoso, the overall commander of the Hunters' guerrillas, in dealing with the various other guerrilla units who were to participate in the Los Baños raid, felt that he brought with him to those planning sessions in the schoolhouse in Nanhaya the assurance from guerrilla headquarters that the Filipinos would indeed be protected after the raid. Ingles knew that this had been "SOP for other raids." The discussions with Colonel Price became so heated that Colonel Ingles remembers it nearly "developed into a shoot-out incident, were it not for the intervention of cooler heads who requested a break of the conference."

At the resumption of that conference, Colonel Ingles tried to convince Colonel Price that the Filipinos would be secure by telling him that he would send a message to the headquarters of the 11th Airborne Division asking for confirmation of their safety once the raid had been accomplished. And to persuade Colonel Price of the validity of his intentions, Ingles decided to leave John Fulton, the peripatetic U.S. radio operator, with Price, so that any messages coming from the 11th would be relayed to Price immediately. This gesture convinced Colonel Price to go along with the plan for the liberation of the camp and to coordinate with and support the troops of the 11th. In retrospect, it is obvious that any assurance Colonel Ingles thought he had from either the guerrilla headquarters or the 11th Division headquarters did not materialize. It is also quite clear that if the 11th Airborne had promised assistance it would have delivered it.

General Swing's mission at Los Baños was clear: free the internees and return them to U.S. control. He had not been directed additionally to "seize and hold" the area in and around the Los Baños Internment Camp. If he had been assigned that mission by his superior headquarters, he would have planned the operation differently. It would not have been a "raid." General Swing would have provided the commander in the field with sufficient infantry to seize and hold the area, enough artillery to support that infantry, sufficient logistical means to support combat operations in the area for days, and enough medical, communication, and transportation units to maintain the force for an extended period of time. His suggestion to Burgess, when he was flying in a Cub airplane over the amtrac loading area near Mayondon Point, that Burgess consider holding the area that he then occupied, was an impromptu proposal made on the spur of the successful moment.

If Burgess had had any inkling that part of his mission was the protection of the Filipinos in the area after the raid, he would have found a way to do so and he would have planned his operation far differently. Instead, after considerable thought and a fast mental run-through of an estimate of the situation, Burgess made the decision to move out. Once they arrived at the New Bilibid Prison late on the afternoon of the 23d, Burgess could breathe a sigh of a relief: the raid was over, his battalion had accomplished its mission with speed, amazingly low casualties, and results far beyond their pre-raid expectations.

Gustavo Ingles still feels bitter and guilty about the massacre of the innocent Filipino civilians. He said:

> To this day [1984] the relatives of the massacred persons have not forgiven us. I still maintain that because of the failure of the U.S. Army to occupy and give adequate protection to the town of Los Baños, many Filipinos had to die as a result of the liberation of the internment camp. While this was never the intention prior to the raid, it came out that way, as many feared it would, due to the change of plans in the direction of operation for the liberation of southern Luzon.

On the other hand, one might logically question the location and activities of the guerrillas during the Japanese reprisal attacks and why they were not more effective in counteracting the raiding parties of the Japanese Saito Battalion. Hank Burgess expressed his opinion this way (and opened up a lot of debate on the point):

> Had the guerrillas been as effective and numerous during the raid at Los Baños as some now claim they were, the civilians in that area would not have been subjected to mass murder by the Japanese following the raid.

David Blackledge, former internee, takes exception to that position (as do Ingles, Bill Rivers, and John Fulton). Blackledge wrote:

> As Mr. Burgess surely knows, no guerrilla force has ever been strong enough to prevent reprisals against their own populace by an aroused and vengeful professional military force. The tragedy that befell the hapless Filipino civilians around Los Baños is mourned by the internees who were secretly sustained by their efforts before the rescue and by the American soldiers who were welcomed and aided by these patriotic people.

Who was to blame, other than the Japanese, is difficult to assess. The tragedy of the murdered Filipinos is a heartbreaking story with at least two sides, and neither position is clear-cut or unequivocal.

The details of the eventual apprehension and trial of Sadaaki Konishi make a story that reads like pure fiction. The story begins at the Wack Wack Golf Course outside Manila, which was in limited operation in mid-1945. During the war, the clubhouse had escaped destruction, and the Japanese, during their occupation of Manila, had converted a large portion of the golf course into an ammo dump; a Japanese Antiaircraft Battalion secured the area. After the liberation of Manila, U.S. forces established a POW camp on the grounds of the golf course and used the prisoners to dismantle the AA guns, clear the area of ammo, and restore the club to its original purpose. The U.S. forces then opened the club for very limited operation.

In July 1945 Henry Carpenter, a Colgate-Palmolive executive before the war and one of the internees freed from the Los Baños camp, was playing golf on the partially restored Wack Wack Golf Course. Purely by chance he spotted Konishi among the POWs who worked near the course. He reported his observation to the U.S. military authorities; Konishi was subsequently singled out from the other POWs. After the war, in a trial that lasted from 23 November 1945 to 15 January 1947, the War Crimes Commission tried Sadaaki Konishi for his various war crimes.

Konishi's offenses were concentrated into six specifications and were summarized by the Far East Command Board of Review generally as follows:

> Sadaaki Konishi, formerly a Warrant Officer of the Imperial Japanese Army, was charged with violating the laws of war in six specifications, which in numerical order alleged that he ordered and permitted Japanese soldiers under his command to kill a named American citizen, his wife, their infant son, James Gardner, a named Filipino citizen and about fifty unnamed, unarmed, non-combatant Filipino civilians, at Los Baños on 28 February 1945 [Specification 1]; ordered or permitted Japanese soldiers under his command to kill one named and about sixty unnamed, all unarmed, non-combatant Chinese and Filipino civilians at Los Baños on 6 March 1945 [Specification 2]; ordered or permitted Japanese soldiers under his control to attempt to kill two Chinese infants at Los Baños on 6 March [Specification 3]; ordered or permitted the burning and destruction of private Filipino and

Chinese dwellings [Specification 4]; devised, aided, and abetted a policy of gradual starvation at the civilian internment camp near Los Baños between 1 August 1944 and 23 February 1945, thereby causing the death of four named [John Edwards, Conway Moak, George I. Whitmoyer, and Charles N. Magill] American internees and sickness, disease, and death to numerous unnamed American civilian internees [Specification 5]; and ordered and permitted Japanese soldiers then subject to his control to kill George Louis, an American citizen, and participated in said killing at Los Baños on 28 January 1945 [Specification 6].

The war crimes trial of Konishi proceeded in a brawling atmosphere of recriminations, objections by the score, and motions that caused the president of the commission repeatedly to admonish both counsel for the prosecution and counsel for the defense. The Board of Review said of the trial:

A large part of the record of trial is consumed with argument between counsel, with the commission, with objections over admissibility of evidence, continuances, and attacks on the jurisdiction of the commission to act. There were literally hundreds of objections, some meritorious, but generally directed to an apparent desire on the part of the defense counsel to distract the attention of the court from the real issues, to heckle the opposing counsel, and to confuse the commission. Both prosecution and defense counsel offended in this respect. The President of the Commission repeatedly admonished counsel; on one occasion found a counsel in contempt and assessed a fine against him; and on other occasions threatened counsel with contempt proceedings.

The trial ended on 15 January 1947. At 0830 hours on that date, the commission met in Courtroom No. 1, High Commissioner's Residence, Dewey Boulevard, Manila. Before the commission could announce its decision, however, Mr. King, representing Konishi, in response to the commission president's question, "Has the defense anything further?" said, "At this time, gentlemen of the commission, we wish to renew all of our motions that were denied and all of our objections that were overruled during the course of the trial." Colonel Rice, the commission president, replied, "The ruling by the commission is that all motions that have been denied are still denied."

Colonel Rice then said, "The commission has heard, carefully analyzed, and evaluated all the evidence in this case and has based its findings solely upon the evidence. As a result, the commission has arrived at a judgment and sentence in the case of the defendant and will now pronounce the sentence.

"The accused, Sadaaki Konishi, his chief counsel, and the commission interpreter will take their positions in front of the commission." (The accused, counsel, and interpreter then did so.)

Colonel Rice said, "Sadaaki Konishi, the commission, in closed session, and upon secret written ballot, at least two-thirds of the members at the time the vote was taken concurring in each finding of guilty, finds you: Of the charge, guilty." (The commission excepted certain words in each of the specifications and found the accused not guilty of those excepted words but guilty of all of the specifications except Specification 4, having to do with arson. Of that specification he was found not guilty.)

Then Colonel Rice said, "The commission, in closed session and upon secret written ballot, at least two-thirds of the members present at the time the vote was taken concurring, sentences you to 'death by hanging.'"

Colonel Rice continued, "The Military Police will remove the accused." (The accused was then taken from the courtroom by the Military Police.)

Colonel Rice further said, "The commission will adjourn sine die." (The commission then adjourned at 0845 hours.)

Konishi, for all his sadism, malevolence, crimes, hostility, and hatred of Americans, apparently had a change of heart in his waning days. After the war, Fr. John P. Wallace, a U.S. Army Catholic chaplain, provided Catholic services for Los Baños and Luzon POW Camp #1, which was located about ten miles from the town of Los Baños. In May 1983 he wrote to Sister Miriam Louise Kroeger, a Maryknoll nun and former internee of Los Baños, about the fate of Sadaaki Konishi:

I have a record of baptizing a Japanese War Criminal by the name of Sadaski [sic] Konishi. I baptized him on June 17, 1947, and he was executed the same day. It was my custom to baptize shortly before the execution to eliminate the need for Confession as I could not understand Japanese. I visited this person repeatedly and instructed him in the Catholic faith through an interpreter. His embracing the Catholic faith was genuine and sincere. He told me that he had been impressed by the example of Catholic sisters and priests whom he had encountered during the Japanese Occupation of the Philippines. I do not remember whether or not he was the commandant of Los Baños Concentration Camp as we never talked about their past as War Criminals. They considered everything they did as justifiable.

The baptismal record spells the first name as Sadaski. But the other data on the record conforms to the records of Konishi of Los Baños—particularly his date and place of birth. There can be no question that Sadaaki Konishi went to his death by hanging on 17 June 1947.

CHAPTER XII: Mosscomes

(The principles of war: Mass-Objective-Security-Surprise-Command-Offensive-Maneuver-Economy of Force-Simplicity)

T hat's the story of Los Baños—a bittersweet tale of an obscure event that happened in a remote area of a faraway island more than forty years ago. It is a bitter tale for the victims, relatives, and friends of the Filipinos who were slaughtered by the Japanese; it is a joyous tale for the liberated internees. It was a memorable experience, an upbeat adventure, a triumph for the men of the 11th and the guerrillas who were part of the raiding force. In this one case the raiders did not measure success in terms of body kill or terrain seized; they gauged it in terms of people freed and saved. Therein lies a tremendous difference.

The raiders had every right to be proud of their accomplishment. In just a few days' time, with little prior notice, they mounted a well-conceived, hit-and-run attack against considerable enemy opposition—at least there was the potential for enemy opposition that could overwhelm them. They moved by air, water, and land some twenty-five miles behind the enemy lines; they freed, organized, and moved out some 2,122 exuberant, disorganized men, women, and children; they eliminated the Japanese garrison, killing at least 70 of the enemy and scattering the rest of an estimated 250-man force; and they suffered the loss of two guerrillas killed and six wounded in the fight along the perimeter of and within the camp and three 11th Airborne soldiers (one of whom was the commanding officer of B Company, 637th Tank Destroyer Battalion, an attached unit) killed with the overland force in and around the Lecheria Hills area. Only two U.S. troopers were wounded in the raid on the camp itself.

In retrospect, one might consider that the raid was "daring," "hazardous," "courageous," and "valiant." But to General Swing and Hank Burgess, it wasn't. They did not consider it risky or foolhardy. General Swing would not launch a "risky" or "foolhardy" operation; he would attack only when he had assurances of success. He was by no means timid; that's the last adjective one would use to describe General Swing; but he was not stupid or foolish either.

When asked, "Why did you think that we could succeed in the face of such odds?" Hank Burgess replied:

> This is a question that gets General Swing's goat and mine too. As a lawyer, I would comment on the question that it "assumes facts not in evidence, is without foundation, and begs the question."
>
> What odds are you talking about? What were the facts on that 23d day of February 1945? Don't the facts determine the odds? If you look at the facts, any "odds" were in our favor, and not in the enemy's, all for the following reasons:
>
> 1. The attacking troops were combatwise, disciplined, and well led. They could fight and had been proving it, first in Leyte, then door-to-door in Manila, up the wide avenues and over the rolling ground toward Nichols Field, and on to Fort McKinley.
>
> 2. *All* operations would be conducted under the umbrella of at least twenty-seven fighters at *all times* for ground support, and more fighters were on call if needed. The fighters would stop any effective counterattack against us by the Japanese 8th Infantry Division. The roads would be denied the Japanese by the constant aerial patrols.
>
> 3. The 1st battalion would have at least three to five hours behind the lines to do what they wanted without any large-scale counterattacks.
>
> 4. We *knew* the camp and how to neutralize it. . . .

5. The Japanese garrison consisted of older men, many were wounded veterans, no longer fit for frontline duty; the commander was a weak officer, and the morale was reportedly low.

6. Only forty or fifty men at the camp would be armed at the moment of the attack.

With that kind of information, how can it be said that the odds were against us?

All that may be true as one looks back on it; now, in retrospect, the mission was clear and relatively simple; but before the raid the mission, carried out twenty-five miles behind Japanese lines, was fraught with danger and uncertainties; the situation was not so obvious. There had always been the possibility for calamitous results if the plan had been less well thought out or if it had been executed with indecisiveness, anxiety, or trepidation.

It is very doubtful that the planners and the executors of the raid on Los Baños ever gave even a fleeting moment's thought while planning the raid to the Principles of War as they learned them in the various service schools throughout their careers. With a backward glance, however, at the development and execution of the Los Baños mission, one can see that the Principles of War were very much followed by the developers and executors of the plan, even if they were not consciously aware of them at the time. MOSSCOMES is an acronym used by the students at service schools to help them remember the Principles of War.

M = Mass. This principle holds that the attacker concentrates his force at the point of decision so that the enemy is overwhelmed at the decisive point. In spite of the fact that the very strong Japanese 8th Division was in the general area of Los Baños, the 11th planners put the mass of the 11th troops at the point of decision: the Los Baños Internment Camp, where the attacking forces would outnumber the defenders. Doug Quandt did not give a thought to the historic battle of Leuctra in 371 B.C., where the Thebans fought and defeated the Spartans by massing their forces at the critical point of decision, thereby defeating the Spartans, who overall outnumbered the Thebans. Even so, Doug Quandt, in his planning, used the same Principle of War.

O = Objective. Any fighting force must have a clear-cut, specific, very definite objective before it engages in battle. The Los Baños task force knew exactly what its mission was: move to the internment camp, free the internees, and bring them back to safety. That was all, an objective which was clear-cut and understood by all the troops; it was attainable.

S = Security. Any operation must be carried out in an atmosphere where one's intentions are kept from the enemy until the time of attack; even then, the main attack should be camouflaged as long as possible. At Los Baños, in spite of the noisy tractors on water and on land, in spite of the movement of the Soule Task Force down the west side of Laguna de Bay, in spite of the paratroopers' preparations at Nichols Field, and in spite of the massing of the amtracs at Muntinlupa before the amphibious attack, the enemy was completely in the dark about the goal and mission of those forces. To maintain security, the troops were not informed of their part in the operation until the last possible moment.

S = Surprise. The corollary of security is surprise. Because the operations of the 11th just prior to the raid were secure, they were able to surprise the enemy. This principle was one of the most significant in the entire operation. The Japanese were caught, literally, "with their pants down"; they had no prior knowledge of the raid.

C = Unity of Command. Although Colonel Soule was nominally in command of the entire operation, General Swing made clear before the raid was launched that Hank Burgess was the commander on the ground within the area of the Los Baños Camp itself and until the Soule Task Force arrived at the camp. Since the Soule Task Force never did get to the camp, Burgess was the commander there, even with the authority to convince the 672d Amphibian Tractor Battalion commander, a lieutenant colonel, to remain with the 1/511th until the internees had been evacuated, then to make a second lift to pick up remaining internees and the 1/511th.

O = Offensive. Obviously, only offensive actions achieve decisive results. There can be no question but that the Los Baños raid was an offensive action, and it achieved decisive results. The commander "exploited his initiative and imposed his will on the enemy," as an instructor in tactics at Fort Benning might say.

M = Maneuver. A commander must position his forces to place the enemy commander at a relative disadvantage. He must take advantage of the enemy's weaknesses to outmaneuver him, to cut down his own losses, and to inflict maximum casualties on the enemy forces. Maneuver, of itself, alters combat power. Certainly at Los Baños the attacking forces maneuvered by land, sea, and air to position themselves at the greatest advantage and to overwhelm the enemy at the decisive point. (They didn't attack the Japanese 8th Division; they attacked the guards around the camp.)

E = Economy of Force. This principle is the corollary of the principle of mass. It means that at points other than the point of decision, the commander deploys only the minimum essential forces. The Soule Task Force was large enough to hold off for a time an attack by elements of the Japanese in the Lecheria Hills–Dampalit River area, but it was not so large that it drained essential forces from the 11th, either from the attack on Los Baños or from the continuing attack on Manila and other areas in the 11th's continuing zone of responsibility.

S = Simplicity. This principle holds that commanders must keep their plans as simple as possible because battle is extremely complex anyway, and the unexpected often becomes the norm. The 11th's plan for accomplishing its mission at Los Baños was simple: get in, gather up the internees, get out. That the 11th used three elements—land, sea, and air—did not overly complicate the operation. The 11th's units were trained in air and ground operations. It was a simple plan executed by battle-tested troops. (One might suppose that the ill-fated plan for liberating the American hostages held by the Iranians in Teheran was not particularly simple.)

In short, the Los Baños raid followed the time-honored Principles of War, as important to military operations today as they were when they were first codified and enunciated by Clausewitz in the eighteenth century.

What military lessons were learned from the raid?

1. The commander of the raiding force must have a clear-cut mission, the support of the major command (the 11th Airborne Division), and the authority to plan and execute his mission with little outside guidance and interference. This is a restatement of the time-honored rule of leadership and management: Give a man a job and let him do it.

2. The troops used in such a mission must be highly trained, motivated, thoroughly briefed, self-confident, enthusiastic, and combat-ready. They were.

3. Once the commander is on an objective, he must have the authority to make necessary decisions and to make them stick.

4. An independent operation of this sort must be decentralized to the commander on the ground.

5. Administration, reports, and status accounts must be kept to a minimum. In this case the raiding force was even without written operations orders until after the attack.

6. The chain of command must be effective. When something unexpected occurs, the commander on the spot must have the power to make decisions.

7. Communications outside the raid area need be only the minimum essential to the accomplishment of the mission. Too much communications capability only invites interference by "higher headquarters."

8. When a commander is faced with a critically important mission in which speed is essential (in this case to prevent further harm and a rumored catastrophe to the internees), he must coordinate all his reserves and focus attention and assets on the most important mission.

9. For success in battle, the planning must follow—even intuitively—the traditional, time-tested Principles of War and the planning sequence detailed in the "Estimate of the Situation," another portion of the gospel as preached at the service schools.

10. The biggest lesson learned was probably that if you have a distinct mission, reliable intelligence, well-trained troops, responsible and decisive commanders, and a winning spirit, success can be the only result.

Hank Burgess can have the last word:

In my opinion the fighting ability, morale, self-confidence, and the successes of the 11th Airborne, and of the 511th in particular, had reached such a level by the time of Los Baños that the troops involved could do anything so long as they could retain the initiative and not be trapped into a fixed position, a situation for which they were not equipped or adequately supported with engineers, artillery, and quartermasters.

Epilogue

Where are they today? What happened to the cast of characters of the Los Baños story?

What follows is a partial accounting of most of the principals mentioned in the book. I have arranged the list alphabetically because it is impossible, or at least foolhardy, to attempt to list them in any order of importance.

Adevoso, Eleuterio L. ("Terry" or "Magtanggol".) In Tagalog, Magtanggol means Avenger. Adevoso took the name to "avenge" the death of his close friend, Miguel Ver. Ver was one of the founders of the Hunters and was killed in a Japanese raid on a Hunters' camp in the Sierra Madre on 1 July 1942. After the war, Adevoso became very active in Filipino politics. He was the Secretary of Labor in the cabinet of President Magsaysay and later became the Economic Coordinator during the presidency of Macapagal. He was also the Secretary General of the Liberal Party founded by President M. Roxas. He died on 22 March 1975 after having spent 666 days as a political detainee during the period of martial law declared by President Marcos.

Anderson, Donald G. Lives in Davis, CA, where he manages a lumber company.

Blackledge, David W. In 1984, retired from the U.S. Army as a Colonel. Lives in Carlisle, PA. Currently Assistant Dean for Admissions and Financial Aid at the Dickinson School of Law in Carlisle, PA.

Burgess, Henry A. Joined the Wyoming National Guard in 1937. Graduated from Harvard in 1940. Entered University of Michigan Law School, September 1940. Came on active duty when the National Guard was activated in February, 1941. Originally a platoon leader in Troop E of the 115th Cavalry (Armored cars) which was designated the recon company for the 11th Philippine Infantry Division being activated in the Philippines. Troop E left San Francisco in November of 1941 on the Army Transport Tasker H. Bliss. On 7 December, after a few days at sea, the War Department ordered the transport to return to San Francisco. In 1943, Burgess joined the 11th Airborne Division. Shortly after the war, he married Mary, finished law school, returned to Sheridan, Wyoming, served in the Wyoming House of Representatives and Senate, and, as County Prosecuting Attorney, closed down gambling which had been wide-spread in the county for many years. Today, he is a prominent lawyer and rancher (his spread covers some 40,000 acres) in Sheridan, Wyoming.

Calhoun, Alex. Retired to San Francisco. Deceased.

Castillo, Marcelo S. ("Middie") Retired as a brigadier general in Philippine Army; lives in Manila.

Chenevert, Alan H. Following the war, attended the University of Miami and then became a partner in a small construction firm in West Palm Beach. Recalled to active duty in March, 1951, and served successively with the 11th, 82d, and 101st Airborne Divisions. Retired as lieutenant colonel in September 1968. Thereafter, worked as general manager and project manager in major construction projects in Virginia and North Carolina until 1977 when he retired to Titusville, Florida.

Coleman, Arthur J. After the war, went to work at Letterkenny Army Depot, Chambersburg, PA, as a production controller of ammunition and maintenance. Retired from Letterkenny in 1979.

Edwards, Benjamin Franklin. After his liberation from Los Baños, he spent a few weeks with the recon platoon of the 11th in its bivouac area near Paranaque and then returned to the States. He married his wife, Ruth, in Chicago on 30 June 1945. In March 1946, he and his wife returned to Manila where he resumed his pre-war job with Pan Am. In November of 1948, he accepted a more responsible job with CalTex Petroleum Corporation and served with CalTex in Manila, Saigon, Hong Kong, and South Korea until 1977. He retired in 1977 to his home on eight acres of forested land on Bainbridge Island, Washington.

Fulton, John. Discharged from the Army on 25 December 1945. Returned to college and took his graduate work at Columbia in modern British literature. After college, he first worked as a tech writer for Curtiss Wright Aviation. Then he taught English at the University of Idaho until he returned to New Jersey in 1956 to teach at William Paterson College of NJ. Survived a bout with cancer in 1954. Is a fan of J.S. Bach and occasionally sings with the Masterwork Chorus—concerts in Carnegie Hall and Lincoln Center. In 1984, after his retirement from William Paterson College, he bicycled across the country. He left the Olympic Peninsula near Kalaloch, Washington on 1 July and arrived in Asbury Park, NJ on 23 September—in time to celebrate his 63d birthday on 25 September 1984.

Gray, George. Served a career in the Foreign Service and then retired to Las Vegas. Deceased.

Guerrero, Honorio K. Former Commanding Officer of the 45th Hunters ROTC Regiment. After the war, became one of the top officials, Deputy Collector, of Philippine Bureau of Internal Revenue. Now retired from government service; lives in Manila.

Hettlinger, Walter. Retired from the U.S. Army as a lieutenant colonel. Lives in Fayetteville, NC.

Hunters. After the war, the various ex-Hunter guerrillas strove to maintain the camaraderie which had been born and nurtured among them during the difficult days of the Japanese occupation of the Philippines. It was a proud organization then—proud of its resistance to the Japanese, proud of its considerable assistance to the Americans when they returned to the Islands, and proud of the singular accomplishments of its individual fighters. It grew from the original band of thirteen ex-cadets to over 30,000 guerrillas operating in eleven provinces of Luzon by 1945. After the war, the pride remained, and the members sought to serve their country during its reconstruction period. After liberation, the Hunters banded together in fraternal, patriotic organizations throughout Luzon which developed community projects for the welfare of all of the citizens, set up scholarships for the sons and daughters of ex-Hunters, and adamantly opposed any form of authoritarianism. Many of them continued in the Army or entered politics. For example, Rigorberto Atienza became the Chief of Staff of the Armed Forces of the Philippines; Frisco F. San Juan became chairman of the Presidential Complaints and Action Committee during the presidency of Ramon Magsaysay; Jaime Ferrer became board member of the Rizal Provincial Board and is now a member of the Philippine (Batasan) Congress; Raul Manglapus became undersecretary of Foreign Affairs and later Secretary of Foreign Affairs under President Garcia; Jovito Salonga became a Senator for the Liberal Party and is now the president of that party; Juan Ponce Enrile is now the Minister of National Defense under President Marcos; Effren Plana was the commissioner of Internal Revenue under Marcos; Edmundo Reyes is now the Commissioner of Immigration in the Marcos administration. Today's ex-Hunters, like the American Legion, VFW, and other veterans organizations in the U.S., are dedicated, nation-loving, and freedom seeking patriots. The Hunters have been at least a "thorn in the side" of the Marcos regime.

Holzem, Jim. Currently residing in Edinbuerg, TX.

Ingles, Gustavo C. After the war, became an electrical engineer and worked overseas in Okinawa, Japan, Korea and Viet Nam. Presently, president of the St. John's Trading Company in Manila, a firm which fabricates stainless steel food service equipment for hotels, restaurants, and hospitals.

Iwanaka, Yasuaka, Major, Japanese Army, Commandant of Los Baños camp on 23 February 1945. Fled to the hills near Mt. Maquiling as soon as the raid on the camp started. On 6 or 7 March, 1945, he and several of the other guards who escaped from the camp went to Alaminos near Lipa and joined the Shimbu 35th Corps. He was apparently killed later during the 11th Airborne's attack on Mt. Malepunyo in April of 1945.

Kennington, Robert E. Retired from the Army in 1961 as a colonel and worked for a number of years for an insurance group as a claims representative. Although he was a lawyer before he entered the Army, he spent most of his career with infantry units. Retired again in October 1976 and lives in Sonoma, CA. Travels and researches steamship history.

Kreuger, Walter A. General U.S. Army. Deceased. Commanded Sixth Army to which control of the 11th Airborne Division passed on 10 February 1945 and under which the Division made the raid on Los Baños. At first, General Kreuger was dubious about the merits of the raid, but in his book, *From Down Under to Nippon*, he said: "A rescue operation (Los Baños) involved considerable risk. But intelligence reports indicated that the plight of the internees was desperate and the risk was justified. The whole operation was a complete success because of the careful planning and brilliant execution. It reflected great credit upon all concerned."

Kroeger, Sister Mary Louise. Remained in the Philippines until 1950. Then spent seven years in the States doing development work. Taught at St. Bernard's School in St. Louis for four years, then studied for three years before returning to the Philippines where she taught Muslim students at Notre Dame High and Junior College in Datu Piang, Cotabato. Currently, she is the Purchasing Agent for her Community and lives at the MotherHouse in Maryknoll, NY.

LaFlamme, Ernest H. USMA Class of 1937. Retired as a colonel in 1962. Died in Manchester, NH on 6 August 1980.

Lahti, Edward H. USMA Class of 1939. Retired as a colonel in 1962. Currently living in Herndon, VA.

Maryknoll Sisters Maura Shaun, Antoinette, Frederica, and Andrew and Mother Ethelburga have all gone "to their eternal rest." Sister de Chantal is a resident in the Maryknoll Nursing Home, Maryknoll, NY.

Maria del Rey Danforth, MM Maryknoll nun. After Los Baños, returned to the States and earned a Masters Degree in Journalism from Columbia; travelled and wrote books on mission life; produced a Sunday Morning TV Show on NBC in New York; helped make a movie with Jane Wyman. In 1981, returned to Davao in the Philippines, established and currently operates a Training Center for young people who have lost limbs or who were paralyzed. At 76, she says she is "white-haired and a bit arthritic, kind of forgetful, but as the Psalm says: 'still full of sap, still green.'"

Mason, Harold. (The Moose). Retired to Chesterton, Indiana. Operated on for a tumor on the back of his head which

impaired his vision, but did not keep him from Division reunions (he attended them all from the first one in 1973) or remi-
niscing about firing a pack-75 from the back of an amtrac afloat
on Laguna de Bay. Died in Chesterton on 20 January 1985.

McCarthy, William R. Maryknoll priest. His mother died
when he was three years old, and he dropped out of high school
in his junior year. For several years, he worked in the wholesale
heating and plumbing supply business and later studied law.
Thereafter, he entered the Maryknoll order and was ordained
to the priesthood on 16 June 1940. His first assignment was to
the Maryknoll missions in the Philippines. After his release from
Los Baños in 1945, he returned to the States. In 1946, he was
assigned to the Maryknoll parish in Lima, Peru, where he spent
many years. He celebrated his fortieth anniversary to the priesthood in 1980. Currently, he is assigned to the Catholic Foreign
Mission Society of America in New York City.

Mesereau, Thomas. West Point Class of January 1943. Re-
signed from the Army in 1953 as a lieutenant colonel. Worked
in the restaurant and food service business in New York and
California. Currently lives in Laguna Beach, CA.

Miles, Prentice Melvin ("Pete"). Died of a heart attack in
Manila in 1962.

Muller, Henry J. Retired from the Army as a brigadier general. Owns and operates a garden supply company in Santa Barbara, CA.

Nash, Grace. Continues to write and teach music in Scottsdale, Arizona.

Nelson, Mary Harrington. Married a U.S. government employee who had been interned with her in Los Baños.

"Oscar"-Rosendo Castillo. Lives in the Philippines. In 1978,
when members of the 11th Airborne Division made their first
"Return to the Philippines," Oscar was on hand in Manila to
greet the returning veterans of the Division and especially Jim
Holzem.

Okomoto, Daikichi. Civilian Interpreter at Los Baños. After
the raid, escaped to Mt. Maquiling. Thereafter, assigned to the
2d Battalion (Suicide Battalion) of Fujishige Division. Battalion
surrendered on 19 September 1945. Okomoto detained in POW

Camp near Colombo, Luzon, until he was returned to Japan on 1 July 1947. Now living in Kyoto, Japan. Age 82.

Pierson, Albert. Assistant Division Commander of the 11th during the war. Now a retired major general currently living in Washington, DC.

"Price" (Romeo Espino). Post-war Army Chief of Staff of the Philippine Army. Retired as a four-star general in 1981. He and his wife, Helen, currently operate a small hotel in Manila.

Quandt, Douglass P. USMA 1937. Served in the Korean War as Assistant Artillery Officer of X Corps. Attained the rank of major general and retired in 1966. Lifelong bachelor. Died in San Francisco 30 March 1973.

Quesada, Francisco B. ("Kit"). After the war, worked for the Philippine government on tourism and wrote a book on the subject. Led the Filipino delegation to the International Conference on Human Rights in Helsinki in 1971. Currently a colonel in the California State Guard. He is active in the California State Military Reserve and serves as the Division G3 and Training Advisor of the 2d Infantry Brigade at Fort Funston, CA. Member of the National Guard Advisory Committee to the San Francisco County and City Board of Supervisors. Lives in San Francisco.

Ringler, John M. Colonel U.S. Army Retired. Served in the U.S. Army for thirty years, twenty-four of which were with airborne units. (This is a near record.) After World War II, served with the 11th Airborne in Japan and Fort Campbell, KY. Served as an advisor in Viet Nam 1957–1958 and with the Green Berets at Fort Bragg from 1966 until his retirement on 30 June 1970. In 1971, joined the State Department as an advisor to the Vietnamese National Police and served again in Viet Nam until the summer of 1973. Now fully retired and lives in Fayetteville, NC, near Fort Bragg, NC, "The Home of the Airborne."

Rivers, William R. Served with Transocean Airlines in Oakland, CA, from 1946–1961; then became President of International Air Service Company 1961–1967; next, Marketing VP of National Airmotive, 1967–1975. Retired in 1975; spends his time traveling around the world.

Skau, George. In August of 1945, shortly before the surrender of the Japanese, General MacArthur's headquarters ordered the 11th Airborne Division to proceed by air transport from Luzon to Okinawa to Japan to commence the occupation of Japan once the formal surrender had been accomplished. Martin Squires was on one of the planes at the Lipa Airstrip on Luzon, on which had been loaded part of the Division Recon Platoon. Skau could not find a seat on that plane so he ordered Squires off so that he, Skau, could be with the lead elements of this platoon arriving in Okinawa. As the plane neared Naha, Okinawa, the Japanese kamikazes were attacking ships in the Naha harbor. The ships put up a smoke screen to try to hide themselves from the kamikazes. Unfortunately, the smoke obscured the landing strip at Naha, and the C-46 carrying Skau crashed into the cliff below the strip killing all 31 men aboard.

Smith, Jasper Bryan. Joined the Military Police after his service with the 672d Amphibian Tractor Battalion. Retired from the Army and now lives in Anderson, Indiana.

Soule, Robert H. Served as assistant division commander of the 11th Airborne Division during the occupation of Japan. Promoted to major general and served as Military Attaché to China during the reign of Chiang Kai Shek. Retired from the Army as a major general and died in San Francisco some years ago.

Squires, Martin. Married Margaret Whitaker, ex-internee of Los Baños in 1947. Worked for 27 years for Boeing Aircraft as an aerospace engineer and Quality Control Engineer. Retired in January 1984.

Swing, Joseph M. USMA 1915. Retired from the U.S. Army in 1954 as a lieutenant general; spent his last three years of active duty commanding Sixth Army at the Presidio of San Francisco. Served as U.S. Commissioner of Immigration and Naturalization, 1954–1961. Died in San Francisco on 9 December 1984 at age 90.

Vanderpool, Jay D. Completed thirty years service while in Viet Nam and retired in 1976 as a colonel to his home in Sarasota, FL. Serves occasionally as a consultant to the Defense Department.

Whitaker, Margaret. Returned to the U.S. after her release from Los Baños and entered Western Washington University, Bellingham, WA. In 1946, after returning to her dorm room, she found a note from a young man who had seen her picture in the local paper which had identified her as having been an internee in Los Baños. The young man who sent her the note was Martin Squires. They were married in 1947. She is now retired from her school teaching position.

Zervoulakos. Fred. Currently living near San Francisco.

Appendix A

Sister Miriam Louise Kroeger, one of the Maryknoll nuns from Baguio, described life in Los Baños—at least, in Vatican City—in poignant terms. Her testimony seems to deserve being reproduced in full. Sister Kroeger survived and lives at the Maryknoll House at Maryknoll, New York.

"Our new home at Los Baños had formerly been the Agricultural School, and 100 of us were stationed in one of the nipa barracks that had been used as a stockade for the cattle and horses. Perhaps it was a blessing after all that the Japanese had not permitted us to take more than two pieces of luggage as there was no room to put any more. Incidentally, the baggage was to include no food.

"A fence was erected between us and the other 1,800 prisoners who had preceded us to Los Baños. Our group included 2 bishops, 1 monsignor, 140 priests, and more than a hundred Sisters. The Protestants numbered about 200 missioners. Masses were celebrated every day, and we had the privilege of receiving the Blessed Sacrament; the 'tabernacle' in which it was kept was one of our suitcases. Outside of religious freedom, the existence in camp was a systematically arranged plan whereby life for the internees would eventually become one of that beyond the grave.

"The water system was so regulated that about the only time you would be able to get any water was at midnight or later. Half-sick, starved, nerve-racked prisoners dragged themselves out of bed to wash their clothes and at the same time to use their one and only container to get a little water with which to wash the 'dishes' the next day.

"Medicines which had been sent by the Red Cross were confiscated by the Japanese, and we were left easy victims to the various epidemics which had had such a devastating effect upon the people, mentally as well as physically—malaria, dysentery, infantile paralysis, skin diseases, etc.

"During the last few months, our food consisted of two cups of lugao (a paste made of four-fifths water and one-fifth rice), one cup of which was served at nine o'clock in the morning, and another cup at four in the afternoon. [Vatican City was on a different meal schedule than the internees in the main part of the camp.] This was filled with worms, sand, and stone. In the beginning we cleaned the rice before it was cooked, but later we were so weak that we hadn't the energy to do even that. The rice was than prepared with all the foreign elements in it. Some people removed the worms from the cooked rice, but when they finished eating, they were still so starved that they ate the worms which they had previously put aside. The Japanese permitted us to pick the weeds about the barracks. These we boiled and ate with our lugao. Personally, though, I never gathered the weeds for myself as I felt the energy expended was not worth the harvest. Some thought that the greens would counteract the beriberi of which everyone was a victim. That was not true, as some of those who ate the most weeds had beriberi in its worst form.

"No lights were permitted in the camp. This restriction alone was a source of torture, and night traffic in the camp finally became such that our committee had to establish traffic rules whereby everyone kept to his right to avoid the others whom he could not see coming from the opposite direction. Not being able to read at night was another keen punishment; magazines and newspapers were never seen.

"With the ever-increasing bombing of the islands by the Americans, the camp enclosure became more rigid and the Japanese more difficult to deal with. The final touch came when we were confined to our barracks twenty-four hours a day. When the planes were overhead, we were forbidden to show any emotion; disobeying such a directive meant death by gunfire. As we well knew, there would be no hesitation about shooting. Our men had been warned that anyone found leaving the camp would be shot on sight. The next day at dawn a starving man was found trying to get food over the fence and was killed instantly. Later, another man was returning with a pack of food on his back; he was shot but did not die. When the priest asked permission to see him, the Japanese refused. We saw this man being carried out beyond the gate and heard a shot fired later. The body was turned over to us for burial.

"The deaths were reaching such a number that the grave-digging crew had to be doubled in order to prevent the bodies from remaining unburied too long. To watch our men at such work was a gruesome ordeal. Their skeleton frames were clad only in patched shorts, and as they dug laboriously in the claylike soil, their bones moving painfully in harmony with each slow-motion swing of the pick, one wondered if in reality they weren't digging their own resting places. Beriberi was of such long standing that it was beginning to endanger everyone's life. Death also resulted from eating weeds that were not considered digestible. Intestinal obstruction resulted. Operations were performed under the worst possible conditions. As the patients had no resistance and the doctors had no medicine, death generally was the only alternative. One man who was mentally disturbed tried to eat his mattress and mosquito net. He died. In fact, all of the more than 2,100 could watch the progressing symptoms of the disease in themselves and wonder how much longer they could endure.

"Despite conditions, we did our best to celebrate Christmas of '44. One of the Canadian brothers made Nativity figures out of clay, with a dirty pink blanket as a backdrop. From our tin cans that were no longer usable, we cut bells and animals to hang on the 'Christmas tree.' It was at times such as this that the Japanese would become very irritated. For all the force and power that lay behind them, they were never able to dampen our spirits. More than once they told us that we were not to be happy because we were prisoners of war and as such had nothing to be merry about. That was one order we never obeyed.

"Various pleas were made to the Japanese for food, even just a little salt to put in our lugao, but to no avail. The bishop asked that we make a public Novena to our Lady of Lourdes, aware that our plight was really desperate. When the Novena ended on the Feast of Lourdes, February 11, 1945, there was no apparent answer to our prayers that had been so imploringly said. However, the bishop felt that a favorable answer was at hand even though we saw no actual proof of it.

"Finally, the Japanese stopped giving us even the lugao ration. Instead, they doled out unhusked rice; most people were too weak to remove the hulls. In spite of the doctors' warnings not to eat the whole kernal, some did eat it. Death was the result.

"Finally, the weed patch was closed to us. Bishop then directed that we have exposition of the Blessed Sacrament with public recitation of the Rosary throughout the day. Personally, I was so weak that I couldn't even move my fingers from one bead to the other, so I just wrapped the rosary around my wrist and sat out the time."

APPENDIX B

Los Baños Internment Camp

(40th Anniversary Program: Los Baños Liberation, February 23, 1985.
Hunters ROTC Association Inc. 1985)

AMERICAN

Adams, Elbridge M.
Adams, Gustav Adolph
Adams, Owen
Adams, Welba S.
Adrian, Kathleen Halloran
Adrian, Michael Joseph
Agnes, Sister Inelda
Agnes, Sister Regina
Ahern, Hilary
Aimee, Sister Marie
Aiton, Joe E.
Aiton, Felicimo L.
Aiton, Josepha D.
Albert, Daniel Louis
Ale, Francis Harvey
Allen, Robert Coleman
Alness, Mark Gerhard
Alphonsa, Sister Mary
Alsobrook, Anthony Leonidas
Amstutz, Elda
Ancilla, Sister Marie
Anderson, Charles Richard
Anderson, Charles Stewart
Anderson, Theodore Maxwell
Anderson, Oscar .William
Ankney, William Edgar
Antoinette, Sister M.
Andrew, Sister Mary
Apelseth, Clement Anders
Appleby, Blanche

Aquinata, Sister M.
Arana, Bernardina
Arana, Esther
Arana, Cesar
Arick, Melvin Ray
Arida, Jodat Kamel
Armstrong, Robert Worthington
Ashton, Sidney
Assumpta, Sister M.
Augustus, Sister Mary
Avery, Charles William
Avery, Henry
Axtman, Boniface
Ayres, Glen Edwin
Babbitt, Winfred Howard
Backman, Herbert
Bagby, Calvin T.
Baker, Rowland John
Balano, Felix
Baldwin, Rena
Barnaby, Catherine
Barnes, Charles Irwin
Barnes, Evelyn Crew
Barnes, Richard Porter
Barter, Fred
Bartgis, Fred
Barth, Phyllis Ludwig
Bartlett, Mildred Glaze
Bartlett, Sydney Stockholm
Barton, Roy Franklin
Bateman, Jack
Bateman, John James

Bateman, Sallie
Bauman, William McComb
Baxter, Cecil Marie
Baxter, Sidney
Bayley, Harold Raymond
Bayouth, Khallel Assad
Beaber, H.
Beata, Sister M.
Beaty, Truman Carlson
Bebell, Clifford Felix Swift
Beck, Emsley William
Beck, Francis Harold
Becker, Frank Emil
Bee, Edwin Joseph
Beeman, Frank Robert
Beeman, Maude Rona
Beeman, Narvel Chester
Beeman, Raymond Richard
Beeman, Wallace Earl
Begley, Charlie
Beigbeder, Frank Michael
Bennett, Frank Cantillo
Benninghoven, Edward Robert
Berger, William Harris
Bergman, Gerda Ottelia
Besser, Leo
Bezotte, Fred
Billings, Bliss W.
Binsted, Norman S.
Binsted, Willie M. G.
Birsh, Charles
Bissinger, George Henry
Bissinger, Winifred Allen
Bittner, Joseph
Blackledge, David
Blackledge, Helen
Blackledge, Robert
Blair, Herbert E.
Blair, Susan
Blake, Lila
Blake, Mary
Blake, Owen A.

Blakeley, Mildred M.
Blalock, John
Blanchard, Harold Mason
Blanton, Charles Maxwell
Blanton, Dale Lincoln
Blechynden, Claire Louise
Blue, Harry Coleman
Bogacz, Francis
Bogle, Edwin Carmel
Bolderston, Constance
Bollman, Benjamin B.
Bollman, Elsie K.
Bollman, J. W.
Bollman, Lynn B.
Bond, Leo
Bonham, Rex
Boomer, Louise Charmian
Boomer, Joseph
Boston, William
Boswell, Eleanor Madaline
Bousman, H.
Bousman, James
Bousman, Martha
Bousman, Nona
Bousman, Tom
Bowker, Bayard Jordan
Bowie, Harold Dewell
Bowie, Leah Lourdes
Bowie, Paquita Rodriguez
Boyce, Leila Susan
Boyce, Viola Ceres
Boyd, Joseph
Boyens, Ernest
Boyers, James Simon
Boyle, Philip
Bradfield, Elizabeth Shortridge
Bradley, Brant
Bradney, Reuel
Bradanauer, Frederick W.
Bradanauer, Grace A.
Bratton, Charles Henley
Brazee, Albert John Jr.

Brazee, Nancy Agnes Erwin
Brendel, Oswood Roland
Brigitine, Sister
Brink, John William
Brink, Maude E.
Brink, Myron
Brink, Pamela
Brink, Robert Arlington
Broad, Wilfred
Brock, Joe O.
Brockway, Alex Grove
Brockway, Merna Morris
Brook, Walter Leroy
Brooks, Horace
Brown, George
Brown, Harry John
Brown, Helen Margaret
Brown, Katherine Ellis
Brown, Mary Martha
Brown, Nell McAfee
Brown, Ray
Brown, Richard Sefton
Brown, Roy H.
Browne, Leslie
Browne, Pilar
Browne, Robert
Brush, John Burk
Brush, Lois Bogue
Brushfield, Elizabeth
Bryan, Arthur
Bryan, Edgar Robeson
Bryan, Winifred
Bucher, Anna L.
Bucher, George Scott
Bucher, Henry H.
Bucher, Henry H. Jr.
Bucher, Louise S.
Bucher, Priscilla J.
Buckalew, Donald Howland
Buckles, Frank Woodruff
Budlong, Vinton Alva
Burke, Harry Taylor

Burkman, Charles Harris
Burlingame, Walter Michael
Brunham, Edward Frank
Burns, Francis
Burns, James
Burns, James (2)
Burrell, Louie Grant
Burton, Edith Ganz
Burton, Harry Royal
Burton, James Edward
Butler, John Nicholsen
Butler, Linnie Marie
Cadwallader, Helen
Caecilius, Sister M.
Cain, Claude Oliver
Cain, Thomas
Caldwell, William A.
Calhoun, Alexander Dewey
Calvert, John Ellis
Calve, Elisa Warbaugh
Cammack, Larue
Campbell, Guilford E.
Campbell, Leo Lee
Campp, Anthony L.
Canson, John
Capen, Morris Noel
Caritas, Sister M.
Carlisle, Mabel Burris
Carlson, Alvin
Carlson, Imogene Ina
Carlson, Lawrence
Carlson, Mark
Carlucci, John (Boniface)
Carpenter, Henry
Carson, Hilton
Carter, Roland van
Carty, George B.
Carty, Eleanor May
Carty, Jean Pearl
Casanave, Andres
Casanave, Emilio
Casanave, Grete

Casanave, Pedro Jr.
Casanave, Pedro Andres
Casanave, Peter A.
Casanave, Rachel Olive
Casanave, Teresa E.
Casanave, Theodore
Casey, Edward
Cashman, Michael
Cassel, Henry D.
Cassell, Marie
Cassell, Marion Reedy
Cassell, Maurice Arnold
Cassidy, John Patrick
Catherine, Sister M.
Cease, Forrest Lee
Cecil, Robert E.
Celeste, Sister M.
Chambers, Bunnie Sr.
Chambers, Bunnie Jr.
Chambers, Isidra
Chambers, Katherine
Chambers, Maria
Chantal, Sister M. de
Chapman, Corwin Clyde
Chapman, Mary Frances
Chapman, Virginia Dewey
Chase, Leland Preston
Chatman, Littleton
Cheek, Jesse Willard
Chester, Harold Dean
Chester, Pearl Eileen
Chestnut, James Edward
Chew, John Hamilton
Chichester, Robert Oxley
Chickese, Ernest
Childers, Ralph Leroy
Christensen, Edward
Christensen, Joseph
Christie, A.
Chisholm, Robert
Cillo, Thomas
Clare, Joseph-Mother M.

Clark, Andrew
Clark, Rush Spencer
Claude, Henry Louie
Clayton, Noel
Clifford, Carl Gaines
Clifford, William Dennis
Clingen, Herbert Signer
Clingen, Ida Ruth
Clingen, Robert Fraser
Cobb, Laura May
Coffey, Henry A.
Cochran, Donald Lewellyn
Cofer, Newton
Coggeshall, Roland Roberts
Cogswell, Gladys Jessie
Cole, Birnie
Cole, George Edward
Cole, Minnie
Coleman, Barbara M.
Coleman, Marjorie K.
Coleman, Marshall L.
Coleman, Patricia C.
Colin, Paul J.
Collier, Leonard Hooper
Collins, Joseph Davis
Collins, Thomas James
Colman, Sister
Conant, Ellsworth Thomas
Conant, Juanda June
Conant Myra Belle
Cone, Hector Anthony
Congleton, Lucy E.
Conner, Herman Burt
Connors, John
Conway, Joseph Michael
Constance, Sister M.
Cook, James William
Cook, Maude Rose
Cook, William Sherman
Cook, W. Thomas
Cooper, Alfred D.
Cooper, Hugh Price

Copello, Thomas George
Copper, Robert Gamble
Corbett, Daniel
Cornelison, Bernice
Cort, Marcus Robert
Corwin, Alvah Oatis
Crabb, Josephine Rosalie
Craven, Louise Broad
Craven, Osgood Coit
Crawford, Joseph Claypole
Crawford, Robert Allan
Crawford, Virginia Hale
Crist, Ann Bennett
Crist, Lynn Levi
Croft, Selma Marion
Croft, Patty Gene
Croft, William Frederick
Croisant, Everett Albert
Cromwell, Robert Horace
Croney, Dorothy Fain
Crooks, William
Crosby, George Howard
Crothers, Ellen N.
Crothers, John Young
Cullens, James Wimberly
Cullum, Leo
Cumming, Clarence Warder
Cumming, Patrick
Cummings, Ernest
Cummings, Milton Weston
Cunningham, Frederick Noel
Curavo, Leonard Alexander
Curran, Elmer Hege
Curran, Howard H.
Curran, Hugh McCollum Sr.
Curran, Hugh McCollum Jr.
Custer, Theodore Hart
Dahlke, Gustav A.
Dahlke, Inga Hedwig
Dakin, Bess May
Dakin, Charles Austin
Dale, Billie Ann

Dale, Donna Lee
Dale, Edna Lee
Dale, Frank Emmit
Dale, Melvin Eugene
Dale, Roberta M.
Damrosch, Elizabeth H.
Damrosch, Leopold
Damrosch, Leopold Jr.
Danie, Amelia Louise
Danie, Antony Joseph
Davey, Laura Emily
David, Sister M.
Davidson, Abraham
Davidson, Arthur Dewain
Davis, Marian Electra
Davis, Maureen Neal
Davis, Roger William
Davis, Rosella A.
Davis, Sun Ye
Dayton, Earl Tresiliam
Deam, Mary L.
Dean, Harry Wilson
Decker, Louis
De Coito, Louis
De Coito, Ann I
Decoteau, Joseph
Dedegas, Basil
Deihl, Edith Jolles
Deihl, Renzie Watson
De la Costa, Frank A.
De la Costa, Jan
De la Fuente, Pelegrin
De Loffe, John
De Martini, Louise V.
Deppermann, Charles
Depue, Rodney Albert
Detrick, Herbert J.
Detrick, Lulu H.
Detzer, Linus William
DeVries, David Andrew
DeVries, Gene
DeVries, Gladys L.

DeVries, Henry William Sr.
DeVries, Henry William Jr.
Dewhirst, Harry Daniel
DeWitt, Clyde Alton
Dick, Thomas William
Dincher, Frederick
Dingle, Leila
Dingman, Arthur
Divine Child, Sister Mary
Doig, Leroy Dorry, Jr.
Doino, Francis
Dominica, Sister M.
Dorothy, Sister
Dow, William
Dowd, Austin
Dowling, Richard
Downing, Donald Clark
Doyle, Emily Norma
Doyle, Joseph Desmond
Downs, Darley
Dragset, Ingie
Dreyer, Karl Olaf
Drost, Leonard
Dudley, Earl C., Sr.
Dudley, Earl C., Jr.
Dudley, Susie Hall
Dugas, Alfred Frederick
Delaney, Frank Lorraine
Dustin, Herbert Warren
Dwyre, Allen Louis
Dyer, Althea C.
Dyer, Harlan L.
Dyer, June L.
Dyer, Mary
Eanswida, Mother M.
Earl, George Richard
Eaton, Gertrude Mary
Eaton, Leon Schultz
Ebbesen, Frank E.
Eddy, Arthur Louis
Edwards, Benjamin Franklin
Edwards, Herbert Kenneth

Edwards, John
Edwards, Mary Constance
Eison, George Simon
Ekstrand, Martin Eugene
Eldridge, Lawrence
Eldridge, Norma
Eldridge, Paul H.
Eldridge, Retha
Eleanor, Sister Frances
Elizabeth, Sister M.
Elliott, Francis Roy
Ellis, Adele Marie
Elstner, Josephine Elmer
Elwood, Joseph Donald
Emerson, Ause
Epes, Branch Jones Sr.
Epes, Branch Jones Jr.
Epes, William Fitzgerald
Erdman, Joseph James
Erickson, Eric Oscar
Erickson, Harry Eric
Evans, Bertha Rae
Evory, Harold William
Ewing, Margaret Greenfield
Ewing, Roy Emerson
Fairweather, Barbara Hayne
Fasy, Carroll
Fawcett, Alfred Edward Sr.
Fawcett, Alfred Jr.
Feely, Gertrude
Felicidade, M. Mary
Felix, Harold (Raphael)
Fernandez, Carmen Mary
Fernandez, Gregoria
Fernandez, Joaquin Jose
Fernandez, Juanina Mary
Fernandez, Mary Louise
Ferrier, John William
Ferrier, Theresa Diana
Fidelis, Sister M.
Fielding, Ralph
Fisher, Arthur George

Fisher, Frederick Russell
Fisher, Ruth Lincoln
Fishman, Alvin William
Fittinghoff, Nicholas Alexander
Fleisher, Henry
Fleming, Joseph Lamar
Fletcher, Charles Falkner
Flint, Alvin Lovett
Flint, Sarah Viola
Florence, Paul Billington
Flores, Joe Tatani
Florez, Juanita R.
Florez, Julietta Lee
Florez, Ramona Samilpa
Fluemer, Arnold William
Fonger, Leith Cox
Fonger, William Henry
Ford, Charles Emery
Ford, Henry Tagros
Ford, William Munroe
Forney, William Thomas
Fowler, Ernest A.
Fox, Frank Christopher
Fox, Henry
Fox, James Joseph
Fox, James Roy
Fox, Mattea
Fox, Vincent Altizo
Francisco, Louis Joseph
Frantz, Daniel David
Fraser, Elvie
Frederica, Sister M.
Fredenert, M. M.
Freeman, Edward Francis
Freeman, Frances Mary
Freeman, Jo Fisher
Fricke, Herman Henry
Fricke, Dorothy
Friedl, Joseph
Fuller, Sumner Bacon
Gabrielson, Carl William
Gaffke, Albert A.

Gaillard, John Gourdin
Galassi, Dominico
Gallaher, Robert Franklin
Gallagher, Harry Joseph
Gallapaue, William Earl
Gallit, Henry Emil
Galway, Howard
Gardiner, Clifford A.
Gardiner Elizabeth A.
Gardiner, William A.
Gardner, Claude Dennis
Garmezy, Samuel
Garrett, Elwood Llewellin
Garrigues, Dwight N.
Gavigan, Tripp G.
Genevieve, Sister Rose
Georgia, Sister M.
Gesemyer, Arthur K.
Gesemyer, Georgie C. Sr.
Gesemyer, George C. Jr.
Gewald, Myrtle F.
Gibson, Alvin Harvey
Giles, Vinton Sela
Gilfoil, Katherine
Gilfoil, Katherine N.
Gilfoil, Lydia Alice
Gilfoil, Mary Louise
Gilfoil, Patricia Ann
Gilfoil, William Scott
Girard, Edward
Giucondiana, M. M.
Gisel, Eugene
Gladys, Sister M.
Glunz, Charles
Glunz, Henrietta H.
Godfrey, M. M.
Goebel, Otto John
Goldman, Edmund
Golucke, Louis Harold
Goodwin, Martin Luther
Gordenker, Alexander
Gordon, John J.

Gorzelanski, Helen Clara
Gotthold, Diana
Grady, Virginia H.
Gray, Bernice Louise
Gray, Edward James
Gray, George
Grau, Albert
Graves, Arthur
Greer, Henry
Griffin, Elizabeth G.
Griffin, Frank
Grishkevich, Vitaly Ippolit
Grode, Leo
Gross, Morton Robert
Guicheteau, Arnold J.
Gunder, Jack H.
Gunnels, Robert Lee
Guthrie, Mary J.
Guthrie, Richard S.
Guthrie, Romelda A.
Guthrie, William E.
Haberer, Emanuel Julius
Hacker, Leonard
Hackett, Alice
Hackett, John Alexander
Hageman, Marshall N.
Hale, J. Willis
Hale, Velma M.
Haley, Arthur Edward
Haley, James
Hall, Norman Shannon
Hallett, John Bartlett
Ham, Hugh Mack
Hammill, Dena M.
Hammill, Richard L.
Hammill, Rogers N.
Hammond, L. D. Lloyd
Hamra, Adeeb Joseph
Hancock, Lawrence Kelly
Hancock, Mary Edna
Hannings, Richard Edward
Hanson, Donie Taylor

Hanson, Rolf Hinnen
Hard, Herbert William
Hard, Marie Lucille
Hardy, Beverly Earl
Harms, Lloyd Frederick
Harper, Anita Mae
Harper, Arthur Edward
Harper, Betty Jane
Harper, James Albert
Harper, Steven Phillip
Harrah, Orville
Harrah, Rose Marie
Harrell, Richard Maxted
Harrington, Mary Rose
Harris, William S.
Harrison, Phillip Francis
Harshman, Albert N.
Harshman, Anita Wichman
Hart, Herbert Henry
Hart, Joseph Chittendon
Hartnett, Ernest
Hatcher, Benjamin Carlile
Hause, Charles David
Hausman, Louis Michael
Haven, Lewis Quincy Jr.
Hayme, Carl
Haynes, Albert
Headley, Donald Grant
Healy, Gerald
Healy, John
Heath, George Eddy
Hebard, William Lawrence
Heery, Joseph Marion
Heesch, Henry John
Heichert, Murray Baker
Hell, Jan Howard
Hellis, Herbert Dean
Henderson, Barclay C.
Henderson, Dorothy Gardiner
Henderson, George William
Hendrix, Daisy
Hennel, Charles

Hennesen, Maria Alexandrina
Hennesen, Paul
Herndon, Alice Patterson
Herndon, Rees Frazer
Hertz, Harold Emerson
Hess, Arlene F.
Hess, Hudson S.
Hess, Lois Ellen
Hess, R. Bruce
Hess, Robert R.
Hess, Victor Glen
Hess, Viola Ruth
Hibbard, James F.
Hicks, John Thomas
Highsmith, Jerome
Hight, Allen H.
Hiland, George S.
Hildabrand, Carl
Hileman, Arthur Daniel
Hill, Alva J.
Hill, Jay Ward
Hill, John
Hill, Martha M.
Hill, Samuel W.
Hinck, Dorothy A.
Hinck, Edward M.
Hinck, John A. Jr.
Hinck, Mary L.
Hinck, Robert
Hindberg, Walter
Hinkley, Jay Augustus
Hinsche, Otto
Hobson, Henry
Hochreiter, Charles J.
Hodge, Julia M.
Hodges, Catherine Taylor
Hodges, Harry Mead
Hoffmann, Winifred
Hogenboom, David Lee
Hogenboom, Leonard Samuel
Hogenboom, Ruth Groters
Hogenboom, Stephen

Hokanson, Marie Corp
Hokanson, Mons
Holt, Jack Berger
Holt, Truman Slayton
Holy Name, Sister M.
Honor, Dorothy Y.
Honor, Herbert C.
Honor, Herbert Jr.
Honor, Vera O.
Hood, Thomas Dewitt
Hook, Emil V.
Horgan, Gregory
Hornbostel, Johanna Mario
Horton, Frank
Hoskins, Colin Macrae
Hoyt, Jackson Leach
Hubbard, Charles R.
Hubbard, Christine
Hubbard, William Augustus
Hudson, Clay Menafee
Hudson, Lewis Clifton
Hudson, Primitiva Bertumen
Hughes, Harry Bloomfield
Hughes, Hugh John
Hughes, Russell
Hughes, Samuel Alexander
Hull, Edwin Miles
Hunt, Darcy Swain
Hunt, Phray O.
Hunter, John Jacobs
Hyland, Walter
Harpst, Earl Michael
Iddings, Paul Loren
Immaculate Concepcion, S. R. M.
Innis, Charles
Innis, David
Innis, David James
Innis, Donald
Innis, Frances
Innis, Joseph
Irvin, Tom B.
Irvine, Bessie

Irwin, Henry
Isabel, Sister M.
Jackson, Myrtle
Jacobs, Louis Welch
Jacobson, David
James, Elizabeth
Jamieson, William
Janda, Marie Wagner
Janda, Robert Lee
Jarlath, M. M. of S. T.
John, Rees Hopkin
Johnson, Cherokee Chickasaw
Johnson, Frederick Arnold
Johnson, Henry S.
Johnson, Ralph Murdoch
Johnson, Seneca O.
Johnson, Thomas W.
Johnson, Walter
Johnston, Doris
Johnston, William W.
Jones, Andy
Jones, Bernard Edwin
Jones, Charles Ernest
Jones, Elvis Everett
Jones, Ethel L.
Jones, Frank Dehaven
Jones, Muriel Gertrude
Jones, Robert Berian
Jones, William Henry
Jordon, Thomas Mark
Julian, Frederick
Juravel, Carl
Jurgenssen, August John
Jurgenssen, Jennie Grace
Justin, Sister M.
Kahler, Stannie Daniel
Kalkowsky, Adam Edward
Kapes, David
Katz, Anne
Katz, Frances Valerie
Katz, Isabella
Katz, William Allen

Kahn, Maurice
Kaminski, Nicodemus
Kavanagh, Joseph
Kay, Joseph Kerop
Kailen, Ernest
Kelley, Daniel James
Kelly, Harold Maxwell
Kemery, Mona Mae
Kemp, Oley C.
Kern, Helen
Kerr, Joseph
Ketchum, Gladys Esperanza
Keys, Harold Harte
Keys, John Dewitt
Kidder, Lucia Booth
Kidder, Stanley Rast
Kiene, Clarence Kirk
Kiene, Mildred Evelyn
Kienle, Alfred
Kilkenny, Edward Michael
King, Carl Philip
King, Josephine Cook
King, Mary Barbara
Kingsbury, Stanley Carlos
Kinn, Leo
Kinney, John Thomas
Kinsella, John Sylvester
Kitzmiller, Blaine John
Kitzmiller, Owen
Kleinpell, Robert Mensson
Klippert, Edward
Knaesche, Herman
Knowles, Sambuel Etnyre
Koestner, Alfred U. S.
Kolodziej, Antonio
Kramer, Amelia
Kramer, Donald
Kramer, Effie
Kramer, Georgette
Kramer, Harry
Knutson, Gilman Darrell
Koons, Harry Montford

Koons, Thelma Donnelly
Krause, William Owen
Kringle, Harry
Kuhlman, William Henry
Kundert, Paul Denton
Lacey, Betty
Lacey, Kristin
Lacey, Sharon
Lacey, William Edward
Lacy, Merrill Ghent
LaFouge, Edward Rudolph
Lam, Bo Ming
Lamb, William Lee
Lambert, Frederick Dankilla
Landis, Audrey Blanche
Landis, Frederick
Landis, Patricia A.
Landis, Richard
Landis, Roderic
LaPointe, William F.
LaPorte, Margaret
LaPorte, Otto
Lappin, Leslie Everett
Lauriat, Frederick
Lautzenheiser, Ora Ezra
LaVigne, Ernest Henri
Lawry, Gordon Langford
Lawton, Betty Estelle
Lawyer, Jerome
Leary, John (Jack) Thomas
Leary, Paul
Lederman, Daniel Bishop
Lee, Charlotte Kingsbury
Lee, C. W.
Lee, David
Lee, Elfred M.
Lee, Fred M.
Lee, James Milton
Lee, Margurite
LeForge, Roxy
Leighton, Ethel Packard
Leisring, Lawrence

Leitch, James Elmer
Leland, James Arthur
Leland, Rosamond Cooper
Leland, Shirley Mae
Leonarda, Sister M.
Lesage, Alphons Gerard
Lessner, Eva
Lessner, Hilda
Levy, Ruben
Lew, Wah Sun
Liggett, James Paul
Liles, Lawrence Poland
Limpert, John William
Lind, Niles John
Linn, Harold Adolphus
Lochboehler, Bernard
Logan, George Lafayette
Lombard, Harold Webster
Lombard, James Dino
Lord, Montague
Louis, George James
Lovell, Glenn Howard
Lovell, Ruth Patterson
Lowry, William Arthur
Lubarsky, Saul
Lucy, Sister Mary
Lundquist, Carl Axel
Luckman, Elsie Marion
Lyon, Herbert
McAfee, Clauda
McAfee, Leo Gay
McAfee, Robert
McAllister, Margaret
McAnlis, David
McAnlis, Jean
McAnlis, Josephine
McAnlis, Ruth
McAnlis, William
McBride, John Henry
McCaffray, Arthur
McCalister, Jacob
McCandlish, William Foster

McCann, James
McCarter, Edward Lee
McCarthy, Floyd Arthur
McCarthy, Marian Florence
McCarthy, William Ransom
McCarty, Leroy
McCarty, Edward Charles
McCloskey, Robert E.
McClure, Carl Hamlin
McClure, Ryanna
McCoy, May
McCoy, Oscar Gervius
McCune, Joseph Gerhardt
McDonough, Charles A.
McEntee, Samuel Sanders
McGaretty, Howard Carson
McGovern, Lee
McGrath, Peter William
McGrew, Kinsie
McGuiness, Joseph
McGuire, Grace Ann
McHugh, Patricia Willis
McIntosh, Melville Ethelbert
McKay, Jean
McKee, Robert
McKeown, Hugh Michael
McLey, Harold J. G.
McMann, Frank Patrick
McMann, James
McMann, John
McManus, Ambrose
McMullen, Joseph
McNamara, Francis Robert
McNicholas, John
McSorley, Richard
McStay, John
McStay, John Curry
McVey, Bunnie Cecilia
McVey, Charles David
McVey, Grace Alice Mary
McVey, Mary Cecilia
Mabry, Frank M.

Mabry, Opal Marie
MacDonald, Alyse Louise
MacDonald, Bob
MacDonald, George
MacDonald, Helen
MacDonald, John
MacDonald, Kenneth
McDonald, Margaret
MacIntosh, James
MacKinnon, James Bowie
MacLaren, Donald Ross
Madigan, Francis
Madsen, Elmer
MaGee, George Lyman
MaGee, Mary Elizabeth Sr.
MaGee, Mary Elizabeth Jr.
MaGee, Philip Donald
Magill, Charles Newton
Mahoney, John Joseph
Makepeace, Lloyd Brenecke
Malmstrom, Charles Clarence
Mangels, Franz
Mangels, Henry Ahrends
Mangels, John F.
Mangels, Margaretta Hermine
Mangels, Nieves
Mangels, Nieves Chofra
Mankin, James Percy
Manser, Daniel Leonard
Marcella, Sister M.
Margerita, Sister M.
Margulies, Ruben
Marion, Sister Cecilia
Marsden, Ralph Walter
Martin, Clarence
Martin, D. P.
Martin, Edgar
Massey, Charlotte
Masson, Philip
Matthew, Sister Rose
Matthews, William Jerome
Maura, Sister Bernadette

Maurashon, Sister
Maxcy, Joseph
Maxey, Wilburn
Maxwell, William Allen
Mayer, Harry O'Brien
Meagher, Bernard Joseph
Meagher, Zora Simmons
Mee, Louis
Meinhardt, Ruth
Melton, Jesse Edgar
Merrill, Robert Heath
Merritt, Isaac Erwin
Messinger, George Marion
Metz, Carmen Adoracion
Meukow, Coleman Arian
Meukow, George Osakina
Meukow, Nina Ruth
Meukow, Walter Trendel
Meyer, Gus Henry
Miles, Daniel Walter
Miles, Prentice Melvin
Miller, Charles Henry
Miller, Dorothy Veronica
Miller, Gilbert Charles
Miller, Helen
Miller, John Joseph
Miller, Maxine Margaret
Mills, John Andrew
Millward, Samuel James Jr.
Miravalle, Andrew Nino
Miriam, Sister Agnes
Miriam, Sister Louise
Miriam, Sister Thomas
Missmer, George Washington
Missler, Carl Edward
Mitchell, John
Mitchell, Thomas
Mitchell, William Thomas
Moak, Conway Columbus
Mock, Charles Gordon
Mollart, Stanley Vincent
Monaghan, Forbes

Montesa, Anthony Joseph
Montesa, Edward William
Montesa, Henrietta F.
Montesa, John Phillip
Montgomery, Antonia Cantilo
Montgomery, Ethel Denise
Montgomery, Everett Verden
Montgomery, Fern Asunsano
Moore, Charles F.
Moore, Emma G.
Moore, George
Moore, Joseph Oliver
Moore, Joseph W.
Moore, Leonard C.
Moore, Mae Dancy
Moore, Patricia E.
Mora, Ernest Joseph
Mora, George Castro
Mora, Iberia Ortuno
Moran, Lawrence Richard
Morehouse, Francis B.
Morehouse, Phyllis Brenda
Morehouse, Winifred Louis
Morison, Walter Durrell
Morning, John
Morris, Leroy
Morrision, Carson C.
Morrision, Helena V.
Mortlock, Frank Oliver
Moss, George Herbert
Mudd, Maurice
Mueller, William Fred
Muldoon, Anthony Gregory
Mulry, Joseph
Mulryan, Alma Steiger
Mulryan, James Raymond
Munger, Henry Weston
Munger, Louralee Patrick
Murphin, William
Murphy, John Joseph
Murray, William Elmer
Myers, Kenneth Robert

Myers, William Tyner
Naftaly, Lillian Saidee
Naftaly, Nancy Nataly
Naido, Joseph
Naido, Ruth Louise
Nance, Dana Wilson
Nash, Gail Blackmarr
Nash, Grace Chapman
Nash, Ralph
Nash, Ralph Stanley
Nash, Roy Leslie
Nash, Margaret Alice
Nathanson, Nathaniel Arthur
Nau, Catherine Ludwina
Neal, James
Neal, Pauline
Neibert, Alice Julia
Neibert, Henry Edward
Neikam, William L.
Nelson, Thomas Page
Nelson, Valley
Newcomb, Walter Cattell
Newgord, Julius Gerard
Nicholas, John Middleton
Nichols, John Randolph
Nichols, Leonard David
Nicholson, John
Nicholson, William
Nicol, Celeste Claire
Nicol, Charles Bertram
Nicol, Fedora Mary
Nicol, Jacqueline Winifred
Nicol, Normal Arthur
Nicoll, David
Nicholson, James Francis
Nokes, Wilbur Charles
Norton, Alfred
Nuger, Isaac
Nuttall, Edmond
O'Boirne, Vincent
O'Brien, John Robert
O'Brien, Michael Wilbur

Obst, Thomas James
O'Conner, Clarence
Ode, Carsten Linnevold
O'Hara, Kathleen F.
O'Hara, Lorraine Betty
O'Hara, Michael Joseph
O'Hara, Michael Joseph Jr.
O'Haver, Goldie Aimee
Ogan, William Clarence
Olivette, Sister M.
Olsen, Lillian Agnes
O'Malloy, John Bryan
O'Neill, James
Oppenheimer, John
Osbon, Bert Paul
O'Shaughnessy, Martin
Oss, Norman Alfred Jr.
O'Toole, John Patrick
Overton, Elbert Monroe
Owens, Hoyle Williams
Pacheco, Michael Angelo
Paget, Cyrus
Paige, Eldene Elinor
Palmatier, Ellery Leroy
Palmer, Clarence Hugh
Palmer, Mildred Ailene
Pangborn, Wallace
Parham, Archer Brandon
Parker, Bertha F.
Parker, Bertha Helena
Parker, Helen Dorothy
Parker, Roy Lester
Parker, Wilbur Clarke
Parquette, William Stewart
Parish, Edward John Jr.
Passmore, Fred J.
Patricia, Sister M.
Patricia, Sister Marie
Patterson, Myron
Pauli, Ralph
Pawley, Charles Thomas
Pearson, Cecil Leroy

Peck, Lawrence Leroy
Peek, Elvin Roland
Penny, Harold Ray
Pepper, Charles John
Perfecta, Sister
Perkins, Willie Ray
Pearlman, Max O.
Perry, Walter Lee Gihon
Pflug, Emma
Phillips, Eleanor Marie
Phillips, Howard Lester Sr.
Phillips, Howard Lester Jr.
Philp, Dorothy Suzanne
Pickell, William H.
Pickens, Henri B.
Pickering, Camille Elaine
Pickering, John Kuykendall
Pierce, Margaret Helen
Pirassoli, Charles William
Pitcher, Susie Josephine
Plowman, Claire Elizabeth
Plowman, Elizabeth Oxford
Plowman, George Harden
Pohl, Gordon Robert
Pollard, Harriet Emma
Pond, Helen
Porter, Lloyd Thomas
Posner, Irving
Precino, Thomas
Preiser, Rosa Christian
Preston, Rose Marie
Price, Walter Scott
Priestner, Joseph
Purnell, John Ferguson
Purnell, Lillian Cottrell
Putney, Harry Bryan
Quillinan, Frank William
Quinn, Grant
Raleigh, Daniel Mead
Rand, Grace
Rast, Beni
Ratcliffe, Jesse Walker

Raymond, Mona
Reardon, Francis
Redard, Alexander James
Redempta, Sister M.
Reich, Bertha Harris
Reid, William Robert
Reilly, Matthew
Reinhart, James H.
Reith, Joseph
Repetti, William
Repikoff, John
Reuter, James
Rey, Sister Maria del
Reynolds, Ralph Leonard
Rhudie, Ada Woodsworth
Rhudie, Oscar Peter
Rice, Williard Lamont
Richards, Edwin Franklin
Richards, Mary Fielding
Riddle, Henry Hampton
Rider, Frank Jackson
Riffel, Dorothy Ann
Riffel, Esther N.
Riffel, Gordon William
Riffel, Retta Leona
Riffel, William E.
Riley, Charles
Rively, William
Rivers, William Richard
Rizzuti, Oarm
Robert Marie, Sister
Roberts, Elizabeth
Roberts, Galien Sofia
Roberts, Odin Gregory
Robertson, Joseph H.
Robie, Merle Steel
Robinson, Charles A.
Robinson, Graham Post
Robinson, Leslie D.
Robinson, Roberta May
Rodgers, Frances
Roebuck, Brooks Waldo

Scott, Lyle Cecil
Seals, Margaret Mildred
Sechrist, David P.
Sechrist, Harold
Sechrist, John W.
Sechrist, Marguerite
Shaffer, William Robert
Shapiro, Herman
Shaw, Herbert Wesley
Shaw, Kate Sibley
Shaw, Walter Ray
Sherk, David Robert
Sherk, Gerry Ann
Sherk, Margaret Coulson
Shimmel, Edith
Shoemaker, Abbott Paul
Shropshire, Harry Wesley
Shurdut, Joseph Moses
Siena, Sister M.
Silen, Elizabeth Jean
Silen, Joan Bradford
Silen, Margaret Elizabeth
Silen, Shirley Ann
Silloway, Merle
Simatovich, Nicholas Joseph
Simmons, Ernest Edgeworth
Sklenar, Anthony Joseph
Small, Elizabeth Studavant
Small, Frank Sylvester
Small, Helen Elizabeth
Smallwood, Robert
Smith, Alfred Whitacre
Smith, B. Ward
Smith, Dewey Woods
Smith, Harry Josselyn
Smith, Harry Thurston
Smith, Joseph John
Smith, Paul L.
Smith, Stephen L.
Smith, Viola R.
Smith, Willard Horace
Smoyer, Egbert M.

Snead, Elizabeth B.
Snead, Mary Carol
Snead, Paul Kindig
Snead, Paul Laurence
Sniffen, Genevieve Marie
Sniffen, John Mark
Snyder, Gaines
Snyder, Mary Lucille
Snyder, William Raymond
Soares, John Stanislas
Sottile, Frank Joseph
Spatz, Oswald
Spear, Earl Franklin
Spencer, William Meek
Spencer, William Robert
Sperry, Henry M.
Stacy, Gertrude Rosie
Stahl, Alfred Joaquin
Stancliff, Leo
Stark, Clarence Theo
Starr, John Bernal
Stearns, Mary Jean Stephens
Steffens, Raymond Harold
Steven, Oswald Barnard
Stevens, Leslie Eugene
Steward, Basilia Torres
Stewart, John Norman
Still, Dorothy
Stiver, Edna Theresa
Stiver, Joseph Alfred
Stocking, Charles Samuel
Stokes, Henry Milton
Stoll, Eugene Leo
Stoneburner, Edna
Strong, James Walter
St. Thomas, Federico Jr.
Stuart, David Lennox
Stubo, Knutty Christian
Stumbo, John David
Stump, Irene J.
Stump, Lawrence
Stumpf, William Jerome Jr.

Sturm, Stanley Marcellus
Sudhoff, Raymond George
Sullivan, Edward
Sullivan, Russell
Suro, Reuben
Swanson, Ruth Pauline
Sykora, Frank
Tabor, John
Tapia, Edwin Joseph Jones
Taylor, William Leonard
Taylor, Willis L.
Tekippe, Owen
Terrill, Thomas Star
Terry, Albert Henry
Terry, Carol Louise
Terry, Joseph Edward
Teurnee, Maurice Conrad
Theophila, Sister M.
Theudere, M. Mary of S. P.
Thomas, Antonita B.
Thomas, Dollie Mae
Thomas, Florence A.
Thomas, Howard Wilton
Thomas, Robert Lee
Thompson, David Bill
Thompson, Floyd Addison
Thompson, Leslie Daniel
Tinling, Don
Titlow, Marian Phillips
Todd, Carrie Edwina
Todd, George Jr.
Todd, Noel
Todebush, Ralph Bernard
Tootle, Mildred Caroline
Torkeson, Edward
Treubig, John F.
Tribble, Jesse Lee
Trogstad, Martha Bowler
Tuck, Ernest E.
Tuck, Helen G.
Tuite, Thomas
Tulloch, James Garfield Jr.

Tulloch, William James
Tutten, Daniel Eugene
Ullman, Frank
Ullman, Tamara Alexis
Urquhardt, Edward J.
Urquhardt, Maud J.
Urquhardt, Stanley P.
Vandenplas, Pierre Gaston
Vanderburg, Charles Osborn
Vernick, Joseph Barry
Vicroy, Sigle Allen
Villar, Charles Herman
Vincent, Louis Lester
Vitalis, Sister Mary
Vogelgesang, John
Von Hess, Jack C.
Voss, William Frederick
Vinson, Olivert Castille
Vinson, Thomas Chalmers
Wagelie, Cunval Andreas
Wagner, John Robert
Wagner, Rudolph
Wahlgreen, Beulah King
Walker, Alfred Francis
Walker, Harold
Walker, Orian Love
Wallace, Frank Byron
Waples, James Francis
Ward, William Vines
Wareham, Johnson Matthew
Warner, Carl
Warner, Mary Delilah
Warren, Fred Prince
Warren, Harry Pre
Waterstradt, Albert Edward
Wathen, John David
Webster, Walter Jr.
Weems, Alexander Murray
Weibel, Mary Eileen
Weil, Charles William
Welborn, George
Welch, Leo

Wells, James
Wells, Jessie
Wenetzki, Charles Eduard
West, Glenn Key
West, Hester D.
Wester, Arthur W.
Westmoreland, Graham Bradley
Westmoreland, Victoria Maria
Wheeler, Hiram Albert L.
Wheeler, Ida Ellen
Wheeler, Robert Antony
Wheeler, Robert J. M.
Whitaker, Evelyn Eddy
Whitaker, Helen Elizabeth
Whitaker, Jocelyn Alfred
Whitaker, Margaret Evelyn
Whitaker, Septimus Tom B.
White, George Henry Jr.
White, Nathaniel Walker
Whitesides, John Garrett
Whitmoyer, George Irwin
Wichman, Daniel Lee
Wichman, Douglas
Wichman, Ernest Hermsen
Wichman, Gladys Caroline
Widdoes, Alice S.
Widdoes, H. W.
Wienke, Carl Ludwig
Wienke, Carmen Aurora
Wienke, Edward Peter
Wienke, Elizabeth Carmen
Wienke, Frederick Johan
Wienke, Marcie Christina
Wienke, Theresa Victoria
Wienke, Violet Alma
Wilcox, Lyle
Wilcox, Wendel
Wilder, Charlie
Wiley, Samuel
Williams, Clyde Scott
Williams, Gordon L.
Williams, Greta R.

Williams, Jack
Williams, Leona H.
Williams, Roy Harold
Willmann, George J.
Wills, Hugh Clarence
Wills, Ida Gertrude
Wills, Jane S.
Wilson, Anita Marie
Wilson, Edward John
Wilson, Harold Norman
Wilson, James Reese
Wilson, Jesse Smith
Wilson, John
Wilson, John Brownlee
Wilson, Wilbur Scott
Winn, Charles Robert
Winn, Ethel May
Winship, S. Davis
Winsor, Christine
Wislizenus, Claire Alberton
Wittman, Arthur Carl
Wolff, Charles
Wolfe, Carrie A.
Wolfe, Leslie
Wolfgram, Ida Mae
Wolfgram, Leroy Herbert
Wood, Joseph Palmer
Woodin, Charles Wesley
Woodrooff, William Dickey
Woods, Robert Gordon
Woodworth, Ruth A.
Workman, Doris Therese
Workman, George Welman
Workman, Helen Marie
Workman, Katherine Marie
Workman, Lillian Ann
Workman, Mildred Josephine
Worthen, Helen Margaret
Worthen, Thomas Roy
Wright, Lourdes Dizon
Wright, Randall William
Wright, Tobias Henry

Yankey, Mary Louise Curran
Yankey, William Ross
Yarborough, Alta Lenna
Yarborough, Henry Edward Jr.
Yard, Lester Hollaster
Yartz, John
Yearsley, Helen Ellison
Young, Robert Alexander
Young, Roman
Young, William H.
Zervoulakos, Alfred Gregory
Zigler, William McKinley
Zillig, Martin

BRITISH

Aaron, Jean Margaret
Aaron, John David
Aaron, John Maurice
Airiess, Eric Mather
Aitkens, John Reginald
Albine, Sister
Aldred, Herbert
Allen, Constance
Allen, Elizabeth
Allen, Margaret
Allen, Phillip
Anderson, David
Andrews, Nadia
Andrews, Ronald V.
Arnovick, Mary M.
Arnovick, Charles
Arnovick, George M.
Azevedo, Olga
Azevedo, Beatrice
Bairgrie, Alexander
Baigrie, Bertha
Baildon, Aimee
Balfour, William
Balis, David
Balis, Jenny
Barnes, Katherine

Barnes, Kenneth
Barnes, Robert
Barnes, William Frank
Barr, Fiona
Barr, Margaret
Barr, Ronald
Barrett, Cecil
Beck, Arthur Charlesworth
Beebee, Walter Willis
Beeman, Sarah
Behenna, Dorothy
Bennett, Lillian
Bentley, Edward
Birchall, James Richardson
Black, James
Blair, Leslie
Blechynden, Lindsey DeClarke
Boddington, Dorothy
Boddington, Richard John
Bonner, Norman Ellis
Bosch, Edward Henry Brett
Boswell, George James
Bradshaw, John William
Brambles, James Christopher
Brambles, Margaret Lillian
Brambles, Ralph Douglas
Brambles, Elizabeth
Brambles, Grace
Brambles, Patricia
Brambles, Ralph
Bramwell, Edward Kennedy
Bramwell, Helen L.
Breson, Lillian
Brewster, Charles
Brooks, Anna
Brooks, Cyril H.
Brooks, Kenneth S.
Brooks, Leonard C.
Brooks, Rose E.
Buckberrough, Rosa
Buhler, Charles
Burn, Robert

Burn, William Angus
Bush, Edward Stanley
Cameron, John Fraser
Corley, Thomas Ekstrom
Celestine, Sister M.
Chapman, Maurice Bonham
Chong, Charles
Christian, Frederick
Clark, Wallace Robert
Clarke, Esther Millicent
Clarke, Evelyn Victoria
Cohen, Florence Frances
Corfield, Isla
Corfield, Gillian I.
Coxon, Jane Margaret
Crabbe, Kenneth Murray
Creech, Henry
Crewe, James
Curtis, John Shearme
Dalgleish, Mabel Emily
Dalgleish, Mabel Margaret
Da Silva, Augustus
D'Authreau, John Harold
Dickson, Elsa Fanny
Dodd, Gloria Lydia
Dodd, Reginald Morris
Dodd, Zina Andreevna
Dolores, Sister Maria
Donald, William
Dos Remedios, Henry Joseph
Douglas, William
Doull, Agnes
Doull, William
Dow, James Frederick
Drysdale, Thomas Douglas
Duncan, Ian Murray
Dwyer, Thomas
Ethelburga, Sister M.
Gertrude, Sister Lane Fox
Fairweather, James Edwin
Falkner, Angeles Martin
Falkner, James Albert

Falkner, Ronald D.
Fitzgerald, Desmond S.
Fox, Catherine Mary
Fox, Christopher Charles
Fox, Charles James
Fox, Lawrence
Fox, Patrick James
Fox, Stephen George
Frampton, Amy Beatrice
Frampton, Muriel
Freckleton, Thomas
Geddes, Eric
Geddes, Jean Frances
Gillett, Bertram John
Gordon, Mary
Gordon, Matthew Dobie
Grant, Helen Gordon
Gray, Irene Betty
Green, Louisa
Green, Michael John
Greenland, Lucy Violet
Griffith, Owen Ambrose
Grimmant, David Henry
Haigh, Annie
Haigh, Jesse
Haigh, Renee Mary
Haigh, Victor Alfred
Hails, Henry Forster
Hallowes, Elsie Mary
Hamblett, James
Hanson, Frank Raymond
Hardcastle, Charles Otterson
Harris, William Francis Geo.
Hayes, Jean
Hayes, Kathleen Elizabeth
Hayes, Michael Aloysius
Haymes, Maxwell Freeland L.
Hearn, Martin Everard
Hill, Rowland George
Hodges, Arthur J.
Hodges, Eleanora
Hoey, Richard C.

Hoey, Ruth C.
Hollyer, William George
Horridge, George Redvers
Hughes, Donald Francis
Humphries, John Hugh
Hurley, Patrick
Hutchison, David Dick
Irvine, Jean
Ismail, Sheil Salim
Jackson, James Gregory
Jamieson, Stewart
Jaques, Stanley Heath
Jay, John Leslie
John, Dorothy A.
John, Helen M.
John, Kathleen Elizabeth
John, May
Jones, Henry Victor
Jordon, Kathleen Agnes
Kane, John William James
Kay, Aubony Taylor
Kennedy, Eileen
Kennedy, Erna V.
Kennedy, Kathleen M.
Kennedy, Robert C.
Kennedy, Robert C. Jr.
Kew, Cecil
King, Agnes Isabel
King, Charles Forrester
Kotliar, Betty
Lee, Ansie
Legg, John Alexander
Leith, Henry Earl
Leith, Mair
Leith, Rosemary
Leyshon, Frank Howard
Ligertwood, Charles Liddell
Lloyds, Edwin William
McClure, Lawrence Maxton
McGinness, Thomas John
McGregor, Robin
McKerchar, Ian

McLeod, Hugh
McMaster, John Wilson
McMaster, Norah Helen
McWhirter, Hugh Fergus
MacIntyre, Norah Peal
MacIntyre, Ronald
MacKay, Kathleen Mary M.
MacLaren, William Hart
MacLean, Hector James Hilder
MacLean, Margaret
MacWilliam, Jean Cowan Shanks
MacWilliam, Richard Niven
MacWilliam, Scott
Malcolm, Harry Redd
Malpas, William Richard J.
Mann, William Ronald
Mather, William Gladston
Maxima, Sister M.
Medina, Elfrida Elizabeth
Meadows, Gordon
Miller, Charles Walter
Miller, David Carlton
Miller, Patricia Ann
Miller, Robert Walker
Miller, Vera Alexandra
Moore, Calvert Hildabrand
Morley, Howard
Morris, Robert Owen
Morrison, Geoffrey Lionel
Morrison, Robert Alexander
Naismith, William Cunningham
Nathanson, Jean L.
Nathanson, Marie Emsley
Nelson, Archibald Graham
Newgord, Esther
Newsome, Peter Noel Vesey
Nicolson, John
Norton-Smith, Kenneth James
Oliver, Violet Lillian
Palmer, Bertha Lucy
Palmer, John Blything
Palmer, Ronald Singleton

Parker, Herman Vercomb
Parquette, Rosemarie Dorothy
Paterson, James
Paterson, Mary D.
Patey, Walter Bruce
Patricia, M. M.
Pedder, Gerald Herbert
Pedersen, Gwendolyn Florence
Perry, David Henry
Philomena, Sister Marie
Piatnitsky, Olga Pavlovna
Piercy, Arthur
Pollard, Arnold
Pollock, Yvonne Celia
Pope, Harvey Collie
Porter, Robert John
Price, Arthur
Price, Elizabeth Sible
Price, William Samuel
Prismall, Allen
Proudfoot, Alexander
Prout, James Ormand
Quinn, Bernard Alphonsus
Redfern, Foster
Reich, Joseph
Reid, George William
Richardson, William Bryan
Robertson, Howard Laird
Roche, Barbara Pavlovna
Roche, Mary Roberta
Rodda, Hababah
Rodgers, Albert G.
Rodgers, Marcus G.
Rodgers, Rosa N.
Royston, John
Rushton, Violet Edith
Rushton, George
Ryde, Sonia
Sawyer, Paula Adelatie
Schelkunoff, Vladimir Peter
Scott, David Alexander
Serephins, Sister Mary of the

Sinclair, Jeffrey Whitfeld
Small, William Valentine
Smith, George Albert
Smith, Joan Marie
Smith, John Alwynne George L.
Smith, Louis
Smith, William A.
Smith, Arthur Linton
Spackman, Harold C.
Spackman, Winifred D.
Steel, James Laurie
Stephens, Sydney
Stratton, Joseph Grant L.
Strong, Martin
Symonds, John
Templer, Angela Mary
Templer, Ann Hazel
Templer, James Robert
Templer, Jennifer S.
Thomson, Elizabeth Marie
Thomson, Robert Allison
Tomkin, Anna Georgvina
Tonkin, Marguerite Janet A.
Tonkin, Mathew McNair
Tonkin, William Charles Geo.
Turner, William
Tyre, Alexander James
Watson, William
Watt, Effie Margaret
Watt, Olive Charlotte
Watty, Lewis Thomas
Webb, Frank Hardy
Whittal, Henry Cecil
Wightman, Arthur John
Wightman, Eglington John
Wightman, Ethelgiva Frances
Wightman, Irene Nellie
Wightman, William Dana
Willder, Katie Agnes
Williams, Hugh Hosking
Williams, John Joseph
Williamson, Margaret

Wilson, Ian Thurburn
Wilson, Walter James
Windle, Wilfred Edwin
Wood, Charles John
Wooding, Wilfred
Wright, Arthur
Wulfildan, M. M.
Yewen, Nina Efgenieva
Zacharias, Hans

BRITISH AUSTRALIAN

Bargallo, Amelia
Bargallo, Salvadora
Best, Francis
Blanchard, Mary
Byrne, Joseph
Cruice, William
Deane, Patrick
Dougherty, John Hercules
English, Leo
Gygar, Andrew
Holt, Bridget Trist
Holt, Edna May
Hughes, Allen John
Jackson, Gordon
Kemp, Joy Elizabeth
Laycock, William Murray B.
Laycock, Kathleen
McCarthy, Charles
McGuire, Mary Kathleen
MacMaster, John Dunlop
Nield, Frederick Bodin
O'Donnell, Gerard
Pinkerton, Stanley Corey
Pinkerton, Velma
Richards, Thomas Robert
Ridley, John Edwin
Sagor, Amy Lida
Sexton, Francis
Smith, Flora Beryl
Taylor, Betsy Doris

Taylor, Charles
Thomas, George Frederick
Walsh, Francis

BRITISH CANADIAN

Abarista, Sister Mary
Alphonse, de Ligori
Angeline, Sister Mary
Ann Celine, Sister Saint
Ann Marie, Sister
Arcand, Ulric
Begin, Joseph
Benoit, Mother Mary of Saint
Bernard, Sister M.
Bleau, Albert
Brouillard, Rodrigue
Charter, Catherine
Charter, Luckey Kathleen
Charter, Thomas Henry
Christophe, Soeur Saint
Clotilde, Sister M.
Dalmis, Michael
Desmarais, Camille
Everista, Mother
Frician, Sister M.
Gabriel, Sister De-Anuncion
Gabriel, Sister S.
Geofferey, Joseph
Gustav, Sister Saint
Harper, Ella Mae
Hodgson, Francis Xavier
Holloway, Glen Irwin
Humphries, Robert Maxwell
Jarry, Andre
Jepson, Leon Baynes
Joseph de Bethlehem, Sister
Lawton, Herbert
Loptson, Adulsufinn Magnus
Loptson, Faith C.
McCullough, Henry
McKenzie, Catherine

McKenney, Warren Evans
Madeline Marie Barrat, Sister
Marie de Preciux Sang, Sister
Mathiew, Soeur Saint
Maurice, Sister Mary
Mooney, Luke Henry
Murphy, William J.
Nicol, Arthur Louis
Paget, Kathleen M.
Paget, Margaret E. J.
Paget, William H. W.
Palmer, Blanche Evelyn
Philp, George Ansel
Pierre Claver, Sr. S.
Rene, M. M.
Rosemonde, M. M
Shaw, Alice Florence (Beyes)
Victorice, M. M. of Saint
Williams, William C.
Ymer, M. M. de Saint

NETHERLANDS

Aalten, Hans van
Albana, Sister N.
Alarda, Sister M.
Aldenhuysen, Godfred
Alice, Sister M.
Alphonsa, Sister M.
Anastasia, Sister M.
Bathildis, Sister M.
Bieschop, Roosegaade J. Philip
Blans, Thomas
Blewanus, Gerard
Boggiam, Max
Borght, Francisco van der
Bos, Maria Theresa
Burer, John
Cajetani, Sister M.
Canisia, Sister M.
Coenders, John

Corsten, Andrew
Croonen, Joseph
Decorata, Sister
DeHaan, Isaac
Dekker, John
DeWit, E.
Donata, M.
Dyk, Francisco van
Egonia, Sister M.
Engelen, Felite van
Es, Roelof van
Evangelista, Sister M.
Fransen, Martinus
Gentila, Sister M.
Glansbeek, Reiner van
Groonen, Josef
Groot, Petrus
Hagen, Jan van
Hartog, William
Hendricks, Nicholas Wilhelmus
Houben, Arnold
Intven, Joseph
Janssens, Alberta
Janssens, Marius Cornelus
Jonkerguuw, Hubertus Josephus
Joseph M.
Jurgens, Constans (Bishop)
Keet, Teodoro
Kemperman, Richard
Kilb, Antony
Loo, Cornelio van der
Lutgardis, M.
Magdala, Sister M.
Margretta, Sister M.
Mees, Gregory
Mees, William
Michels, Derk Aw.
Modesta, Sister M.
Notenboom, Jacobus Cornlis
Odyk, Anton van
Oomen, Antonius Paulus
Opstal, Van William

Polycarpa, Sister M.
Raben, Karel Hendrik
Reimers, Christian Hendrik
Reoinjen, Henricus van
Ruyter, Jan
Schaeffer, Johannes Henricus
Slangen, Peter
Sleegers, Henry
Smits, Adrianus
Steyger, Adrianus
Tangelder, Gerardo
Timp, Pedro John
Tonus, Cornelio
Trienekens, Gerardus F.
Van der List, Petrus J.
Van Overveld, Antonio
Van Vlierden, Constant Matthys
Verhoven, Joseph
Vincent, Jacobus
Vlasvelo, Pedro
Vrakking, Johan
Werff, Alice Catherine
Werff, Milagros Herrera
Werff, Pieter Hildebrand
Werff, Wanda Oliva
Werkhoven, Jacobux
Willemina, M.
Willemsen, Bernardus J.
Zegwaard, Francis Henry

NORWEGIAN

Aanonsen, Nels Marion
Abrahamsen, Blarne William
Christensen, Yugvar Kjell
Eilertsen, Thomas
Einarsen, Ruben Helmer
Monsen, Olaf
Oyen, Nils
Pedersen, Erling Bjoern
Petersen, Knut Selmer
Petersen, Trygve

POLISH

Adelski, Borys
Bieniarz, Edward
Gang, Samuel Sam
Hirschorn, Marcus
Keller, Harry
Krzewinski, Ludwig
Lerner, Helen
Lounsbury, Irene Olshenke
Mingelgruen, Wilhelm
Neuman, Rudolph Ham
Propper, Norbert
Rabinowicz, Icko
Rabinowicz, Mordchal
Sackiewicz, Alexander
Sackiewicz, Wladyslaw
Sielski, Wladyslaw
Sielski-Jones, Yadwiga Teresa
Soroka, Samuel Chaim
Strzalkowski, Henry
Szpigielman, Marek
Wahraaftig, Oswald
Werbner, Izydor

ITALIAN

Bulli, Angelo
Coll-Mellini, Helen
Ghigliotti, Giuseppe
Ghigliotti, Lourdes
Gircognini, Lorenzo
Gircognini, Manuela
Gircognini, Maria Lisa
Gislon, Antonio
Giuseppefranco, Altomonte
Mellini, Rudolph
Vigano, Angelo
Vigano, Camilla
Vigano, Tuillo
Vigano, Augusto
Vigano, Federico
Vigano, Maria

Appendix C

Los Baños Internment Camp
February 28, 1945
(From the personal files of Ben Edwards)

As of February 23rd, the day the Los Baños Internees were rescued, the following is reported for the record:

DEATHS: *George Irwin Whitmoyer:* Age 49, American, died on February 17th of tuberculosis.

Guilford L. Campbell: Age 77, American, died on February 18th of beriberi and heart disease and goiter.

Charles Newton Magill: Age 68, American, died on February 19th of beriberi.

Herbert E. Blair: Age 65, American, died on February 20th of beriberi.

H. E. Burton: Age 68, American, died on February 22nd of beriberi.

BIRTHS: For the record, the birth was reported, on February 20th, of Lois Kathleen McCoy, to Mr. and Mrs. Oscar McCoy, American.

FIREWOOD: It was reported that after many requests, the authorities did permit the camp to send work crews into the old camp for three consecutive days to obtain firewood for the kitchen.

EXTRA FOOD: The committee approved that extra food be given to those men digging graves and building coffins, this extra food to take the form of a noon meal. This was agreed upon because of the long hours of this work needed, due to the high incidence of deaths.

NOTICES: On February 17th and again on February 19th, due to the insistence of the Japanese, the following notices were issued:

2/17—"Everyone is again urged not to make any form of demonstration and not to congregate in groups when planes are heard or seen in the vicinity of the camp. The Lieutenant in charge of the Garrison has given us numerous warnings in this connection and the Committee believes that failure to comply with these instructions is dangerous to us all. Also, internees are again requested to keep calm and remain in their respective cubicles when shots are heard or when there is any evidence of military action near the Camp. To do otherwise will only jeopardize the safety of the group as a whole.

2/19—In spite of repeated warnings issued by the Committee, several internees were slapped and threatened by Japanese sentries for standing in the open while planes were passing overhead. Internees must realize that the present is not the time to take such warnings lightly. The Authorities even object to internees standing watching planes passing overhead. It is strongly urged that everyone remain in their cubicles or under cover on such occasions as it is feared that more drastic means may be taken by the Authorities.

ROLL CALL: At the Roll Call on February 19th the following persons were missing and are presumed to have left camp:

> Benjamin Franklin Edwards, American, age 25, barracks 12.
> Prentice Melvin Miles, American, age 39, barracks 12.
> Alfred Gregory Zervoulakos, American, age 20, barracks 11.

CONFERENCES WITH COMMANDANT: For the record, there are attached hereto summaries of the conferences held at the Commandant's Office on February 20th and 21st on the subject of food conditions in camp, with particular reference to the issue of palay.

FOOD: On February 19th the Authorities released additional rations of rice to the Camp, presumably sufficient to cover a four-day period. However, many of the sacks were short in weight, and actually only a three-day ration was furnished, and that a very limited one. Four sacks of palay were issued, which it was subsequently necessary to release to internees for individual husking and preparation, so that the individuals could cook for themselves.

The rations issued and the rice position of the camp for the four days February 20 to 23rd were as follows:

Ration—4 days at 7 sacks per day—28 sacks of 50 kos.—
1400 kilos in Stock—actual weights—

Rice—2 sacks at 50 kilos	—	100 kos
8 sacks at 40 kilos	—	320 kos
		420 kos.

Palay—40 sacks at 29.45   —   1,178 kos.

50% allowance for husking 580 kos   1010

Required to make up 4 days' ration   390 kilos
                                                        Rice

In that connection, the Committee on several occasions protested to the Commandant against the issue of palay, since the palay was furnished without any warning and the internees had no means of preparing it and no fuel for cooking it. The Authorities insisted that palay was the only thing which could and would be made available to the internees, and stated quite frankly that if we desired to eat, we would have to make the best of what they could supply us. During the later days extremely small amounts of the supplementary food were brought into the Camp by the Japanese, with the result that internees had not more than the 150 grams of rice in the form of palay.

Late in the evening of the 22nd, the Commandant asked that seventeen men be provided to go outside the Camp to unload additional supplies of palay. A working detail was provided and the men brought back with them that evening 35 sacks, which were turned over to the Japanese with the hope and expectation that the grain would be released the following day to internees.

M. B. Heichert   Chairman   D. Croney
                                Recording Secretary

Appendix D

New Bilibid Prison,
Muntinlupa, Philippines
February 28, 1945

General Douglas MacArthur
Commander in Chief
U. S. Armed Forces in the Far East

Dear General MacArthur:

It is the unanimous desire of the former internees, who are now at this Camp, to express their sincere appreciation for release from the hands of the Japanese Army at Los Baños.

We request you to convey our deep feeling of gratitude to the officers and men of the military units which participated in the action last Friday.

Even the untrained observer was conscious that such an operation could only be achieved by the perfect coordination and timing of the Air Corps, paratroops, amphibious units and the guerillas. Its success, which was effected without a serious injury to any of the 2,121 internees, speaks eloquently for the generalship and ability of the U.S. Armed Forces under your command. We are proud of them and we thank you.

Very respectfully,

ADMINISTRATION COMMITTEE
(CIVILIAN INTERNEES OF LOS BAÑOS INTERNMENT CAMP)

Murray B. Reichert, Chairman	A. D. Calhoun, Member
L. L. Watty, Vice Chairman	R. E. Cecil, Member
George Gray, Secretary	Clyde DeWitt, Member
	W. F. G. Harris, Member

Appendix E

New Bilibid Prison
Muntinlupa, P.X.
20th Feb., 1945

General Douglas MacArthur
Manila.

Dear Sir:

Acting on behalf of the four hundred odd British nationals rescued on the 23rd February from the internment camp at Los Baños, we wish to convey our thanks to all who were involved in that magnificent operation and in particular to the officers and men of the 11th Airborne Division as well as the guerillas employed.

The whole affair was a perfect example of American daring, originality and mechanical efficiency and the speed at which it was carried out resulted in the internees being conveyed to safety before realizing to the full the extent of the danger involved or indeed the potentialities of the situation in which they had been living.

As a tangible expression of our appreciation we would very much like to present to the 11th Airborne Division as a war trophy our most treasured possession which is the Union Jack Flag flown in Los Baños Camp on our so-called "Freedom Day", 7th January 1945, and if this has your approval, we propose to make the presentation at the concert which has been arranged for Friday, 4th March.

In conclusion, we wish also to convey our most appreciative thanks to all those who assisted by receiving us at New Bilibid Prison and who have continued to care for us magnificently since that memorable day.

Yours respectfully,

L. T. Watty

W.F.G. Harris

British Members of Los Baños Administrative Committee

Appendix F

March 13, 1945

The Officer Commanding
Company B
1st Battalion, 511th Infantry Regiment
11th Airborne Division, 14th Corps, 6th Army

Sir:

On behalf of approximately four hundred and twenty British subjects formerly interned at Los Baños Internment Camp, I am writing to ask you to express to the men of Company B our sincere appreciation and gratitude for our rescue which was effected by them on 23rd February last.

The gallantry, daring and coordination which made the rescue possible, without one civilian casualty, will, we feel, give the action a place in history which will never be forgotten.

As a tangible mark of our gratitude to the men who risked so much for us we are sending you a Union Jack which we ask you to present them as a trophy.

This flag was originally given to a member of the British Community by an Officer of the Australian Mercantile Marine who rescued it from his ship which was sunk in Manila Bay. Thereafter it was smuggled into Santo Tomas Camp and later into Los Baños Camp. It successfully evaded several searches of quarters by the Japanese, and on 7th January, 1945, when the Japanese temporarily left us free in Los Baños, it flew over the Camp side by side with the Stars and Stripes. When the Japanese returned it again went into hiding until 23rd February.

I relate the history of the flag in order to indicate that we value it. It was in fact our most treasured possession in Camp, and, as such, we give it to your men, confident that it could not be in better hands.

We wish you and your men the best of good fortune wherever the trend of this war may take you in the future.

Sincerely yours,

L. T. Watty, Vice-Chairman
Administration Committee
Los Baños Internment Camp

Bibliography

Abernathy, Col. William C., U.S.A. (Ret.). Letters to the author, 9 January 1985 and 19 February 1985.

After Action Report, Mike I Operation, U.S. Army, Headquarters XIV Corps, 29 July 1945.

After Action Report, Operation Mike VI, Luzon Campaign, 31 January–30 June 1945, 11th Airborne Division, 24 January 1946.

After Action Report, "The Los Baños Operations," General Headquarters, U.S. Philippine Island Forces, Hunters-ROTC Guerrillas, 18 March 1945.

Airborne Division TO&ES, 1944

Anderson, Charles R. "Diary of the Living Dead." *Chicago Times*, 17 March 1945.

Bailey, Maj. Maxwell C., U.S.A.F. "Raid at Los Baños." *Military Review*, May 1983.

Blackledge, Col. David W. Letters to *Voice of the Angels*, 30 June 1982 and 15 June 1983.

———. Letters to the author, 7 January 1984 and 19 April 1984.

———. Col., U.S.A. (Ret.). Letter to *Voice of the Angels*, 8 October 1983.

Brooks, Ford. Letter to Alan Chenevert, 4 August 1983.

Burgess, Henry A. "Reminiscences of the 11th Airborne Raid on Los Baños," unpublished, 1981.

———. Nine letters to the author, 20 May 1982 through 7 November 1984.

Chenevert, Lt. Col. Alan H., (U.S.A. Ret.). Eight letters to the author, 1983–85.

Coleman, Arthur J. Three letters to the author, 1984.

Colley, David P. Article in *Allentown Morning Call*, 7 December 1981.

Combat Log, 1st Battalion, 188th Glider Infantry, Luzon P.I. 22–25 February 1945.

Combat Notes, Numbers 5 and 7, ACSG3, Headquarters Sixth Army, 1945.

Cullum, Leo A., S.J. Letter to Ben Edwards, 11 July 1984.

Deacon, Kenneth J. "Engineers in the Los Baños Raid," *The Military Engineer*, March–April 1958.

Devlin, Gerard M. *Paratroopers*. New York: St. Martin's Press, 1979.

Edwards, Ben F. Twenty-five letters to the author, 10 September 1983 through 14 March 1985.

———. Personal Report: "Los Baños Internment Camp, Philippines, Escape and Liberation, 21 November 1983.

Ellis, Steve. "Los Baños Freedom Day." *VFW Magazine*, February 1979.

Extracts from Public Trial of Sadaaki Konishi. Various exhibits filed under RG153, Box 1105, File #40–1896.

———. Testimony of Sadaaki Konishi at LUPOW #8, 28 November 1945.

———. Rumor regarding escape of war criminals in charge of Los Baños Prison Camp, 10 July 1945.

———. Q and A of Osamu Yoshimura at LUPOW #1, Cabuyao, Luguna, 23 November 1945.

———. Perpetuation of Testimony of Edward James Gray, 29 May 1945.

———. Q and A of Matilda Liam Chu (killing of Ang Kai and bayoneting of two children left for dead).

———. Perpetuation of Testimony of Paul Lauren Iddings, 14 September 1945.

———. Testimony of Paul Hennesen.

———. Review of opening statement of prosecutor, Mr. O'Neill.

———. Charges, ramifications, pleas, findings, sentence adjudged 15 January 1947.

———. Proceedings and Authentication of Record, 18 January 1947.

———. Opinion of the Board of Review, 11 August 1947.

———. Approval of sentence, Headquarters Philippines Ryukyus Command, 25 February 1947.

Farrell, Frank W., Lt. Gen., U.S.A. (Ret.). Letter to *Voice of the Angels*, 1977.

Flanagan, Maj. Edward M., Jr., "The Angels, A History of the 11th Airborne Division," Washington, D.C.: Inf Journal Press, 1948.

———. Lt. Col. "The Los Baños Raid," *War Story*, March 1958.

———. Lt. Gen, U.S.A. (Ret.). "The Los Baños Raid," *Army*, June 1983.

Field Order No. 7, Headquarters XIV Corps, U.S. Army, 17 February 1945.

"Freed Manila Exults." *Maryknoll Magazine*, Summer 1945. Author unknown.

Fulton, John. Five letters to the author, 1984; letter to *Voice of the Angels*," January 1984.

———. Letter to *Voice of the Angels*, 30 May 1983.

———. Letter to *Voice of the Angels*, 15 May 1984.

Garter, Mel, Col. U.S.A. (Ret.). Three letters to the author, 1985.

Heichert, Murray B. Letter of appreciation to eleven U.S. Navy nurses for their assistance in operating Los Baños hospital. 28 February 1945.

———. Administrative committee chairman's roll call report to Japanese Los Baños commandant, 19 February 1945.

———. Report: "Summary of the Events Leading to the Rescue of the Los Baños Internment Camp on 23 February 1945."

"History of 11th Airborne Division Reconnaissance Troop." Unsigned and undated.

Holstein, Lee. "Leyte Operation," *Voice of the Angels*, 15 September 1983.

Holzem, James. Letter to *Voice of the Angels*, 1977.

Ingles, Gustavo C. Letters to the author, December 1984 and January 1985.

———. "Los Baños." Letter to *Voice of the Angels*, 12 December 1983.

Kennington, Maj. Robert E., Infantry school thesis on "The Operations of the Los Baños Force," 1948.

———. Col. U.S.A. (Ret.). Two letters to the author, 1984.

Kroeger, Miriam Louise, Maryknoll Sister. Letters to the author, 29 March 1983.

———. Report written in Baguio, 1 November 1945.

Levenson, Edward, "Veterans Reunite, Recall WWII Rescue Mission." *The Sentinel Weekender*, Carlisle, Pa., 25 February 1984.

MacArthur, Douglas. *Reminiscences*. New York: McGraw-Hill, 1964.

Manchester, William, *American Caesar*. Boston and Toronto: Little Brown, 1978.

Mason, Harold. Letter to the author, 21 February 1983.

McCarthy, William R., MM. "The Angels Came at Seven." Maryknoll publication, 16 June 1980.

Nash, Grace Chapman. "The Gallant Buccaneer of Los Baños." *Reader's Digest*, February 1959.

———. "That We Might Live." Scottsdale, Ariz.: Shano Publishers, 1984.

Nieva, Antonio A. "The Liberation of Los Baños." *Voice of the Angels*, 15 March 1984.

O'Callahan, Rose Marie, Maryknoll Sister. Letter home undated but shortly after rescue.

Okamoto, Daikichi, Japanese interpreter, Los Baños Camp. Letters to Ben Edwards, 22 April 1984 and 8 May 1984.

Pierson, Albert, Maj. Gen., U.S.A. (Ret.). Letter to the author 12 January 1985.

Quandt, Colonel Douglass P. "Fifth Wheel." *Voice of the Angels*, 15 September 1983.

———. "Salute to General Swing." *Voice of the Angels*, 1983.

Quesada, Francisco B., U.S.A. Col., (Ret.). Letters to the author, 19 September 1984 and 6 November 1984.

———. "Hunters-ROTC Guerrillas Mark 42d Anniversary," 1982.

———. "Notes on the Los Baños Internee Camp Liberation," undated.

———. "Terry's Hunters." First Edition, undated.

———. "Daring War Operation Remembered." *Voice of the Angels*, 23 February 1980.

Ringler, John M., Col., U.S.A. (Ret.). Letters to the author, 22 April 1983, 19 August 1984, 7 September 1984.

Rivers, W. R. Four letters to the author. 1983–84.

Smith, Jasper Bryan. Letter to the author, 5 August 1983.

Squires, Morton. Five letters to the author, 1984–85.

Swing, Joseph M., Lt.Gen., U.S.A. (deceased). "General Swing's Diary." Record of his trip in 1943 as American Airborne Advisor to General Eisenhower, Allied Force Headquarters, Algiers, Algeria.

Tutay, Filemon V. "Liberation of Los Baños." *Philippines Free Press*, 18 February 1950.

Vanderpool, Jay D., Colonel, U.S.A. (Ret.). Four letters to the author, 1984.

———. Letter to David Blackledge, 17 March 1982.

Vogelgesang, John, S.V.D. "A Christmas to Remember." Divine Word Missionaries, Winter 1984.

Wallace, John P., Col., Chaplain Corps, U.S.A. (Ret.). Letter to Sister Miriam Louise Kroeger, 21 May 1983.

Walsh, Louise A., Col., U.S.A. (Ret.). "The Raid on Los Baños." *The Static Line*, December 1980.

Watty, L.T. British representative, Los Baños administration committee, letter of appreciation to B Company, *511th PIR*, 13 March 1945.

Williams, George J., S.J. Article in Manila newspaper, February 1947.

Index